Developing Management in Schools

K B Everard

Basil Blackwell

© K. B. Everard 1986
First published 1986
Reprinted 1987 (with corrections)

Published by Basil Blackwell Ltd
108 Cowley Road
Oxford OX4 1JF
England

British Library Cataloguing in Publication Data

Everard, K.B.
    Developing management in schools.
    1. School management and organisation—Great Britain
    I. Title
    371.2'00941   LB2901

    ISBN 0–631–14831–0

Typeset in 10 on 12pt Sabon by Oxford Publishing Services, Oxford
Printed in Great Britain

Contents

		Page
Preface		v
Acknowledgements		vii
1	Introduction	1
2	School Management Observed	6
2.1	The managers	6
2.2	The organisations	12
2.3	Ethos, philosophy and management style	21
2.4	Problems of managing schools	33
2.5	Financial management	50
2.6	Qualities needed for school management	54
2.7	Selection	58
2.8	School reviews	60
2.9	Staff appraisal	64
2.10	Training	69
2.11	Change, development and innovation	75
2.12	Encounters with industry	79
2.13	Encounters on management courses	84
2.14	Findings of other observers and commentators	101
2.15	Comparison with Western Europe	116
2.16	School management: salient features	118
3	Industrial Management Compared	126
3.1	The nature of management	126
3.2	Components of management	130
3.3	Good practices	134
3.4	Appraisal	143
3.5	Developing managers	159
3.6	Resource management	174
3.7	Organisational problems, change and development	180
3.8	Should schools learn from industry?	186
3.9	How schools can learn from industry	192
3.10	Evaluation of management training	197
4	School Management Development	203
4.1	The education service hierarchy	204
4.2	Advisers and inspectors	207

4.3   Consultancy provision   209
4.4   Support within the school   211
4.5   Professional associations and networks   212
4.6   Management training provision   214
4.7   Education management provision   218
4.8   Higher education institutions   225
4.9   Private sector institutions   227
4.10 Publishers   229
4.11 The National Development Centre for School
      Management Training   232

Appendix 1 Particulars of schools visited   237
Appendix 2 Research methodology   239

Bibliography   245
References   254
Index   261

Preface

This book has its origins amongst some uncomfortable feelings of ignorance and insecurity on my part. Just before I retired early from ICI in 1982 (we had a falling rolls problem), my colleague, Bob Finch, the Schools Liaison Officer, asked me on behalf of the Centre for the Study of Comprehensive Schools to write a report on what such schools could learn from industry about management. That report (Everard 1984) has sold many copies. However, little did its readers know that I had only thrice set foot in a comprehensive school, yet here was I – one of those despicable industrialists to boot – telling them what they could learn: a vulnerable position indeed! I knew little about the management problems of schools, though after 15 years of being an education and training manager, and hence much involved with both management training and organisational change, I felt I did know a thing or two about management and organisation development in industry.

Anyway, no-one called my bluff, but when the publication of the report led to invitations to help train heads to manage, I felt I ought to take a closer look at their world if I was to speak appropriately to their condition and to help them to learn from industry whatever was wholesome and of good report. But how? An advertisement placed by the Leverhulme Trust suggested a way: I successfully applied for a research grant to study the problems of school management and this enabled me to pay visits to 20 schools over a period of two years. Talking to heads and other staff and seeing some school management in action, I was able from my ex-industrial perspective to draw some comparisons with the problems that industry faces. At the same time I became involved with the design of a one-term management training course at the University of London Institute of Education, where I became a consultant, tutor and later Visiting Fellow. Working with the rest of the course team was an enriching experience. Training on four of these courses at the Institute and contributing to other school management courses at Keele, Leeds and Warwick Universities, as well as at Bulmershe, Roehampton, Newham and other colleges, enabled me to meet several hundred heads and senior staff *in statu pupillarii* and to experience with them some of the problems they had in learning not only management, but how to train others to manage more effectively – for that was the main object of my involvement in the ULIE one-term courses.

Even before I left ICI, I had become involved in both management education and education management, since I was on the CNAA Committee for Business and Management Studies and its two boards, the Postgraduate Courses Board and the Educational Organisation and Management Board (formerly Panel), of which I was one of the original members. This brought me into close contact with award-bearing courses on management, not only for industrialists but also for teachers. Informal contacts with the National Development Centre for School Management Training at Bristol (NDC), the Association of Teachers of Management at the Polytechnic of Central London (where I was a Visiting Professor while still with ICI) and the Centre for the Study of Comprehensive Schools (CSCS) at York helped me to enlarge my perspective on the developing management scene in schools, while my honorary chairmanship (till 1984) of the British Association for Commercial and Industrial Education (BACIE) enabled me to remain in touch with developments in the industrial scene. Finally, I have kept close to the training of young people through my chairmanship of the Development Training Advisory Group, a consortium of Brathay Hall, Endeavour Training, the Industrial Society, Lindley, Outward Bound and the YMCA. These agencies do a great deal to round off the education that young people receive in schools and also provide leadership training for managers; the learning processes contrast with those in much of secondary and tertiary education. This, then, is where I come from.

Surveying this whole scene convinced me of the value of building learning bridges across the gulf that separates teachers in their management role from those in industry, commerce and the public service outside education whose job it is to make their organisations more effective. My first book, *Effective School Management*, with Geoffrey Morris (Everard and Morris 1985), was aimed at heads and other teachers who have to help run their schools; this one looks beyond – at the processes, systems and structures that support the development of management in schools. At the risk of seeming arrogant, perhaps I can express the difference in the parodied words of a verse I came across recently:

No teacher I of boys or smaller fry,
No teacher I of teachers, no not I;
Mine was the distant aim, the longer reach:
To train men how to manage men who teach,
And help to train to manage, those I teach.

Muffle the sexist ring; then you know what I have been trying to do for the last four years, and why I came to write this book.

I have encountered the usual problems with the absence from the English language of words that avoid the gender issue. More than ever I am conscious in my encounters with teachers that so many more of them are female than is the case with industrial managers. It now worries me to write 'he' when I mean 'he or she', but it would worry me more to adopt the clumsy mention of both genders throughout the book; so the male pronouns win on a head count.

Another difficulty lies in writing for a mixed readership in primary, special and independent schools, as well as in state secondaries which provided the main focus for my fieldwork, though not for my tutorial activities where primaries are more heavily represented (there are, after all, more of them). A part of what I write applies only to school management in the state sector. Rather than keep inserting provisos, I shall rely on the reader to discern what is particular to the various types of school and what is general to all.

K B Everard,
Welwyn Garden City.

Acknowledgements

This book could not have been written without the co-operation of the necessarily anonymous heads and staff of the schools I visited as part of my research. I am deeply grateful for their hospitality and time that they gave me, and for allowing me to publish the findings; and to ILEA for allowing me access to some of their schools. I also thank the many heads and other teachers who came on courses that I have tutored and who have (no doubt unwittingly!) added to my stock of material.

I am glad to acknowledge permission to publish material obtained from other investigators, particularly Messrs Bowden, Duffet, Dwyer, Gray, Phillips and Weindling. My publishers, Basil Blackwell, have kindly allowed me to include in section 3.7 lengthy excerpts from Andrew Pettigrew's excellent book on ICI, *The Awakening Giant.*

There are many colleagues in education to whom I owe a debt of gratitude; in particular John Welton, Pam Young, John Sayer and Derek Waters at the University of London Institute of Education have given me much encouragement and inspiration, though they are not, of course, to be held responsible for my views. Similarly I owe thanks to Harry Gray of Lancaster University, Ray Bolam and his colleagues at the National Development Centre for School Management Training at Bristol, and Frank Stoner and others at the Centre for the Study of Comprehensive Schools at York University.

Finally, I wish to thank the Leverhulme Trust for their grant towards the expenses of my research, though I owe my personal sustenance to my ICI pension. I count it a privilege to have had 30 years' employment in this company, and thereby to have acquired a wealth of experience of developing management, which I am now able to share with schools.

Chapter 1

Introduction

Management is not a subject taught at school, nor (except for classroom management) in initial teacher training, but it has to be learned in later life by those keen to advance their professional careers in schools. So with industry: although I spent four years studying for my first degree to become a qualified chemist, I received no instruction in managing the three laboratory assistants whom ICI assigned to me in my first research job; and subsequently I had only about a week's formal management training before I first became a departmental manager. Moreover, I had no special knowledge of education when I was appointed to run an education department with a secretarial training school, an apprentice training school and a residential management training centre. Of course I survived, just as heads survive when they suddenly find themselves in charge of 10–100 staff and buildings worth over £1 million. At least, however, they know they can teach; I had to learn whether I could train.

It can be done; many do it; but can it seriously be argued that the professional practice of chemistry should take four years' formal preparation, of teaching, two, of medicine, five or more, yet of management, next to nil? It is not as though the higher echelons of management present a less demanding role than those of a conscientious teacher, chemist or even a doctor; the intellectual challenge, the emotional drain and the calls on one's interpersonal skills are of the same order, if not greater, in a complex organisation like a large secondary school full of boisterous adolescents.

What distinguishes learning to be a manager (such as a head) from learning to be a teacher, a chemist or a doctor is that, whereas these latter learn systematically in a lecture room or laboratory, many managers have learned haphazardly in their ordinary workplace. This is slowly changing as formal management training takes root, but it is still essentially true that management (except in the forces) is mostly learned by picking it up, whereas other professions learn by being taught over a period of years. Doctors', teachers', chemists' learning is a *managed* process; managers' learning is mostly left to chance.

Some may find this unremarkable and argue that management is not a profession anyway; that it does not lend itself to systematic, as distinct from adventitious, learning; and that its successful practice is more the result of possessing a particular combination of innate personal qualities than of mastering trainable skills. Hence one may *develop* into a manager, by God's good grace, but one cannot *be developed* by someone set in authority, like a teacher or more senior manager. This is not my view, although I accept that in-built aptitudes strongly influence trainability.

Organisations like schools and firms, together with their employees, surely deserve better than to be governed by 'amateurs', however naturally gifted they may be. A systematic process is needed for developing management in schools, in firms, in hospitals and elsewhere, because the problems that naturally occur in such organisations impair their effectiveness and unless they are managed properly, the pupils, the customers, the patients suffer – and, of course, the employees. Her Majesty's Inspectors repeatedly provide evidence of unsatisfactory management in schools; for example, (HMI 1985) they report that in almost one third of the schools visited poor leadership and management were adversely affecting the quality of the work, the levels and deployment of resources and the take-up of INSET. In nearly half the schools visited the organisation of learning was judged unsatisfactory in some lessons and the management of resources in primary schools was faulted; they identified poor management by headteachers in a quarter of the country's primary schools, though secondary heads came out rather better.

It has taken a long time for the British to take management development seriously in civilian life; the Americans, the Germans, the French and the Japanese seem to believe in a more professional approach. Even the backward Chinese have been taking matters in hand; their Communist Party congress decreed in 1979 that Chinese management would be upgraded. By the time I visited the country to study management only three years later, no fewer than 1.6 million of them had been trained on management courses by a cascade process not dissimilar in concept from the DES 3/83 school management training initiative, with its 'OTTO (one-term training opportunity) graduates' training less experienced heads on 20-day basic courses; there was, however, a slight difference in the scale of operation (Everard 1983). Thus in the first year, some 800 teachers attended DES 3/83 courses roughly in the proportion of 3:1 on basic and OTTO programmes; by 1986 the National Development Centre expected that 3500–4000 teachers would have done so. However, the 104 Local Education Authorities (LEAs) employ some 31 500 headteachers, 27 000 deputies and 70 000 heads of departments etc. with middle management responsibilities, that is, 128 500 managers in all. So only about 3 per cent of the eligible population will have attended these programmes over the three years of their availability. Figures from the Hughes report (Hughes, Carter and Fidler 1981) showed that only one per cent had attended award-bearing management courses, though 14 per cent had been on a non-award-bearing course at some time. Evidently the vast majority of teachers in managerial positions have not been formally trained for that aspect of their jobs.

While course attendance statistics provide one indicator of the extent to which systematic management development occurs, there are more important, albeit less objective, criteria than that. I shall argue later that the process of developing management is not to be equated with sending people on courses; it has to be regarded as an integral part of a whole set of policies, processes and practices that support an over-arching objective – that of improving the effectiveness of the organisation in the pursuit of its fundamental aim. The last chapter examines the main support systems and suggests that most of them are distinctly rickety. Indeed, the whole book is aimed as much at the directors and managers of the support systems and agencies as at the heads and senior management of schools, for all these (including the growing number of industrialists who are becoming involved with schools, whom I hope the book will enlighten about school management problems) are part of a web of support for developing management in schools. If current initiatives in this direction are to be effective and enduring, then the strategies of the various agencies concerned need to be mutually reinforcing.

One way of assessing the overall system for developing management in schools is to compare it with that which exists in industry, making due allowance for the difference in the sets of problems that industry and education each have to address. Another major theme of the book is therefore to draw this comparison. Chapter 2 examines management problems and practices in schools; Chapter 3 does so for industry and describes its philosophy and approach, with particular reference to one firm, ICI, which not only provided the bedrock of my own experience of these matters, but also enjoys a good reputation as a well-managed organisation. Indeed, its personnel management policies are embedded in a tradition of good practice that pre-dates its formation; one of the constituent companies, Brunner Mond, was held up as a paragon of humane and progressive management even in the last century. Latterly ICI has become recognised as a leader in the management of complex change (Pettigrew 1985). However, it is certainly not the intention of this book to argue that industrial management (even as exemplified by ICI and other progressive firms) is superior in all respects to that of schools and therefore that its practices should be transferred, hook, line and sinker; all I would invite readers to do is to seek out, take on board and adapt the approaches that they consider to be relevant and better than their own. Section 3.7 in particular will show that problems abound in industry, despite good management, which are not dissimilar from those in schools. The issue is not that management is incompetent because organisations have problems, but rather that there are degrees of competence in tackling the problems that face all managers. Developing that competence is a vital task for all organisations.

The field of management development is wide, and I have had to be selective in the topics to discuss; this is not intended to be a comprehensive textbook. Instead, I have chosen to devote special attention to those approaches that present the sharpest contrast between schools and industry, for example the use of systematic staff appraisal and the management of change. Here there is much crossing of the learning bridge at the present time, and still more to come. So far the response of teachers who have crossed the bridge is generally favourable; the criticism comes mainly from the spectators who sit watching from the bank, and in Section 3.8 I have a few words for them.

As for the style of the book, it is intended to inform, to provoke thought and perhaps controversy, and to stimulate some approaches to developing management which I believe will help schools to become more effective, as well as more satisfying places in which to work. In reporting the results of my fieldwork in Chapter 2, I conclude most sections with a list of issues to consider. The purpose of these lists is to flag some of the main management issues as matters for reflexion, which will need to be addressed in order to develop a more professional approach to school management. I take most of them up in Chapter 3, when I compare industrial with school management; but I leave some loose ends for others to tie, perhaps by taking the issues as topics for discussion on management courses, and indeed as part of a school review or INSET activity within the school.

I have put in an appendix the description of the research methodology on which most of Chapter 2 is based, so as not to divert attention from the substantive issues that the research illuminated. With so vast a system as the education service, it is difficult to be sure that visits to such a small sample of schools have yielded representative results; I am encouraged, however, by the compatibility of my findings with those of other observers, which I have summarised in Section 2.14. The library research that I have undertaken to find what others have written on the main themes of the book has shown that this is still a relatively untilled field. Comparative research about management and management development in educational and in other institutions is particularly scanty. Far more is written on pedagogical than on managerial or organisational processes, but even in the pedagogical field there is room for more comparative studies of the effectiveness of learning in a school setting compared with that in an industrial training setting. Indeed, I believe that teachers who experience a well-designed process for learning management will realise its implications for the way in which they teach children. Management training has something in common with the 'development training' of young adults, with the Royal Society of Arts' 'Education for Capability' movement and with the more advanced life skills training that is increasingly provided in schools. These all aim to help people to become originators rather than pawns, to make a difference to their world by getting things to happen – a problem solved, a decision implemented, an objective attained.

The last chapter touches on the wider perspective of how to change the whole education system of which schools are a part, in order to make them more effective in accomplishing their primary task. In open systems theory you cannot treat schools in isolation; 'No man is an island'. What happens within schools is influenced by what happens without. We need to think in the heady terms of total systems change. With around a million people employed in the education service (about half of them school teachers), and with a budget amounting to some 11 per cent of the gross national product, the problem of overcoming inertia in such a system and of catalysing, steering and managing change is almost too gigantic to contemplate; and yet the best way of eating an elephant is one bite at a time.

It is by generally developing competence in management and by targetting specific action on key points in the system that strategic change will be brought about. I do not believe that this should be the preserve of the party politicians; there is an important managerial contribution to be made to improving the effectiveness of education. As I write these words in autumn 1985, the forces detracting from its effectiveness and impeding progress towards its improvement were never more debilitating: low morale, industrial action, pupil unrest. Change will come anyway in such a turbulent environment; if it is to be change for the better, it must be *managed*, yet the capability of the education system for managing change is not well developed. As George Walker, chairman of the Centre for the Study of Comprehensive Schools, has pointed out (Walker 1985), 'Unless the government takes the management of change in education more seriously (I do not quarrel with many of its proposed reforms) none of this will happen. Instead, good industrial managers like John Harvey-Jones (whose infectious enthusiasm I shall remember for a long time) will be hindered by a system which has allowed the state schools to decline to a position of almost terminal weakness.' H G Wells wrote: 'Human history becomes more of a race between education and catastrophe.' If education is not to experience catastrophe, there is no time to lose in developing management within it.

Chapter 2

School management observed

The first twelve sections of this chapter are based on the findings from my visits to twenty schools, from Cornwall to Aberdeenshire, to investigate the problems of school management. Most of the schools were mixed comprehensive, but the sample included one primary and three independent schools (see Appendix 1). As well as interviewing the head and usually the deputies and other senior staff, at some schools I sat in on various meetings, assemblies and disciplinary interviews and even shadowed the head for a day. The results are presented under a number of themes, each of which is covered in one of the sections that follow.

During the period in which the fieldwork was carried out (1983–5), I was involved in a number of school management courses, and my conclusions from this experience follow the fieldwork results. Other observers have commented on the same kind of themes as I examined, and I summarise their findings before concluding the chapter with a summary of the salient featues of school management. I begin with the managers themselves.

2.1 The managers

Heads

The sample of heads interviewed, like the hundred or more encountered on management courses, covered a wide range of characteristics and experience. Only one had a formal qualification in management (a DMS); another held an M Ed in curriculum development; some had not even been on any short courses in management. The longest non-award-bearing courses they had attended were the Henley Management College course, lasting ten weeks, and the six-week ILEA management course, which includes a week of 'T-group training' run by the Grubb Institute. Not surprisingly, therefore, the heads do not regard formal courses as having contributed more than peripherally to their competence as managers.

The apprenticeship model is the route by which most heads think they acquired their competence before assuming headship responsibility; they learn from other heads by working as teachers or deputies, and then develop their competence simply by gaining experience in the job. Where the 'master' was outstanding, they felt they owed him an immense debt of gratitude for pointing them firmly along their careers. Sometimes, however, they learned from an anti-model; for example, a head who was so incompetent that as deputies they had to take more responsibility than usual for running the school, and even for 'training the boss'. Their predecessors in office were also not infrequently cited as anti-models. To take the example of the head of a comprehensive school (and here I quote from my visit report):

Among the formative influences in his development was the anti-model of a 'workaholic' head to whom he had been deputy, but who had been 'marvellous with parents'. . . His predecessor at the school had epitomised all that was traditional in a headmaster: an autocrat who kept knowledge to himself, who was held in awe and who, some felt, had allowed the school to stagnate, although he had undoubted qualities in a number of areas. Consequently he wanted to change the image of the school head from the traditional autocrat who kept parents at bay and staff in the dark, ruling the children with a rod of iron, to one who was devolutionary and participative in style. He wanted to be seen to delegate and to encourage this in others.

Experience outside school was sometimes a very formative influence: one head still directed a family business; another had run a business before entering the profession; another had been a salesman in the City; two had been seconded to industry for some months, and had been much exposed to industrial management concepts in shorter bursts; two had been on the staff of training colleges; two had been councillors; one a local education authority (LEA) adviser; and one had learned much by being a trade union official (NUT). There were distinct connections between these experiences and what they did in their schools; thus the ex-adviser was regarded by his staff as having excellent organising skills, and the ex-salesman as being superb on public relations.

At one comprehensive school the head commented on his experience in having formerly been an LEA adviser. One of the most important skills he had learned was in boundary management, having dealt with local politicians. He had been highly regarded in the Authority for this, and his transfer to the school enabled him to capitalise on the skill. He had had many difficult tasks in the advisory role and had seen many different schools in the course of his duties. The area of job descriptions and staff selection was very familiar to him. Above all, he had learned to manage his time, since the pressures of the job made it crucial to set priorities.

A disadvantage of his advisory experience was the dominance of the negotiating style in getting things done; since an adviser has no structural authority, he has to get things done solely through persuasion, whereas in a school it is possible, and sometimes desirable, to exercise the coercive power associated with structural authority. When he took over the school, therefore, he found himself involved in over-lengthy discussions where he tried to be very patient and equable, instead of being sometimes decisive and firm. Since at first he also took classes (before being adviser he had been head of English in a school) his time was over-committed. Yet it was important to him to brush up his teaching skills, for an adviser loses contact with children; managing a class of children is different from managing adults, and he regards himself as better at the latter.

Of particular value was previous experience in a boarding school, either as housemaster or house tutor; several respondents commented on the usefulness of such experience in acquiring general management skills. Experience of grammar schools was also mentioned as useful, as it implanted a sense of quality and performance not so often encountered – it was suggested – in secondary modern or comprehensive schools.

Once appointed, heads normally receive little support; they are on their own, mostly feel lonely and isolated, and are expected to find their feet as best they can. Some looked back on their induction as a baptism of fire.

1   At a comprehensive school in an area where the LEA is noted for cheeseparing, the head arrived to find he was without a secretary and soon the occupants of two senior posts left. Several months' delay occurred before these posts were filled; meanwhile the new head had to cope with a 50 per cent teaching load, since very tight staffing ratios are operated by the county. His predicament attracted a little sympathy but no immediate action. He had been appointed, he thought, to arrest a downward decline in the school, which brought with it the threat of amalgamation, so there were plenty of immediate managerial tasks to do. He thought a head could manage either by compass or radar; because of the circumstances he found at the time, he had chosen the compass, setting a general course and steering it, and withstanding the alarming bumps against the rocks he scraped on the way. Another head might have gone for radar, feeling his way forward, consulting all the time, and avoiding the hidden rocks; and so might he if the school had had a more favourable image. Certainly he felt that his training had been inadequate for the task he was expected to do, as was his induction into the school.

2   At another comprehensive school a house head of four years' standing who had pastoral responsibility for a fifth of the school was asked whether there were features of the way the school was run which added to the stress of pastoral work. He replied that it had become more supportive in the last three years. The former head had been in post for 21 years and the change of head after all this time had brought a feeling of insecurity and uncertainty, heightened by economic cuts and falling rolls. This had shown up as an increase in the number of discipline problems and a lowered morale among the staff. The new head's first year had not been a happy one for him or the school. Although he had set new aims, he was perceived as being somewhat indecisive, whereas his predecessor had always made cut-and-dried decisions. He had felt very isolated, as though a chasm separated him from his staff. Matters had come to a head when the 70 staff, led by the chairman of the common room, had decided to put a paper to him outlining their concerns. He had taken this feedback in a constructive way and spent more time in getting round the school and talking to staff. Both he and the staff had valued this greater openness and wanted to see it sustained.

Although three heads were active in their professional associations or in other extramural professional roles (for example, as a member of an examinations council), there was little sense of collegiality among their professional colleagues; overwork and feelings of rivalry usually militated against effective peer support, though there were two heads who courageously swapped places for a week (see p. 62). Considering the relatively easy access through the parent or governor network to other professional managers, it was surprisingly rare to find managerial support from outside the teaching profession; nevertheless, those who had built such contacts found them of great value. Equally rare was pastoral support from an LEA adviser or officer, and no-one mentioned (as sometimes happens in other professions) a college or university lecturer as a mentor.

The use of job descriptions to define the role of a head is by no means universal; except for conformity with the law, accountabilities are usually unspecified. Those heads who had job descriptions had usually written their own. There were no formal systems of performance appraisal, but one head got her own staff to appraise her and another had tried (unsuccessfully) to get his LEA adviser to do so. One chairman of governors was mentioned as providing useful counsel and excellent support, though his predecessor had done little but criticise and intervene unhelpfully on ideological grounds.

At a voluntary controlled all-ability school, the head described his role as a very isolated one, with few opportunities to test himself against the way in which other heads managed. He kept asking himself self-evaluation questions, for example, was he as good as he ought to be? How competent was he at conducting committee meetings? He had not received formal management training, so he had had to learn the skills by himself or by watching others. He would very much like to sit in with peers and see them in action, but he had no opportunities for this. However, he had only two years to go before retirement, so this wish was mainly out of interest. He habitually shied away from formality; he had no formal system of staff development and appraisal. However, he had felt the need for it and had taken the opportunity offered by growth in the school, and the decision by the LEA to appoint an addition to the senior management team, to put the new deputy in charge of staff in-service development and training.

Much criticism has been levelled at the methods for selecting heads (the POST report: Morgan, Hall and Mackay 1983); this study has shown that neither is there room for complacency in the way they are prepared for headship, developed and supported.

Other senior managers

In the tier below head there was also much variety, but some stereotypes were discernible. Several schools had what Alistair Mant has called the 'backbone manager' (Mant 1969) – people who were neither high fliers nor also-rans, but anchor men and women. Typically they have been in the same school for many years, know it backwards and have earned the respect of staff and pupils alike. Their activities consist of tasks delegated downwards from the head as too routine or time-consuming (for example, timetabling), or upwards from the staff as too difficult, or requiring co-ordination and clout. There is a flavour of adjutant about the role. Their skill lies in their relationships; they hold the ring as mediators between an innovating head and a suspicious staff, trusted by both. They keep the common room sweet. Pupils see them as disciplinarians, firm but fair. Some are pillars of local society, perhaps parish councillors or lay preachers. They no longer have aspirations to become heads; these days that is a job for a younger man or woman. Of systematic management training, they have had none – or, if they have, they were unenthusiastic; their learning has come from life.

The other stereotype is the younger, ambitious, energetic deputy, often in charge of staff development or curriculum development, actively scanning the *Times Educational Supplement* for headship vacancies in other schools (or deputy headships in larger or well-regarded schools). They are in charge of their own development, seeking opportunities for secondment and going on courses, sometimes at their own expense. They are to be found in the vanguard of change in the school, working happily with like minds among the staff, and patiently coaxing the hidebound to try something new. Their authority and influence stem as much from their competent professionalism as from their position in the hierarchy. Usually they have a fruitful relationship with the head, whose protégé they may well be; they trust one another and use each other's skills. Trickier to handle are their relationships with older colleagues, who may see them as a threat to stability with their novel ideas. But if they manage these relationships well, they can constitute a formidable top management team.

None of the 28 interviewed was formally qualified in management, but one had been seconded to industry for a year, one had come from industry into teaching, where he had been on a six-week management course run by ILEA (also attended by two other deputies interviewed); one was undergoing an Open University school management course, and one a master's course at Liverpool University.

The apprenticeship or 'osmosis' model (working under a good head and watching his approach) was valued by several respondents as a means of learning management, and the one deputy who had been a housemaster in a state boarding school said that this was the best preparation of all for a deputy headship post.

Against a background in which systematic management development was rare and course attendance infrequent, it was particularly interesting to find a young deputy head who came across strongly as consciously managing her own development. Although she had used both a role model and an anti-model, and had been on a few courses which she found 'enormously useful', she felt that she had learned more through habitual systematic reviews of her own performance. She regularly spent time reflecting on it and laying plans for improvement. As a result of this awareness of the learning process she was not only good at coaching others in her school, but she had become involved in running courses on aspects of management.

Without exception, the middle managers interviewed (heads of department, heads of house) had had even less preparation for management responsibilities. One had kept a log of all the problems that came to him in his first week as house head, and he remembered feeling quite overwhelmed by the sheer flood of matters referred to him from below. He had to work out his own salvation, and eventually learned how to cope.

The apprenticeship method of learning management was again in evidence, and reached its height at a boarding school where appointments to housemaster were decided two years ahead, so that there was ample time for the outgoing incumbent to pass on the 'tricks of the trade'.

A housemaster interviewed had been in post for seven years, having previously been chaplain and head of religious education. It was a job akin to that of a general manager, in the sense that a wide variety of tasks came his way. He had had very little training for the job; the tradition was to throw people in at the deep end and let them swim. The management of the catering side had come as a great shock to him. He had learned by experience how to delegate; he had four house tutors to whom he could delegate. Administration and budgets had presented no problems, because his predecessor had been well organised, and had simply passed on his systems and his expertise. Although as a young teacher he had wanted to ask 'How am I doing?', this was not done, or if it was, it would evoke a non-committal reply. He had therefore learned that he was doing all right unless someone came and told him otherwise. The assumption was that once you had been appointed a master, you had arrived, and of course you could do the job.

One head of science had been on a series of a dozen day-long management modules organised by the LEA, but only one of these (in industry) had proved really relevant to the actual problems he faced. Dealing with 'conflicts of personality' in the department was a problem that caused him many headaches.

Three interviewees had had commercial management experience before entering teaching, one in the family hotel business and another as purchasing manager of a well-known food manufacturer; another had run his own business. Together with a teacher who had been in industry, but not at management level, and with a head of commerce who had had two secondments to industry, these five had a grasp of management and organisation processes which enabled them to comment very perceptively on their schools' regimes. Knowledge of commerce and industry gave them a yardstick of comparison so that they knew what was capable of being improved; those without exposure to the world outside school tended to accept ineffectiveness without question. It was just the way things were.

Some issues to consider

1   What are the strengths and limitations of the apprenticeship model of learning how to manage a school?
2   What kinds of additional experience contribute most to the managerial competence of heads and senior staff?
3   Are such experiences given due weight in the selection process?
4   What arrangements should there be for induction of staff into a new managerial position?
5   How can systematic self-development best be encouraged?

2.2 *The organisations*

As is well known to teachers, there is considerable variety in the way schools are organised, but some sort of matrix organisation is usual in the larger schools. As far as the academic curriculum is concerned, subjects are allocated to departments and sometimes departments to faculties, while in the pastoral system children are allocated to groupings such as Upper School, Middle School, Lower School, or to Houses or Halls, and/or to Years, subdivided into Forms. Titles such as Head of Department (HoD), Head of House, Head of Sixth Form and Form Tutor are given to the teachers responsible for managing these units of the organisation.

The senior management team typically consists of the head and up to three deputies, but in the independent sector titles like second or under master (or mistress) are more usual, and are also found in the state sector. Bursars handle financial, estates and personnel management in the independent sector and are occasionallly encountered in state schools, though not at a senior level. Within the senior team, deputies are usually allocated specific responsibilities, for example for the academic curriculum (including the timetable), for the pastoral side and for general administration respectively. Some schools, however, do not like separating the academic and pastoral responsibilities, and others, where they are separate, periodically rotate the incumbents from role to role in order to promote integration. The choice of organisation appears to be mainly influenced by the views of the present or previous head, and at some of the schools visited changes had been made or were contemplated; for example, one head was getting rid of the head of faculty tier, since she thought it unnecessarily distanced her from the classroom teachers. Except where a school was expanding or contracting, or where there was a new head, the basic structure of the organisation was not an issue that evoked much comment, and formal organisation charts were seldom to be seen.

It was possible to discern a trend towards making structures sharper and more explicit; some schools were just introducing written job descriptions, at least for the senior staff, and staff manuals were being written which described responsibilities. At the other extreme were some well-established and detailed manuals which read more like rule books; however, these tended not to be well-thumbed documents in daily use, but reference books written for administrative tidiness and kept in a bottom drawer. Some teachers felt that formality had gone too far when manuals ran to over a hundred pages; 40–50 pages were more common.

Meeting structure

There was some variation in the number, nature and frequency of meetings, but the main ones were of the senior management team, usually on a daily or weekly basis, and the heads of departments' meeting, from weekly to twice a term; heads of houses (i.e. the pastoral leaders) also met regularly. Full staff meetings (or common room meetings) took place usually up to four times a term, though in one school the frequency had been more like once a decade; these tended to be more like briefing meetings than consultative councils, and indeed it was by no means the normal practice to have a procedure for joint consultation. Where staff meetings were used for 'consultation', the head saw them as safety valves and said that they were formidable meetings to control. In independent schools there were regular finance committee meetings with the bursar in charge, but normally meetings were chaired by the head or a deputy. Some heads were not enamoured with committees of any sort, preferring to do most of their business on a one-to-one basis.

In a few schools, however, there was a fairly complex infrastructure of meetings and groups, either of 'duty teams', for example, to handle discipline on a regular basis, or of 'working parties' to spearhead new developments. The need for systematic attention to innovation, via working groups, was widely felt, since development issues were apt to get crowded out of operational agenda for regular meetings. Moreover, cross-departmental groupings were found to be very helpful in breaking down the isolation of the different departments.

Although it was normal practice to take minutes of most of the formal meetings, the rather scrappy, scribbled nature of these often left much to be desired. Typed sets of minutes were sometimes posted in the staffroom, as a vehicle for communication. Schools may not always be aware of the standards of precision in recording decisions etc. in other organisations:

The warden of a village college had spent a period on secondment to the international planning department of an oil company. What most impressed him was the precision and economy of language that characterised the papers produced by this department for the board. He came away determined to evaluate more carefully what he wanted to say and to set standards for others in the college that reflected what he had found to be so valuable an aspect of communication.

The structuring of time

One of the distinguishing features of schools as organisations is the way in which time is structured and fragmented. Not only is it rigidly divided into three terms with long intervals between, but within the day it is parcelled out into quanta of sometimes astonishingly short duration. A nine-period day of 35 minutes per period is typical, though at one school visited there was a four-period day. At another, a modular system of considerable flexibility had been introduced:

The senior deputy principal and director of studies had responsibility for the timetable, for curriculum co-ordination, for liaison with parents on choice of options, and for liaison with the local technical college. His mathematical background no doubt helped him to devise, as leader of a team of four, an extraordinarily complex timetable, which was graphically displayed on a pin-board about 15 by 6 feet in size, on the wall of his large office. Although the problem of constructing a timetable had defied a number of computer firms that had been brought in to advise, an Apple computer was used to print out the timetable and to analyse it (for example in terms of the number of rooms free in any period). It was also used for option sorting and helped to ensure that almost any set of options could be accommodated (though for educational reasons, some sets of options were disallowed). It was an interactive system, which any staff could use. Its use had led to major savings in planning time, and to the more prompt publication of the final timetable. Even so, and despite advance planning of specialist room allocation, it took the experienced timetabling team three weeks to prepare it.

The philosophy that had led to such a complex planning system was that the needs of the individual student must always be paramount; if motivation was to be sustained, students must feel that they were doing subjects they wanted to study. The management structure must therefore adapt to the consequences of that philosophy. Other schools failed their pupils by not exploiting the possibilities open to them through ingenious timetabling.

The timetable was built up of modules of 20 minutes, which were combined in units of 2, 3, 4 and 6, depending on the demands of the subject being taught. Although the core school day was from 9 a.m. till 3.30 p.m., some classes took place from 8.10 till 8.50, some at lunchtime (12.40 to 1.50) and some from 3.30 till 4.10.

Long though this school day was, no state day-school approached the length of day that was usual in independent boarding schools.

Another school was experimenting with its timetable by giving teams of teachers responsibility within broadly grouped areas for blocks of time within these areas; it was thought that not only would this be pedagogically more sound, but it would also simplify, by delegation, the construction of the timetable.

Seemingly excessive fragmentation of the day was justified on the basis that children cannot concentrate on one subject for longer than about 40 minutes. However, there is probably an underlying assumption that the predominant pedagogical process is didactic rather than inductive. When children are actively doing something they enjoy, they can become engrossed for a good deal longer than 40 minutes. Recent experience with the Schools Council Industry Project, for example, has shown that it is quite possible and educative to suspend the timetable for a fortnight on a single task.

As less traditional pedagogical approaches permeate schools, it is likely that the fragmentation of time will be increasingly questioned, and it will require a good deal of ingenuity to construct more flexible timetables.

Involvement of pupils in organisation management

When teachers describe their schools they seldom see the children as part of the organisation (Handy 1984). The organisational framework is set up and managed by the teaching staff, with the children being regarded as the raw material which the organisation transforms. To ascertain whether pupils played any part in managing the school, I usually had to use prompt questions. These elicited the fact that in a few schools there are senior pupil councils; more frequently there are house captains, prefects and other roles allocated to pupils who are thought able to discharge such responsibilities. These included speaking at public functions, setting a lead and example, arranging rosters of prefects' duties (on top of their duties to curb unruly behaviour, deal with anti-social conduct and stop dangerous activities), bringing to the head's attention any strong feelings for improvements in the organisation of the school, and – at another school – engendering a good atmosphere and spirit in the sixth form and being responsible for its discipline, committee organisation and funds, attending a variety of assemblies and taking one per house per term, assisting with first-year discipline, organising prefects and monitors, ensuring house captains fulfil their role effectively, being seen helping with duties, getting to know the non-teaching staff and holding regular meetings with the head and house heads.

Makin has described the use of pupil conferences on the curriculum (Makin 1984); these gave strong pointers to curriculum development, for there was almost unanimous agreement that it was too academic, and an overwhelming impression that the values and traditions of the traditional curriculum were irrelevant to the pupils' needs and an obstacle to a more balanced and productive form of education.

At departmental level, one school, by the use of questionnaires, had involved pupils in a major organisational exercise:

Within his department the head of design studies had carried out a major reorganisation, beginning with a definition of its aims and objectives. It had been based on a professionally designed questionnaire which the pupils had completed in order to give accurate feedback from their point of view about what subjects they took, why they had chosen them, why they dropped them and how they thought of them. The result was an impressive and thorough policy document for the subject group which detailed the group's aims and objectives and listed the responsibilities of every member of the staff.

In general, however, the powers given to 'pupil managers' and their opportunities for participative decision-making are minimal. Since management is a rich source of learning about societal processes, it is questionable whether it is right to deprive pupils of opportunities to experience it. One teacher thought that not only was it wrong, but that the whole organisational régime in the school was miseducative:

A master familiar with industry was fairly outspoken and critical in his views about the education his independent school was providing. He thought that the boys were as deprived as those in the state sector, but in a different way – deprived of experience of reality. In a regime where the head wields more coercive power than a company chairman, boys were given minimum responsibility, even as prefects; there were many things that they could and should organise by themselves, besides voluntary service activities. In this respect the boys were not being stretched. At present, the school was preparing boys to manage organisations in which people did as they were told; this was totally unrealistic when businesses were now having to be managed by consent. A major attitude and cultural change in the school regime was needed to prepare boys for entering into tomorrow's world. The trouble is the built-in inertia in the education system, and the lack of capability to manage change; we needed a Florence Nightingale to transform the regime and give a lead.

Work flow

Any organisation has to handle one-off pieces of work that do not fit into the main routine activity (in schools, teaching). For the head, such work may occupy a major proportion of his time and indeed come to be seen as the main raison d'être of the job. Much of it will consist of dealing with the in-tray and incoming telephone calls. How is such work handled? Some heads, apparently with encyclopaedic memories, deal with it as it comes, mostly by themselves, but sometimes in a one-to-one relationship with another member of the staff (including the school secretary). They do not themselves keep files or records of how this work is dealt with, though their secretaries maintain a filing system of sorts. Other heads are more methodical; they attach a 'work-in-progress' chit to each item of incoming mail, to indicate how it is to be processed by delegation and by monitoring. They have sophisticated office filing systems at hand, and can locate at will any document or record that they need. They work with their secretaries to maintain the system, and are seen by their staff to be well-organised.

One comprehensive school head, with an interest in computers and a well-developed card index of pupil records (including photographs), was gradually transferring data on to floppy disks, but so far most schools seem a long way away from having an electronic office; indeed, in one school the new head was having to introduce for the first time an efficient manual system, since keeping pupil records had not been one of his predecessor's strong points. However, for one bursar such modern technology is more than a gleam in the eye; he has the money to introduce a computer-based information technology system, but he has yet to win the hearts and minds of his academic colleagues, only about 20 per cent of whom have ever touched a computer keyboard. Another bursar had just invested £18 000 in two word processors, with which he was very pleased.

It might be supposed that a school would represent an interesting 'laboratory' of clerical work, and that pupils intending to pursue clerical or administrative careers might get useful work experience by being involved in the operation of work flow systems in the school office. However, it was rare to find examples of this. At a few schools, children were allocated receptionist duties and dealt with all visitors as they entered the school, but at only one was there a young person doing office work. This was in a rural school where a pupil who had recently left had been taken on as a YTS trainee. Although there were union objections to such an arrangement, the head had circumvented them.

At another school, the sixth form pupils had been given the task of writing and producing an 'alternative' school prospectus, which was characterised by a good deal more candour, humour and even-handedness than is usually found in such documents.

The conduct and content of meetings

Most of the senior management team meetings attended were conducted in a convivial 'club culture', with participants being on Christian name terms. However, with larger meetings (for example, heads of departments') there was more formality, with appellations like Mr, M/s etc. being used. At such meetings, some decisions were taken by majority vote, a procedure rarely encountered in industry. Visual aids (for example flipcharts) were not available at any meeting observed.

The sample of meetings attended was too small to justify general conclusions, but some anecdotal notes are worth recording for the questions they raise:

1 The senior management team met every morning and always had an overcrowded agenda. The first item took most of the time; it was to determine whether the school rules permitted boys to wear two ear-rings, or only one, in their left ears. After all aspects of the problem had been ventilated, it was decided that the relevant rule was ambiguously worded. The head undertook to rewrite the rule himself.

2 The head remarked that many of the items coming up at meetings were hardy perennials, common from one school to another. It would be helpful if inspectors could identify such items and play a more constructive role in helping schools to deal with them effectively. Unfortunately, however, the only practicable time for dealing with such problems is in the evening, and inspectors don't work in the evenings (*this is not generally true*).

3 The heads of departments' meeting was held after school, with a deputy in the chair and the head present, together with 15 staff. It was planned to run for an hour, but took 1½, though it was quite effectively chaired. The issues discussed were: (a) Minutes of the previous meeting (a manuscript scribble with no subheadings) – accepted; (b) How to get children to do two hours' homework each evening, when not all wanted to – an exchange of views with no firm conclusion; (c) Bad spelling by teachers (especially of children's names) and poor punctuation in school reports – remitted to a task group to manage; (d) A shadow structure for the school, to take account of the effect of falling rolls on manning and scale points – competently handled, despite emotional undercurrents, and agreement obtained; (e) Any other business – a ragged and inconclusive discussion about the circulation of absence slips; the problem lacked definition and clarity.

4 At a house heads' meeting in an urban comprehensive school, the following problems were discussed:
Staff bulletin. One house head questioned whether the staff bulletin was being properly used. He said it duplicated other paper that was circulated to staff, and some staff simply threw it away unread. Others said the papers duplicated were simply reminders of meetings, without which people simply failed to turn up. There was also a problem of too early a deadline for the bulletin. It was decided to make the bulletin the only document that circulated, to give it the authority of the head's signature and to allocate to a named member of staff responsibility for including all relevant material in it, including the minutes of the previous week's meetings and the agenda for the coming week.
Early dismissal from lessons. Too many classes were dismissed early, especially before lunch, thus creating noise and disturbance. One class was released 15 minutes early. The head said he would personally take this up, and mention it at a staff meeting. One of the house heads present said he dismissed classes early when he was on dinner duty; which did the head want? He refused to do this duty unless he could dismiss his class early. The head decided that the class would not be dismissed early; consequently someone else would have to do the dinner duty.
Running inside the building. The first and second years play tag, and drop litter. There were concerns about safety on stairs and near swing doors. The sanction of

closing the building during break was discussed. The discussion was lengthy and not always to the point. It was decided to speak to the boys about the proper use of the school building.

Fifth form disco. Because of the previous disco having been a disaster the head had decided that the next would be for boys only, since they could be controlled unlike outsiders. Last time a group called Papasound had brought six loudspeakers the size of wardrobes, and this had attracted undesirable youths from outside. The staff felt it was unhealthy for boys to be dancing with one another. It was therefore agreed to invite girls and staff from a neighbouring school along.

Reports. Some school reports had been lost or were being held by staff unknown; if they could not be found, they would have to be written again. The head decided he would have to ask every teacher personally whether he had these reports and he proceeded to do this during the day.

At the meeting, which lasted 40 minutes, there was a good deal of difficulty-stating and not many supported positive proposals, but decisions were made and responsibility for carrying them out assigned, though mainly to the head. There could have been more room for delegation. The first item showed that communication in the school is a problem, as elsewhere.

5   A heads of departments' meeting did not get off to a good start as it was preceded by an incident in which a boy was violently attacked. Earlier in the day, a parent had rung the deputy head to say that she had received threats that her son would be killed (though the two incidents are not necessarily connected). The head of department who had had to deal with the incident was visibly shaken.

The meeting was conducted fairly formally, members addressing one another as Mr . . . The two most important items were recommendations for promotion and a change to mixed ability teaching. On the first item there were four such recommendations, each made by a head of department, then the other heads of department commented on the boy in question. In most cases recommendations were widely supported, but where this was not the case, the matter was decided by majority vote. The discussion took about 15 minutes and was effective because people had come prepared. With about 25 in the room there was scope for time-wasting, but the head, who chaired the meeting, announced in advance when the meeting would end.

The change to mixed ability teaching was sufficiently fundamental as to suggest that agreement would be difficult to achieve, especially as the target was to begin nine months later. It was part of the policy of the LEA, which may have helped to gain agreement, but it was surprising that almost every departmental head supported the change, or at least was prepared to go along with it. Each department was asked in turn to state its view, giving reasons. Two problems that emerged were that parents were thought unlikely to support the change, so their reaction would have to be watched; and there was concern about how the severely disturbed boys would react, as they regarded a low ability stream as a sanctuary.

One head of department remarked that the support was so overwhelming that it was surprising the change had not been made already. It was pointed out that two departments had already successfully introduced mixed ability teaching, and this experience had inspired others to try it. The decision was to introduce it at the start of the next academic year, but to regard the introduction as an experiment from which they could withdraw. The need for in-service training and the development of new teaching materials was highlighted.

The meeting was completed on time and proceeded in a businesslike manner.

One head mentioned the value of setting the time at which the meeting would end and of reviewing each meeting before it broke up; this was a technique that he had picked up from the Teesside Industrial Mission when it ran a number of meetings for heads in the area.

Information flow

A fundamental problem in large complex organisations is how to achieve effective flows of information without overloading the communication channels. When organisations are set in a climate of change, the problem can become acute. The situation gets worse still when teachers withdraw their goodwill during industrial action and refuse to attend meetings at all.

Schools suffer from these problems more than most organisations partly because it is more difficult to assemble staff for communication meetings and partly because their matrix structure requires a great deal of information to be shared. When the grapevine beats the official communication channels, teachers' morale is impaired. This frequently happens.

At a school whose head was noted for good organisation, there was a regular pattern of weekly meetings for exchange of information, set into a school calendar. Agendas were recorded and records kept of discussion and decisions. The school office maintained a school diary, available to all staff for reference, and in addition a sheet was posted in the staffroom outlining the following week's events. There was also a monthly newsletter about activities and trips and a weekly bulletin for circulation to all staff and form groups (for communicating to pupils). This was supplemented by a staff bulletin posted weekly in the staffroom. Pigeon-holes for each member of staff and distribution trays were provided for more limited communication.

Much reliance is clearly placed on paper flow to achieve communication, and certainly a great deal is generated (in one school visited the media resources department duplicates 500 000 sheets per year, i.e. 500 per pupil). Communicators often make the mistake of assuming that the messages they have transmitted have been received and understood by the intended recipients. However, sometimes they never arrive, and teachers pressed for time do not always check their pigeon hole in the staff room.

In a business internal telephones are used for much communication, but in a school not only is the telephone system apt to be very basic, but also the teacher spends little time sitting by it.

I recall visiting a school in Atlanta, Georgia, in 1958, where every room and corridor was connected to an internal public address system;

not only could the head overhear any class being taken, but the system was capable of eavesdropping on conversations in lavatories. This was regarded in those days as one of the benefits of modern technology. Some British schools also boast 'Tannoy' systems but, perhaps in keeping with the style of some heads, the messages can only go one way.

Perhaps in a few years' time schools will be equipped with an electronic communications network, like British Telecom's Gold System, which would enable messages in oral, alphanumeric or graphical form to be sent out, stored and accessed at the recipient's convenience at the touch of a button. Meanwhile, complaints of poor communication are likely to remain hardy perennials in schools.

Some issues to consider

1   What criteria should be used to choose the basic organisation structure of a school (faculty, department, house, upper school, year etc.)?
2   Should there be a separate structure to handle financial, estates and certain personnel management aspects of school organisation, thereby freeing the head for the role of leading professional?
3   Should schemes of organisation be explicit and include role descriptions for staff?
4   Should there be staff manuals, and how detailed should they be?
5   Should there be a consultation system, and if so what should it aim to achieve? What should it avoid becoming?
6   What are the hallmarks of an effective committee structure?
7   What should the minutes of meetings look like, and how should they be used?
8   Is the timetable needlessly tyrannical? How can it best respond to new pedagogical approaches?
9   What is the best way of involving pupils in responsible school management and administration?
10   How should heads organise their work flow? What part should the school secretary play in this? What has 'information technology' got to offer?
11   How can discussion of trivia at meetings be contained, and time for dealing with important development issues be enhanced? Would visual aids help? Could inspectors or others weed out 'hardy perennials'?
12   What changes in schools' communication systems should be fostered over the next five years?

2.3 Ethos, philosophy and management style

The way an organisation is structured is by no means a full description of that organisation. It begs the questions: 'What sort of a place is this? What is it like to work in?'. Words like 'culture', 'climate', 'ethos', 'tone' and 'regime' are used to label this other feature of an organisation, and words like 'philosophy' and 'management style' are used to describe the head's distinctive contribution to it. The 'hidden curriculum' is a phrase sometimes used to refer to the pupils' experience of the school regime.

Reynolds, in reviewing British and American evidence on school effectiveness, concludes that it is the world of relationships and expectations, the informal, unstructured world or 'ethos', that seems to be more important than pupil:teacher ratios, class size, resources spent on each child and the formal organisational framework (Reynolds 1983, 1985a, b).

A feel for the culture can be obtained by reading the school prospectus, particularly if it enunciates the school's aims and summarises its dominant value system. However, prospectuses are not always full statements of how things are; they are more likely to be selective statements of how the head would like readers to think them to be.

Spending a day in a school affords many opportunities to pick up the flavours of what a school stands for, what it is like and what sort of leadership the head gives. A passing remark can speak volumes; so can what happens when the head encounters a pupil. In 1981 I visited an Army Apprentice College run by an officer from the Parachute Regiment. There were some 800 boys, the most recent intake having arrived two months before. As the commandant walked me round the college, we passed a score or so of apprentices. In every case he greeted each boy by name, and usually exchanged a brief conversation that demonstrated that he also knew *about* the boy, his progress and his family. The apprentices responded. By contrast, some comprehensive school heads and the children they met showed not a spark of mutual recognition. Others would demonstrate recognition and use the occasion for a comment, on untidy personal appearance, on ignoring some litter or on the dangers of running in corridors.

Staffrooms and classrooms also speak. There is all the difference between a staffroom stacked with overflowing ashtrays, dilipidated chairs, notice-boards groaning under the weight of out-of-date notices or plastered with political posters, and those that are tidy, comfortable, with indoor plants and neatly displayed announcements, for example about courses aimed at professional development. Classrooms can be dreary affairs, or they can provide a rich visual environment in which children's work is proudly displayed. Corridors in which window sills are decorated with tasteful pottery tell a different story from those that bear a discarded plastic cup or sweet wrapping.

In one school a new head had been appalled by the generally unkempt and shabby appearance of the school. After six months the place was transformed, and junior staff paid unsolicited tribute to her energy in tackling the problem.

The way the staff behave towards one another also carries a message. There was one school where it was not 'done' for staff to offer one another recognition and praise, except that the head was in the habit of giving bunches of flowers to women staff who had done something particularly well. By contrast there was another school, admittedly a small one, which was a model of mature and caring relationships, in which concern for people was well balanced against concern for task. The head had brought this about through personal example, through devolving responsibility and building trust, through enunciating the values by which she wished the school run, and through the use of social events to knit her team together.

The head of an independent boarding school described his approach to innovation as pragmatic; he susses out the ground and outflanks the opposition rather than imposing change. However, in successfully introducing work experience for the boys, he had insisted on this despite opposition, and even the opponents gave it a fair wind. He does not regard schools as democratic institutions, whatever lip service is paid to democracy. Sometimes people snipe at him on the basis of poor communication. What he tries to avoid is a head of steam building up; in a closed community, a small spark can cause a big conflagration, so as soon as he senses that rumours are starting, he quickly provides factual information. He thinks he gets good support from the common room, and that he presides over a remarkably tension-free school.

A somewhat different style was displayed by the head of a comprehensive school:

What people think schools ought to be determines what heads are. Broadly speaking, they are distrusted and are not seen as having much competence. They are also lonely people. They are believed to be amateurs at organising. This head's style is markedly diffent from his predecessor's; he affects a personalised style of management, and likes to arrange things informally. He taught in a London comprehensive during the 1960s, when democratic management was a major issue, but he believes there is a place for strong leadership. He certainly feels his own power as head. He tries to get teachers to work together within collaborative structures of management. Skill at interpersonal relations is highly important in this connexion. He is seen by his staff as Machiavellian, but he laughs with them at this and agrees. In his approach to change, he does not start off with a master plan for getting from A to B; rather it is a question of proceeding a step at a time by stealth, and finding ways round obstacles. Instead of always leading change himself, he gets teachers who are trusted by their colleagues to do so, and they front up his ideas.

One head noted that prospective parents judge a school's ethos from quite small cues; one had told him that she had read the signs of a good school from his choosing not to interview her from behind a desk, but rather by sitting informally beside her and her child.

There are, of course, pitfalls in gauging the ethos of a school from a day or two's visit, supplemented by a perusal of the school prospectus, staff manual, school rules, codes of conduct, minutes of meetings and other documents, even when they purport to describe ethos, principles and aims. Some would argue that, since appearances can be deceptive, sociological instruments such as climate questionnaires should be used.

Indeed, at one school visited, the head had already used the profile of organisational characteristics developed by Rensis Likert at the Institute of Social Research at the University of Michigan, USA, which has frequently been applied in industry (Likert 1967). He concluded that 'without exception the variables in question are both relevant and important to the functioning of a school. As an instrument of measurement the profile may not yield results which it would be wise to accept as proven scientific facts, but it will reveal certain patterns and trends on which careful attention may profitably be focused.'

The result was that the system of management at the school was characterised as 'consultative tending towards participative', with favourable group cohesion and supportive relationships. Other measured aspects of the organisation – leadership processes, motivational forces, communication processes and interaction/influence processes – all had reasonably favourable outcomes, though decision-making, goal-setting, control processes and training were more problematic, and received subsequent attention.

These findings (especially as regards training) were entirely in keeping with impressions gained during a day's visit in interviews with the head and his senior colleagues. Additionally, in a meeting with a cross-section of staff, they were uniformly appreciative of the open style of communication in the school and of the opportunities for involvement in its management. Further corroboration was provided by documents illustrating the consultative management structure and containing such statements as 'The consultative procedures of the school must also be so structured as to ensure that every teacher – no matter how inexperienced – feels that he or she is able to contribute to and participate in the formulation of policy'. The contribution of all staff to the school's ethos was also set out in job descriptions: 'willingness and enthusiasm to uphold the school's ethos and values', which were described in job application documents.

Cross-checks of this kind allowed some verification of inferences about school ethos. However, complete consistency was not always found; the staff handbook at one school contained the statement 'There are no School Rules! This statement is not meant to be perverse and unhelpful; it is meant to indicate the underlying philosophy of the school.' Yet on later pages there were statements like: 'Rings, ear-rings and other jewellery are inappropriate to the school situation and should not be worn. . . No running. . . Girls enter the coaches first.'

Thus, although unlimited resources and unrestricted access for administering sociological instruments and for conducting and cross-checking in-depth interviews throughout the school would no doubt provide a more reliable picture, yet even a day spent in a school can yield a meaningful pattern of clues to the school's ethos, and what managers do to influence it.

The following abridged notes from a full day's visit to a 900-pupil independent day school with junior and prep departments capture some of the features of the school which influence ethos.

The head is relatively young. Her previous experience was as a deputy head; she had specialised in careers teaching. She had had no formal management training before appointment (but had done an MA (Ed)), and did not even feel she had been trained on the apprenticeship model. However, since appointment she had been on a six-week management course at Woolley Hall and two courses at Roffey Park on selection interviewing and counselling skills. Like others on the staff, she had attended an Industrial Society course on leadership. As a result of these courses, she accepted the deputy head's strongly held conviction about the value of training and they both encourage it among the staff. They negotiated an increase in the training budget which has risen from £500 to £3000 in 1985 to a projected £5000 in 1986.

She and the deputy had introduced job descriptions for themselves and, after consultation with staff, for heads of departments and others; these are seen as systematic inputs to appraisal. Although there is no formal appraisal system yet (a staff working party was looking into this), the head and the deputy share the task of seeing all the staff once a year. Training needs are discussed and it is usual for form teachers, who are responsible for pastoral work, to go at some time on the Hamblin course on counselling at Swansea University, or to Bramley Grange.

The head spends about 30–40 per cent of her time on external affairs. Asked what her management problems were, she found it difficult to think of them, eventually saying that the main problem was to keep all the balls in the air and to push things forward. 'Things' included updating the school prospectus, producing a sixth form handbook, developing the curriculum (especially in the sixth form), developing pastoral care, finding time in the curriculum for more life and social skills training and for more craft, design and technology, and encouraging the new heads of the prep and junior schools to implement much needed changes. When prompted, she said she had only once had a problem with an unsatisfactory performer on the staff (who had been at the school for 25 years), soon after she had arrived. It was eventually solved when the member of staff decided to move elsewhere, after the head and deputy had made suggestions for improvement, then issued instructions (which were observed in the letter, not the spirit), then submitted a report to the governors and finally arranged a hearing of the case before the governors.

There were no industrial relations, staff discipline or salary problems; most of the staff belonged to AMMA and almost all the junior staff were on Scale 2 (though not in the junior school). Older members of staff saw pupil discipline as lax, and blamed management for not supporting them.

The school is introducing word processors into English teaching, in addition to the well equipped computer room. In this they have the help of an excellent computer technician, who not only services the equipment but also writes programs for them. Staff are well attuned to living with change, especially as it can be managed at the school's own pace, without interference from an LEA.

Most staff teach 30 periods out of 40, so have time for new developments.

While in post the deputy head had attended three week-long management courses at Brighton Polytechnic and Roffey Park, and also several shorter Industrial Society courses; she had previously run a department, as well as engaging in several extramural activities such as magistracy – clearly a woman of affairs, who had 'learned by doing'. After bringing up her family, she came back into full-time teaching, but found as second mistress that her management skills were not used. Instead she was submerged in trivia and spent her time on junior jobs, while the new head worked an 18-hour day. There was therefore a re-think of responsibilities. It was agreed that the load on the head should be relieved by delegating some of the deputy's trivial tasks to the school office. Other tasks such as exam timetabling and staff substitution were delegated to staff. Another secretary, with staggered hours, was taken on and the telephone system modernised. Although additional secretarial help relieved the teaching staff of some of their clerical tasks, some staff were critical and felt that the money might have been better spent on teaching. For their part the governors were concerned about rising administrative costs.

Both the deputy and the head visit the classes of new staff regularly, make notes, and discuss them afterwards with the teacher concerned. They try to be constructive, offering not too many criticisms at one time. One aspect they watch is whether the teacher treats the children as people, and offers them praise for good work. They also lunch with the girls (5–6 at a time), and although they do not specifically ask them for feedback on the teachers' competence, they do pick things up; also parents tell them, so they get some idea of who the good and the less good teachers are, though there is still scope for improving the review of classroom activity.

One of the heads of department is jointly responsible for co-ordinating the school's programme of personal and social development. Hers is an innovating department, with participative management; that is, all the staff discuss new projects and then make a group decision on how to proceed. While part of her management experience was gained from an anti-model (a teacher who was mentally ill and retired early on pension), mostly she takes her cue on management practice from the head, whom she regards as an excellent manager, always on the lookout for job enrichment experiences to stretch staff ('sharing the treats around'). The head is very good at finding ways round problems – 'getting diehards to crack'. Thanks also to the example set by the deputy head, the department always assesses what it is doing and conducts reviews regularly. It takes much of the stress out of management, makes the team happier and involves them in decisions. Indeed, it is a very close-knit team, despite having three new members. She has been on a team management course, one on interpersonal relationships and the Hamblin course on counselling. She reads a lot on management, for example Adair and D. Johns on leadership, the Schools Council Industry Project reports and the *Times Educational Supplement*. Although she is not over-stretched, since being efficient is a counter to stress, one of her staff is stressed, and she is helping her to set priorities. She makes known her own problems to her staff, and this encourages them to be open about theirs. In transactional analysis terms (she finds TA useful), she is a 'reservoir'.

Another head of department, though she had not been on any external courses, had learned management mainly from a number of experienced heads of departments and lecturers in the various schools and colleges that she had worked in before coming to this school; this gave her a good deal of practical experience. However, she applauded as 'fantastic' a school training day, when many opportunities were available. She defined the qualities of the head as an ability to put her finger on the pulse of what is happening, to look to the future and to be empathetic. The present head, ably assisted by the deputy, formed an excellent team, though there was some apprehension when she arrived, as she was so much younger than most of the staff. She dispensed with some of the rules they used to have, and discipline became more lax. Pastoral care was always good but is now tremendous, which helps discipline.

A third head of department recently organised Industrial Society 'Challenge of Industry' courses in the school. She had found her first term as a head of department traumatic and would have liked more support from colleagues. She had been on two counselling courses and thought the best way of dealing with stress was to raise generally the level of competence in pastoral skills among the staff. The head played a vital role in regulating the pressure on staff.

The last head of department interviewed had attended a very good course at Leeds University about her management role. Amongst other things, it had helped her understand the need for staff to have schemes of work. A head of department not only needed to devise these, but also was responsible for setting the ethos or philosophy in her department. She reviewed regularly the work of the department, finding out what went on and where were the areas of stress. She involved the staff in decisions and had an open relationship with them, so that they all said what they felt. Good schools, she thought, needed firm management.

This was clearly a good school, well managed by an unusually close team of head and deputy. The school has a simple set of four explicit aims. The head is a thoughtful person, deeply committed to her job, able to get the best out of people and widely respected by the staff.

The features of the school's ethos which emerge from this description include an unusually strong orientation towards staff development, backed by adequate funding, monitoring and support of teachers' performance, clear definition of roles (with the interesting complementarity of those of the head and the deputy), encouragement of curriculum development especially in the area of information technology, the participative management style of the English department, a good blend of educational values (a caring community) and efficient, businesslike administration.

Shorter thumbnail sketches of school ethos will help to illustrate the variety in the schools visited.

A A school in which the head, a man alert for detail, knew he had to set the tone but encountered resistance in the entrenched attitudes of some of his staff. To counter this he had evolved clear school aims, which he was trying to promote through the staff: 'The first aim of the school is to care for each child. Secondly the school aims to prepare a child to enter society at large as a happy, responsible person, able to contribute socially and economically to the full extent of his or her abilities. Discipline in the school aims to make the school a relaxed but not a lax place to be. A spirit of co-operation and social responsibility is fostered. It is the task of every teacher to instruct pupils in good manners in the classroom.'

B Another school that made its aims explicit (see Figure 2.1, taken from the prospectus). The head was an orderly administrator with clear vision and strong leadership qualities: 'I have a passion for education but a horror of teaching.'

Figure 2.1 Aims of school B

Aims

Aims are ideals and they are like stars in that though we may not reach them we use them to guide us. If we do not know where we are going, it is likely that we will end up somewhere else!

To recognize the individual's talents of all kinds and degrees and to develop this intellectual, physical and creative capacity.

To ensure that the curriculum serves the individual's needs.

To develop a curriculum which is flexible enough to respond to the sensible needs of students at different ages and stages.

To recognize the legitimate demands of employers, colleges, universities, polytechnics and examining bodies.

To recognize the legitimate demands of society as a whole with respect to adequate numeracy, literacy and other fundamental skills relating to the processes of communication; oral, written and visual.

To enable students to acquire the required education relating to the necessity to earn a living and, when appropriate, to enter into skilled occupations and professions.

To seek to measure the extent to which an individual is being successful in making the maximum use of natural gifts and opportunities.

To be rigorously selective in the material presented to students, bearing in mind the above aims and having particular regard to the following aims:

- The instilling of an attitude to learning that shows it to be a life-long process.
- The stimulation of intellectual curiosity.
- The direction and exercising of the emotions.
- The encouragement of discrimination.
- The development of the art of learning.
- The fostering of a capacity to tackle unfamiliar problems.
- The emphasizing of the need to differentiate between truth and lies and between fact and feeling with the associated understanding of the nature of evidence.
- The growth of understanding of the nature and importance of knowledge plus the involvement with the processes and resources of learning.

To recognize and accept difference in natural endowment and environment and to hold every individual in esteem as of right.

To accept responsibility for identifying the physical, aesthetic, creative, emotional and social needs of each individual student as a necessary starting point to satisfy these needs.

To maintain the school as a caring community emphasizing the central importance of good human relationships based upon sensitivity, tolerance, good will and a sense of humour.

To promote the understanding of the fact that the individual and the community have a reciprocal responsibility and that individual needs must at times be secondary to the greater need of a larger group; that collaboration and co-operation is a two-way activity.

To foster habits of responsibility, self-discipline, initiative, endeavour and individual judgment.

To obtain a positive response to the needs of a changing society whilst emphasizing established fundamental values and standards.

To promote the idea that the school is the servant of the community in both local and national terms and to accept the responsibilities which flow from this understanding.

To secure the active involvement of all people concerned with the school's welfare, staff, students, governors, parents and the Authority, in the continuous re-assessment of the aims and objectives of the school.

C In this school the head was managing the ethos in an unusually systematic way. He had used in the school a tool of behavioural science, the Likert style questionnaire (Likert 1967), and was trying to introduce a more participative culture. He had 'pushed management down the line' so as to try to get the school to run itself, although he had to step in during my visit by using his authority to discover who in the school had been responsible for removing all the chains from the boys' toilets. His staff appreciated his open style, his predisposition to delegate, his clear guidelines, good communication and good organisation. So apparently did his pupils; he was sufficiently confident of the influence of the school's ethos to trust a group of 'yobbos' (his phrase) to use the music room in the evenings unsupervised, and he was not disappointed.

D The head of this school used what he called a 'negotiating' style of management, and was a supreme organiser, to which his staff paid tribute. It had an open-door policy and went out of its way to attract visitors to the school, being prepared to accept outside criticism and feedback as a stimulus to improvement, which was systematised by means of a school evaluation process. Since the pupils imported many social problems from the underprivileged community that the school served, the level of stress was high, and the school was not short of pastoral problems among both pupils and a dedicated, overworked staff. An air of vitality was apparent in the school.

E This was a tough, even militaristic school, with discipline a perennial problem, as might be expected from its catchment area. The way in which discipline was administered by some of the hard-bitten teachers tended to be humiliating, and this exacerbated some of the problems. There was tension between the prevailing ethos and the head's personal style, which was open and self-disclosing; when displayed, it could rivet the boys' attention during assembly. This was a school in transition.

F This was also a school in transition; not only had the head started to open it to the community, but symbolically he had structurally altered his office and got rid of his 'gatekeeper' secretary, so as to make himself more accessible. Unlike his predecessor, he visited the staffroom often, walked the school, and encouraged staff and pupils alike to 'get permission on the hoof' rather than by formal applications to his office. He wanted to make the image of secondary school remembered by his pupils 'an object of warmth and affection, like that of primary schools'. Eventually he hoped it would become a school for all the community and not just for children.

G and H These schools were both characterised by the energy they were putting into building links with local industry – not only to prepare pupils to get jobs in a situation of rising unemployment, but also to bring in relevant management expertise.

I The head of this school managed by example; he was a mobile head, always to be seen round the school and rarely in his office. There was an air of easy informality, which was catching. Good practices were spotted and shared around; he spread them like a bumblebee. Consultation was well-developed, especially before innovation. He encouraged outside visits and visitors alike, delegated freely and 'stroked' his staff frequently when he found good work. It was a well-organised school, with a good public image.

J Likewise this school was strongly led. The new head had a clear vision of what she wanted the school to be like. The staff would be happy and confident. She believed the best way to care for children was to challenge them, not to protect them. The school was run by a system of accountabilities, rather than by coercive power. Decision-taking was to be crisp and clear, negotiation responsive but conducted with firmness. Efficiency and general appearance mattered, and the standard of both would be raised. The school's image would be assiduously cultivated. There would be no nonsense in this school; too much had been allowed in the past, through strong union pressure. The staff were beginning to appreciate, and to value, the nature of the change, and they could see the head earning the children's respect.

K This school, by contrast, was not on the move; it had arrived at where it wanted to be. The aims were explicitly Christian. The task was to educate rather than to teach. It was predominantly a child-based rather than a curriculum-led school, yet exam results were good; children were stretched, staff loyal and dedicated. The head described his style as 'pragmatic'; he was informal and flexible, preferring one-to-one consultation to elaborate committee structures, and he made the decisions.

L and M These two schools, in their different vivid ways, were very much in a state of change, with the past receding fast. The heads both had clear ideas of what changes were needed, and were busily engaged in bringing them about. One of the heads was deploying the paraphernalia of behavioural science applied to organisations; the other took his cue from Montgomery and action-centred leadership. Both were successful in leading their schools to new heights of performance. They have already been described as case studies of an innovative and developmental culture (Everard and Morris 1985).

N and O In these schools ethos was not an aspect that was explored; suffice it to say that, although in a rural area, both schools were alive to change and maintained above-average standards of academic performance.

P This school also boasted high standards, both of behaviour and of academic achievement. It clearly had a philosophy and aims, but these were unwritten and inexplicit; perhaps the phrase 'Victorian values' would sum them up, and the head's style, that of a 'benevolent autocrat', was in tune. Consultative systems were ill-developed. Some staff were (probably rightly) concerned about the growing dichotomy between the school's organisational culture and that of the business enterprises and other institutions in which many of the boys would subsequently seek employment; they thought that the 'wrong vibes' were being picked up, and the boys were in for a rude awakening. Although it would be misleading to call the school stick-in-the-mud, it did have a conservative outlook and was not well-placed for cultural innovation within the organisation.

Q This was a school also in the conservative tradition, reflecting the predominant values of the community and the style of the previous head. However, it was losing ground to neighbouring schools. The new head was therefore attempting to reinvigorate it, by tackling its complacency and opening it up to self-criticism and self-renewal. To do this he was introducing more effective management practices, though not without some pain; one member of staff said 'the school is a less friendly place now that it is run like a business.' Perhaps this is inevitable in a school that asks itself what it is in business for, and when survival is the name of the game.

R This school is a hive of bubbling activity; ideas abound. The culture is one in which development and innovation have become the norm. It exposes itself openly to outside influences by having a major programme of staff secondments, and in other respects also staff development is taken seriously. Much power is devolved. Pedagogically the regime is unusually child-centred for a secondary school, and there was even an example of children taking part in the development of the school's organisation. The school's reputation stood high 'in the trade'. Like school B, its aims were carefully thought out (see Figure 2.2).

Figure 2.2 Aims of School R

Aims

The school should, by its overt curriculum, its hidden assumptions and its style of day-to-day living, seek to help all children to come to terms with themselves both within the interior universe of their own personalities and within the community of other people; it would do this by seeking to foster the growth of individual talents, by providing the maximum opportunity for intellectual, emotional, spiritual and physical development within the school and society, by encouraging and liberating the desire to learn, to respect truth, and to seek wisdom and a capacity to love.

The aim of the school is to help the individual to come to terms with himself and his environment, and to improve both.

Objectives

1 *To dispel ignorance* by helping pupils to acquire socially useful knowledge and skills, such as literacy and effective communication in writing, speaking and action.

2 *To aid the acquisition of judgement* by encouraging the ability to listen, observe, discriminate, and the ability to use inductive and deductive processes.

3 *To enable pupils to come to terms with their physical and emotional development* by encouraging the development of self-control, self-awareness and self-esteem, by the practice of physical motor-skills and the development of self-confidence and a sense of responsibility.

4 *To help pupils to understand critically the cultural and physical environment, and encourage them to improve what can be improved and to learn to live with the rest.*

5 *To foster interpersonal relationships* by showing that living in a community (Hall or class group) entails accepting others, warts and all, rejoicing in their success and supporting them in their failures.

6 *To liberate the desire to be creative* by encouraging creative and recreative pursuits both inside and outside 'school time'.

7 *To fit pupils for the community outside the school* by providing the resources for pupils, as far as they are able, to obtain the qualifications, formal and informal, which society requires.

S This was the smallest school visited but it was not for this reason alone that the staff operated as an impressively well-knit, mature and mutually supportive team. The school practised an open door policy and was closely integrated with the community it served. Its approach to personal development, whether of pupils or staff, was exemplary. The appearance of the classrooms and staffroom bore testimony to the caring, competent and stimulating ethos of the school.

T This school, entry to which was oversubscribed, had a tradition of high academic standards, and was clearly managed with great efficiency, using modern technology for administration and having very well equipped classrooms. It had a businesslike air, yet a human face. Pastoral care was taken seriously, and in its provision of professional development experiences for its staff, it excelled all others.

Some issues to consider

1 What influences the ethos of a school? How can it be characterised, and how changed?
2 What part should the development of an explicit set of school aims play in shaping the school's ethos?
3 Is the head the key figure in determining the school's ethos, or do the collective values of the staff play the major part?
4 What management style on the part of the head is most conducive to developing an ethos supportive of learning and personal development?
5 To what extent should the school's ethos reflect the dominant values held in the community it serves?
6 Should the ethos be compatible with the prevailing ethos of organisations in which most pupils will seek employment?
7 Is a 'businesslike' approach to running a school at odds with 'human' values?
8 Of all the things that the head has to manage and shape, how important is ethos? Is it more influential than the formal structure?

2.4 Problems of managing schools

The primary aim of the fieldwork in my research was to identify problems of secondary school management. One method of doing this is to ask the head and other staff what *they* see to be the salient problems of running the school, and this indeed was one of the standard questions I put to them. However, an outside observer visiting a school may spot more problems than the head is aware of or admits to, because the former can apply yardsticks from his experience outside the school.

Moreover, the word 'problem' is not necessarily one that teachers construe in managerial terms, so they do not always call to mind situations that other managers would clearly see as problems. Additional ways of posing the question were therefore used as the research progressed, for example 'What do you see as the main issues with which you have to contend in your role as manager?' or 'Are there any things to do with running the school which make you lose sleep?'. If these questions failed to produce examples of problems, then leading questions such as 'Is your school short of money or textbooks?' or 'Have you any unsatisfactory staff?' were used.

Those heads who had been exposed to some systematic management development were far more articulate than those who had been pitched unaided into headship at the deep end; the former could reel off a dozen or so substantive problems. Older heads who had been been in the post for a long time appeared to be less aware of gaps between current situations and desirable situations. It was as though their life's work had resulted in their schools reaching the point which they wanted them to attain, so there was no further challenge. Although no retired heads were interviewed, when heads described their predecessors, a remarkably consistent picture came across, of men who had allowed their schools to stagnate, who were autocrats or despots, who ruled their schools (pupils and staff alike) with a rod of iron, who did not consult, who kept to themselves – often in their minds – most of the information needed to manage the school (even sometimes pupil records) and who had no concept of management or management structures. New heads, then, were always conscious of the problems they inherited from their predecessors in office.

The management problems mentioned in the schools visited fell into five distinct categories (Table 2.1) exemplified below. The absence of a 'curriculum' category can be attributed to the fact that problems in this area would be seen as part of their professional rather than their managerial role. Because of the overlap between problems to do with the LEA and those to do with resources, these sub-categories have been combined.

Table 2.1 Categories of problems

Category	No. of schools mentioning (n = 20)	Total no. of mentions (n = 135)
Staff problems	17	62
Administrative	12	30
Resources/LEA	10	23
Discipline	10	17
Salary/reward	9	11

The number of schools admitting to problems in each category is shown in the table, as is the number of occasions when such problems were mentioned, sometimes by several respondents at the same school, or by the same respondent in different ways. Because of the varying extents to which respondents were prompted by leading questions, these frequencies have no more than indicative value. In addition, because the sample of schools visited was neither large nor random, care is needed in generalising about the incidence of common problems in schools at large.

There is probably significance, especially for identifying salient staff selection and training needs, in the fact that staff problems easily outnumber the rest – including problems caused by children. There was a surprisingly low incidence of resource problems, such as shortage of money and textbooks, given the stridency of media comment on the effect of economic retrenchment on schools; almost all those reported resulted from a leading question. Only towards the end of the fieldwork (early 1985) was the unions' campaign of industrial action beginning to have serious effects on schools in the state sector. If my survey had started two years later, the effects of this campaign would probably have merited a category on its own and resources/LEA problems might have become more salient.

Staff problems

Only in this category did heads report problems of an intensity that caused them stress and loss of sleep. The sub-categories and incidence of problems in each are shown in Table 2.2.

Table 2.2 Categories of staff problems

Category	No. of mentions
Unsatisfactory performers	15
Stress	10
Hidebound behvaiour	10
Lack of motivation	6
Withdrawal of co-operation	4
Lack of recognition or support	4
Married Women's Protection Act	2
Industrial relations	2
Style or role incompatibilities	2
Difficulty of obtaining staff	1
Staff attitudes to children	1

Unsatisfactory performers

Few schools reported no serious problems of inadequate staff performance. This is not to say that the teaching profession is full of incompetent people, but that the relatively few there are have an influence on the head's peace of mind and the school's reputation out of all proportion to their numbers.

In one head's view, the greatest weakness he has to contend with is the professional standards of some of his heads of departments which he thinks are below an acceptable level. Heads of departments are primarily subject specialists and see their main objective as exciting the children about the subject. Teaching takes pride of place in their scheme of priorities, and they find it difficult to give adequate weight to managerial or administrative responsibilities. Their vision is narrow; they do not see education in the round; they are unwilling to cross subject barriers; they are extremely diffident about appraising their colleagues' teaching competence. This is seen partly as the result of the fact that their initial training never stressed managerial responsibilities, and partly because of poor selection of heads of departments. In the case of scientists, who can pick up higher salaries elsewhere, this is understandable, but the situation calls for much more intense in-service training to make the best of the teaching staff the school has got.

A similar story came from another comprehensive school head.

He had inherited a number of ageing staff in senior positions (Scales 3 and 4) who had been over-promoted and had lost such edge as they once had, so that they were doing just enough work to get by. He had also allowed himself to be over-ruled by his governors soon after his appointment, when a subject head was selected on their strong recommendation but against his better judgement, who had proved to be narrow and inflexible in approach. A recurrent problem with many of the older staff on Scale 3 was the difficulty of encouraging them to undertake duties outside what they perceived as the mainstream of their activities, namely active teaching. For such teachers, organising school activities and contributing to the general administration of the school were seen as an unwelcome and irrelevant diversion. They felt that they were paid to teach; it was the head and his deputies who were paid to administer. There were also non-teaching staff who had become set in their ways after long periods in their jobs doing much the same thing. When reorganisation necessitated a secretary undertaking additional typing duties to relieve overload elsewhere, this was resented even though she was under-occupied. Particularly with older members of staff, he found that attitudes became very entrenched. When he arrived at the school, he was clear what he wanted to be done, but did not wish this simply to be a matter for diktat. He expected the staff to offer their own views on any matter for him to take into account in reaching the eventual decisions and in implementing them. They, however, said they simply wanted to be told what to do and were not seeking to become associated with the decision. It was hard work for him to bring about a sense of collective ownership of decisions.

In some schools the inadequate performance of staff, usually at head of department level, was experienced as deeply serious, and contributed to the stress of the head's job in dealing with the consequences of incompetence, for example parental disaffection. Heads often felt powerless to influence the situation, which became like a running sore. Their hands were tied, or so they thought, by legislation, by the power of the teachers' unions and by lack of support from the LEA. Some thought the LEA inspectorate had a vital role to play in reviewing inadequate performance. They could see no practicable way of getting rid of unsatisfactory performers themselves, either because incompetence could not be proved, or because they could not face the hassle and odium of trying to make a case for dismissal. However, as other heads showed, this is a counsel of despair; progress in dealing with incompetence is not an impossibility, but it does call for patience and persistence.

Causes of unacceptable performance were seen as:

1   mistakes in original selection, especially where rapid expansion of schools had outstripped the supply of good teachers (often in scarcity subjects such as maths, science and CDT);

2   the effects of comprehensivisation, where adequate grammar school teachers had failed with 'Newsom's other half', or adequate secondary modern teachers were intellectually unable to deal with the more intelligent pupils;

3   victims of over-promotion to jobs in expanding schools, where the teacher had failed to grow with the job;

4   'burnt out' or 'turned off' ageing staff who barely did enough work to get by;

5   failure to accept standards of behaviour conducive to the smooth running of the school, for example coming to work inappropriately attired, or using the school as an arena in which to make obtrusive political or ideological stands (though the mere holding of extreme views clearly did not itself constitute 'unsatisfactory performance').

The principal manifestations of unsatisfactory performance were ineffective teaching of the children and/or inability to control them. Lack of initiative, laziness and neglect of duties were also mentioned.

The response of heads and deputy heads to unsatisfactory performance varied. One head cajoled and put the fear of God into the culprit. Another (in Scotland) appealed to the sense of honesty – an unsatisfactory performer was not giving good value for money. Another moved weak teachers around, until they found that there was something they *could* do. Another gave consistent, clear, oral feedback about all aspects of performance, good and bad, studiously recording on paper every single misdemeanour, and regularly showing the record to the teacher. Another saw to it that the weak teacher's role was precisely defined and that good mechanisms existed for him to observe and emulate good practice in other parts of the school. Another went to some trouble to to set the teacher up in a non-teaching job, which used his hobbyist skills in picture-restoring. Another created a new deputy head role, and got the incumbent to 'carry' the weak performer.

The head of an independent boarding school said that on the whole he had been lucky not to have inherited any unsatisfactory staff. At his previous school, however, this had not been the case, and it was very difficult to deal with these situations because of industrial relations problems. He spoke of one teacher whose resignation he had obtained in 24 hours, by writing a carefully worded letter which he had checked with a lawyer; this had been a man with a responsibility allowance of £3500 but who was simply idle. His technique with the unsatisfactory performer was to lose no opportunity to let him know what he thought of him, both face-to-face and on paper. On one occasion he had been threatened with legal action on the grounds of constructive dismissal, and when the teacher had said he would arrange to be represented, the head said he would too; whereupon the man agreed to take early retirement. On another occasion, a teacher giving unsatisfactory performance had pulled himself back from the brink and had stayed on.

Two schools stood out for the systematic way in which they were tackling the problem of the unsatisfactory performer. One went to a great deal of trouble to define precisely the teacher's role; then any successes in performing the job were identified and disseminated; weaknesses were also identified, and various support systems provided; and the LEA inspector was brought into the situation to provide counsel and advice.

At the other school a deputy head, who clearly had unusual talents in the field of personal development and interpersonal skills, worked very closely with the teacher in regularly reviewing his performance, agreeing with him priorities for improvement, setting improvement objectives and surrounding him with both academic and emotional support. After a frustrating lack of success at first, her patience was eventually rewarded, and the teacher began achieving beyond her expectations. Having once tasted success, he was, at the time of my visit, set fair to cope with his job adequately. Intensive coaching of this kind takes up a good deal of time, however, and there are limits to what can be achieved when the basic aptitude is not there.

'Unsatisfactory performance' is a portmanteau phrase, signifying that the teacher concerned is generally not up to the job. Related to it are three other categories which are described in more specific terms: withdrawal of co-operation, lack of motivation and hidebound behaviour. These are more like 'sins of omission', whereas the general category covers incidents where the teacher does something that the head thinks ill-advised.

Withdrawal of co-operation can amount to downright disobedience, such as a refusal on the part of some staff to take a fair share of duties other than teaching, for example attendance at parent/teacher evenings. Then there were heads of departments who would not collaborate in the head's attempt to introduce consultation procedures in the school; they dismissed consultation as 'just a management game'. Another school had had problems with unofficial strikes. In addition to individual acts of defiance, there were towards the end of the study the orchestrated protests, called for by some teachers' unions, at the government's economic cuts, and at the unsatisfactory outcome of pay negotiations.

Lack of motivation covered situations such as unwillingness to take up INSET opportunities that were offered to staff who needed training; the stagnation of staff whose career aspirations had been thwarted by contraction in the education service, especially those who had been repeatedly passed by for promotion; and the effects of low morale and negative attitudes to the teaching profession. Several heads thought that these were deeply serious problems.

Hidebound behaviour consisted of general resistance to change. Typically, it was the failure of individual teachers to change their pedagogical styles or to adapt in any way to the demands of a whole school curriculum policy. They construed their mission as enthusing children with a liking for the subject they taught, and in this they were often successful, at least with some of the children. The trouble was that they could not relate what they were doing to the wider demands of society, the pupils or the school. Innovations in educational technology and such interventions as the technical and vocational education initiative (TVEI) were opposed as a matter of course. Newly appointed heads were particularly conscious of hidebound behaviour, because it was an obstacle to the reforms and developments they wanted to introduce; nor did it arise only when changes were imposed. In three schools the behaviour was described as a refusal to see or respond to the managerial aspects of their role as head of department; they simply saw themselves as 'leading professionals' in their subject, but not as part of the management team. They had no understanding of nor empathy for the head's role and rejected the sharing of managerial responsibility by saying 'That's the head's problem; that's what he's paid for. I'm paid to teach, and I'm not going to be diverted from that.' Such attitudes are probably more common than they appeared.

Legislation etc

Among the categories where problems were infrequent were two that could seriously impair the effectiveness of the school. The Married Women's Protection Act allows female staff who leave to have babies to claim their jobs back later. It proves for some schools an insuperable problem to maintain the quality of teaching during their absence, since satisfactory short-term replacements are not available. Another problem arose when unions had negotiated some concession, such as time off in lieu of work done after school, which had not been compensated for by taking on additional staff as cover. 'Ring-fence' policies can militate against school effectiveness, when vacancies are allowed to be filled only from within the county where they arise; sometimes this leads to unsatisfactory performers being foisted on a school, when there are excellent candidates from farther afield.

In some subjects and geographical areas problems arise because of the difficulty of attracting or retaining able staff; on the other hand, there are clearly some highly competent teachers at work in districts that can hardly be called salubrious.

As can happen in any organisation, there are occasional problems of style incompatibility, for example when a new head finds himself at odds with one of his deputies, and friction results. This can spread more widely, such as when a head who does not believe in corporal punishment and who dislikes teachers' disparaging attitudes to children, arrives in a school run as though it were a prison or old-fashioned army barracks.

Stress

Finally there are the human problems of stress and the lack of an adequate support system for handling it. This problem seems to be widespread and ought to be a matter for considerable concern. Stress is no respecter of hierarchies; indeed the head is probably as much at risk as anybody, and there were indications at one or two schools visited that the expectation of a stressful life had dissuaded otherwise well-qualified people from applying for senior posts; they shunned the responsibility. Even the staff of well-managed small schools in comparatively well-to-do areas report that a high level of stress is part of the job. In areas of social deprivation, where the pupils import problems into the school, matters are worse. For example, in one school visited, there had been five attempted suicides among pupils in a week, and staff absences were giving cause for concern. Where 'Blackboard Jungle' conditions do exist, it is hardly surprising that teachers with a strong sense of vocation and a caring attitude towards children experience stress. However, even in more normal conditions, the constant exposure to a class of demanding children, the tyranny of the timetable and the endemic shortage of recovery time to catch up with with the pace of events, is bound to lead to stress. The situation is exacerbated both by the low public esteem in which the teaching profession is held, and by the primitive support systems that exist for helping teachers who succumb to stress.

Most heads (though not all) say that they have very lonely jobs, like the captain of a ship; they have no-one but their spouses (if any) to turn to when matters begin to get too much for them. This is not a healthy situation. It is part of what Taylor has described as 'the unacceptable face of headship' (Taylor 1983). He surveyed the onset of stress in a series of interviews with heads, and paints a frightening picture of how it is destroying job satisfaction and leading to 'burn-out'. It builds up from the sheer weight of externally imposed change, adding cumulative burdens as each new demand surfaces before the effect of its predecessor can be absorbed. Political and union activity and abrasive teacher professionalism adds to the pressures, and there is a lack of urgency, in Taylor's view, about displaying concern for the head's emotional wellbeing.

Role conflict, for example between the leading professional and the chief executive role, can induce stress, as can conflict in the roles of the school itself (teaching, custodial, certification, socialising etc.). There are more elements of unpredictability in a teacher's job than in many other occupations, and management by crisis seems to be more prevalent. Ill-disciplined children can be masters of stress creation, and petty squabbles in the staffroom can cause teachers to turn in on themselves. There are many teachers who are badly trained for the jobs they are expected to do, and the resulting sense of incompetence is disturbing and self-feeding. For example, they may be plunged by edict into accepting mixed ability teaching, or new courses such as the Certificate of Pre-vocational Education may call for teaching styles different from those to which they are accustomed. At senior level, political pressures for major change can set the head between the upper millstone of the LEA and the nether millstone of the staff. Lack of information about the future of a school experiencing falling rolls, with all the implications for the teachers' livelihoods, is another problem hitting many schools and causing stress. The arrival of a new head can cause anxiety among the less secure staff.

While some pressure and challenge in a job are features contributing to effectiveness, stress becomes a problem when it starts to disable people and sap their confidence in themselves. Some of the problems of unsatisfactory performance may be the result of stress.

Administrative problems

Under this category over half the schools reported a multiplicity of irksome, time-consuming problems that detracted from the smooth running of the school and caused at times immense frustration. In one way or another they represented failures of the system, partly within the school, but mostly in the local authority's systems.

In one school it had taken a deputy head two months and 50 telephone calls to get a Xerox machine installed and working. In another, pottery kilns had been out of use for a term and a half because of scares over asbestos insulation. Central heating and gas cookers were not working, and workmen to put them right were unavailable. Glass panes were falling out of rotting window-frames on to footpaths in high winds, and no-one could be obtained to make them safe. A swimming pool could not be used because there was a dispute as to who should chlorinate the water. Senior LEA officials were unavailable to deal with urgent matters because they in turn were dealing with the demands of elected members on education committees. Money and time were wasted in buying through the county library books that were on display more cheaply in local bookshops, and no-one would give the head the authority to circumvent the system. An antiquated, labour-intensive telephone installation obstructed measures to improve efficiency in the school office, and junior officials in county hall were blocking replacement. Promises on the part of local authority officials were repeatedly not kept.

Some of the more highly paid teachers realised that they should not have to spend so much time on progress-chasing activities which in an engineering firm would be delegated to some junior, but persistent, technical clerk. Other heads had come to accept, and had ceased to question, the fact that much of their time was spent on solving problems that had been delegated upwards; after all, no-one else had the necessary 'clout'. The more astute heads and one or two heads of departments who had built up a track record for getting things done despite the system, had carefully cultivated their personal relationships with key 'gate-keepers' to LEA resources and services, and managed to play the 'old boy network' in order to achieve results.

Although some schools appeared to operate in an environment of bureaucratic inefficiency and lethargy, which must add to their running costs and detract from their effectiveness, this was by no means true of all. One of the independent sector schools was a model of efficiency as regards maintenance of the fabric and development of better facilities. It was not just a question of being able to afford good ancillary services, because in fact they had to be very careful in spending money; it was more a question of organising themselves to be efficient and creating expectations among the maintenance staff that jobs would be done as required and on time.

Local authorities vary in the extent to which they devolve on to schools responsibility for the fabric; those schools that were allowed to employ local firms direct, rather than council workmen, or better still, had skilled all-purpose handymen of their own, were more content with their lot. Even so, a deputy head who found himself having to deal with contractors without having had training or experience in doing so, confessed that he had a hard time.

In some cases problems arose because it was not clear where the responsibility lay, as between the school and the authority, for dealing with some problem; for example, are curtains part of the fabric of the building (LEA responsibility) or are they equipment (school)?

Administrative problems within the school and totally within its control were also often caused by people's unreliability. I have already quoted the example of a sheaf of reports that had gone missing (p. 19). Those heads who placed value on efficient organisation found it a constant problem that carefully designed schedules for getting a set of interlinked activities completed were thrown out because some staff repeatedly failed to meet agreed deadlines. At another school important messages and instructions in the staff bulletin were not being read. Several schools quoted instances of problems caused by lack of forward planning, for example in arranging for a school journey, resulting in the absence of rail tickets and packed meals. Some problems were caused by lack of co-ordination when different activities took place on the campus, for example when more than one caretaker worked overtime for an evening event, when one would do, or where community centre activities clashed with those of the school.

These kinds of problems took their toll on morale; when issues were constantly brought up at staff meetings and went unresolved, this turned people against meetings because they were unproductive and wasted time. By contrast, there are teachers whose early experience helps them to grapple with administrative problems, without relying on the head's 'clout'.

The head of design studies at one comprehensive school had become particularly interested in management, having himself run a business before entering the teaching profession, and this enabled him to take a critical look at aspects of organisational efficiency. For example, he was working with the Authority to extend powers of virement; he had made out a reasoned case for modernising the whole telephone system in the school and had afterwards demonstrated that substantial savings had resulted; he was now working on the school heating system, to make economies through zone control. Next on his list was the computerisation of the accounts system. He had learned his way round the Authority's expenditure sanctioning system; normally cases for modernisation were accepted if a pay-back period of five years or less could be demonstrated. He saw himself more as a facilitator than a decision-taker, since he did not have the authority to take decisions across the school. These tasks required a distinct expertise, especially in interpersonal skills, in which he regarded most teachers as untrained; as a result, schools had what he called 'Band-aid' management systems. He had concluded that there was a good case for large schools to have bursars, who would look after such administrative matters professionally, and be responsible for maintenance.

Resources and relationships with LEAs

As has already been mentioned, there were surprisingly few complaints about the lack of the financial resources needed to run the school. Indeed, one or two heads hinted at overprovision, in the sense that money was being spent on some things unnecessarily and unwisely, because it was there to spend, and it was thought important always to use up one's budget allocation. Such heads regretted that cost-effectiveness, or getting good value for money, was not an important value in the education system; and one head of department, who had been seconded to industry, explained that schools did not take their budgets very seriously, so that by comparison with industry there was a lack of financial control. On the other hand, a bursar said that teachers were responsible people by nature, and the prevailing attitude towards expenditure in his school was 'frugal', so he sometimes had to press departments to invest in new equipment and textbooks.

LEAs clearly vary widely in their control of educational purse-strings. At one school in a rural area the Authority had to spend a great deal of money in bussing children to school, and this, as a consequence, caused shortages of resources elsewhere, for example in a refusal to fill key vacancies without long delays. Their attitude towards the employment of clerical staff and laboratory technicians can only be described as skinflint. Even in 'rich' authorities there was not a generous provision of non-teaching support staff, from bursar to copy typist, and this led to qualified teachers devoting a disproportionate amount of their time to humdrum tasks such as photocopying.

Another category of under-resourcing is INSET. Several heads with plans for curriculum development were thwarted by paltry allocations for staff training. Even where there is earmarked DES support, as in management training, it was reported that authorities could still contrive to divert grants away from education.

Expenditure on items of direct benefit to children, such as computers, textbooks, minibuses and outings, was widely supplemented with funds raised by parent-teacher associations and the like, even in areas of social and economic deprivation. Heads reported that, if the necessary fund-raising effort was put in, there would always be a generous response.

Those authorities that were experimenting with devolution of financial control were supported by heads, sometimes enthusiastically, despite the additional worries to which such responsibility can give rise. It was felt that powers of virement could usefully be increased in the interests of cost-effectiveness, as there was an interplay between capital investment and the school equivalent of productivity. The case study at the end of the previous section exemplifies this. Moreover, when spending decisions were centralised, they were often taken by LEA officials of low calibre (paid much less than heads) who, never having visited a school, had little idea of the effects of their decisions. One school that had encountered this had invited such offficials to come and look round the school, and it had been an eye-opener for them; it had also seconded a teacher to an LEA audit department, to good effect. Such transfers were, however, rare and the inability of LEA staff and teachers to visualise one another's problems remains a source of ineffectiveness.

Role relationships between heads and their LEA contacts varied from the excellent, through the cordial to the very poor. At the excellent end, the head was a member of the Education Committee, and made it her business to invite education officers and advisers into the school, where they were warmly and hospitably received and introduced to the staff; in that school there were no barriers and a good deal of mutual trust and respect. At the other end one had the impression that a political vendetta was being pursued; certainly the level of trust was disquietingly low.

Relationships between the school and the LEA were described as very poor. The Authority's ethos and bureaucratic procedures ran counter to those of the school, and were a straitjacket on what needed to be done. The preferential appointment of county teachers, instigated by the unions, was a case in point. While it was agreed to be necessary to take on redeployed staff, it was not thought reasonable to do so for other staff. Low trust exists between the LEA and schools, instanced by the LEA insisting on seeing job descriptions before placing advertisements, and wanting the names and addresses of all applicants. Questioned on why heads do not attempt collectively to influence the wider system of which they are victims, this head said that the cult of professionalism got in the way.

In between were the heads who were indeed at risk of conflict with their LEAs, knew it, but who carefully read the signs of shifting political winds, anticipated demands and 'sailed' their schools neatly between the rocks and the shoals.

The kind of conflict situation that could arise is illustrated by staff appointments. Heads might have a clear idea of the job and person specification they needed in filling a vacancy. They would then come up against a ring-fence policy and be presented with a list of throw-outs from neighbouring schools (or so the grapevine told them), who could not hold a candle to applicants from other counties. They could then end up being obliged, in effect, to import trouble rather than talent into their schools, to the detriment of the children.

Sometimes LEA structures could be an impediment to change, as when a school lay on the boundary between one authority and another, each with diametrically opposed policies; one might consistently block, and another rubber-stamp, the advice of the professional educators.

Even in authorities that heads generally praised as enlightened, problems of communication between the LEA and the school were endemic. The grapevine operated more quickly than the official channels, and this had a bad effect on industrial relations. Sometimes there would be partial information, such as a target to close 30 per cent of the secondary schools over the next 15 years, and in the absence of guidance on selection criteria or processes for making decisions, unnerving rumours would spread about a move towards sixth form colleges in response to falling rolls.

One head said that the quality of communication between the LEA and its schools is poor. Instructions to schools arrive too late to improve them if they are inept, as they sometimes are, for example as regards preserving harmonious industrial relations. LEA decisions on staffing are taken behind closed doors and announced late, instead of tapping the considerable accumulated experience in the schools. In major decisions, the county seldom asks heads for advice. The extent to which a head has to 'make himself a nuisance' in order to get anything from the LEA is counter-productive.

Because schools, LEA officials and Education Committees are partners in providing an education service, it is clearly important to develop an effective *modus operandi*. However, in some areas this does not exist, and there are few signs of any initiatives likely to improve the situation; indeed, a climate of contraction following a long period of growth is exacerbating it.

Salaries and rewards

Most of the schools in the state sector, though none in the independent sector, quoted the teachers' salary and reward system as an obstacle to improvement. They envied the supposed greater freedom of their counterparts in industry to use the system as a tool of good management. They were quite clear that the present system is unjust and counter-productive. Teachers are not rewarded according to their contribution, and heads are frustrated by their inability to give tangible recognition to outstanding performance. They also deplore the low level of salaries in the profession. It is felt that there is a considerable element of unfairness in heads' own salary scales, because the demands on the manager of an organisation do not increase with its size according to the same relationship that governs that between salary and size of school. The result of this is claimed to be a growing difficulty in persuading people to accept responsibility for running a large school; able deputy heads, watching the demands placed on their heads, just do not want promotion in a large school.

The scale points system imposes a rigidity on the organisation which can seriously detract from its effectiveness. For example, some staff reorganisation may be needed to solve a problem or to capitalise on an opportunity, yet if the scale point jigsaw pieces cannot be fitted into place, the whole development is blocked. In the independent sector (of which a number of state school heads have had personal experience), this would not happen, because heads have discretion to make sensible adjustments to the normal rules of salary administration. Moreover, when teaching staff are not unionised, no-one raises petty points of principle. Greater freedom to reward excellence appropriately in the independent sector must constitute one reason why the state sector loses some outstanding teachers, though the élitism of the public schools is not everyone's cup of tea. Some heads rue their inability to demote less competent teachers by docking their salaries, believing that this is common practice in industry (even though it is probably less prevalent than they imagine).

What measures can heads take to reward high performance, given also that the effect of contraction is highly geared to promotion opportunities? Some go out of their way to award frequent verbal bouquets. They miss no opportunity to mention meritorious conduct in reports to governors. They publicly praise good deeds in the school. They write commendatory notes. They might give a present (presumably paid for out of their own pockets). Their whole management style is oriented towards identifying and recognising good performance, but only in a sincere way and not by empty flattery. Curiously, however, praise is not always received in the way it is intended; in some school cultures, where good performance is considered the norm, fulsome praise can be embarrassing, and lead to questions like 'What was I doing wrong before, that he now sees fit to praise me?' You cannot win all the time!

Discipline

Half the schools mentioned pupil discipline as one of their problems, and even in a school where it was a minor problem the head remarked 'My nightmare is not having good order and discipline in the school'. The general picture that emerged from the visits, no matter how 'good' the school, was of heads and deputies battening down hatches to contain the explosive forces within. Whether they were reflecting the view that society as a whole is unstable, with the seeds of revolution already planted, is not clear; what did come across is a definite edginess on the part of management that things are liable to get out of control unless they are very careful. It cannot be a comfortable feeling.

At one of the schools that had introduced a staff appraisal scheme, the head reported that pupil discipline was the most frequent issue to come up for discussion at interview. A deputy head had found that the old-fashioned methods of discipline were no longer effective; instead of winning his battles, now all he could do was to try to avoid losing them. Miscreants might go unpunished, but it was vital to gain their attention while they were being told that they had done wrong. The knack required was to judge wisely which misdemeanours were really serious and tackle those firmly; the rest had to be ignored. Presumably there is some order of seriousness in which to rank running in corridors, dropping litter, removing toilet chains, truancy, theft, vandalism and violence – these being examples of incidents at the time of my visits.

In schools where corporal punishment had been in use, teachers felt let down when a new head who did not believe in it failed to beat pupils sent to him for the purpose. In another school, where standards of discipline had slipped, the new head was praised when she introduced corridor patrols and took a firm line by expelling pupils who regularly misbehaved. Also praised was the schoolkeeper who had been an NCO in the services, and who used the personal authority of a sharp tongue to maintain discipline and support the teachers. There were teachers who questioned the efficacy of their colleagues' methods for keeping good order; they thought it wrong to talk down to the pupils, to browbeat them, to impute evil motives without evidence and to operate a militaristic regime.

Some teachers try hard to identify the cause of misbehaviour and do what they can to eradicate it, perhaps counselling pupils how to cope with their less than perfect family circumstances. Another approach is to regroup classes where disruption has become the norm, to break up coalitions of miscreants. One school tried to build up pressure in the peer group to control misbehaviour. Some had units for dealing with children with special needs, to which the gifted, the educationally subnormal and the violent were all sent.

In certain areas truancy was a major headache, and in one school so affected they went to some trouble to develop special curricula to try to interest the less motivated pupils. One head had noticed that subjects like woodwork, which at one time interested most boys, now no longer appealed; and he ascribed this to the intellectualisation of practical subjects, whereby, for example, exam marks were awarded more for the ability to describe in writing what a marking gauge is for, than ability actually to use one.

Other problems

The above-mentioned problems presented themselves directly during interviews with teachers; there were others that could be inferred from the visits yet which were not specifically identified by the schools.

The first to strike me was the absence in many schools of an explicit statement of purpose or aims, and in most schools of any precise objectives. If there was a sense of direction, it did not come across. The managerial task was simply to deal with events as they happened, not to develop and instil a philosophy or sense of purpose to act as a touchstone for activity. In one school where thought had been given to aims, the head had concluded that the pluralistic aims that society expected schools to achieve were incompatible; there was therefore no practicable alternative but to muddle through. Perhaps there is some truth in the view that society expects the impossible of schools, and therefore crisis management is more practical than far-sighted leadership. Nevertheless, some schools, exposed to the same expectations and dilemmas, appeared to know where they were going and could describe what they intended to achieve.

The second problem is the absence in most schools of a capacity to adapt to circumstances at a rate commensurate with that at which circumstances change. They shared the problem of the dinosaur, living in hope that things would return to normal soon. Indicators of the problem were: being out of touch with the world outside school; never having enough time to get together and think; lack of understanding of how you manage change; deeply ingrained habits of thought and practice; coalitions of forces conspiring to resist change; absence of support systems such as third party consultation; lack of basic training or understanding of problem-solving methods; and lack of awareness of organisational processes.

The third problem is contextual; the way in which schools are embedded in and linked to the education service as a whole is sub-optimal. Key decisions, such as appointments of heads, and education policy, are taken in the wrong way with the wrong knowledge by the wrong groups of people in the wrong place. For example, the decision to end selective entry and to move from specialist to comprehensive schools may be justified on grounds of ideology, social engineering, equity and educational values, but if it stretches teachers beyond their capacity to teach or managers to manage, is it the correct decision? It could be, if the decision-makers always willed the means (such as adequate INSET) as well as the ends.

A fourth problem is that of morale. There is a strong undercurrent of discontent in the teaching profession, symptoms of which in the state sector are withdrawal of goodwill, industrial action, and the feeling of being victimised by society and its elected representatives. This is the result partly of the low esteem in which they are held by the public – exacerbated by ministerial pronouncements, unfavourable and exaggerated media comment and by the public postures of the more militant teachers' unions – and partly of a failure to come to terms with deep-seated societal changes and economic trends to which education is particularly vulnerable. Such a situation needs countering with positive attitudes and effective leadership from those in senior positions in the education service. This is not always forthcoming. Instead, the general dissatisfaction is being exploited in an attempt to discredit government policies for dealing with the country's economic malaise and to increase pressure for education (and specifically teachers) to be given a bigger share of the national cake. Even so, teachers' salaries are hardly commensurate with their responsibilities in society.

A fifth problem is mainly financial; at least in the state sector, too small a proportion of the available resources is used to support innovation and development – of curricula, staff, pedagogy and educational technology. The available funds and human resources are over-committed to the support of existing operations, leaving little discretionary resource for dealing with much needed innovation. Even when such funds are made available, as with the introduction of computers and school management training, either there is paltry follow-up support all round or (as with TVEI) a tiny proportion of schools benefit. The issue is how to increase resources for development at a time when overall resources are stagnant or even contracting.

To some extent these five problems are connected and I shall return to the over-arching problems in section 2.15. It is difficult to avoid the conclusion that structural reform is needed, although some schools do seem, against all odds, to overcome most of the problems that the DES, LEAs and Education Committees erect around them.

Some issues to consider

1   Is an analysis of the incidence of problems a reliable guide to priorities in improving school management and organisation?

2   How can the interests of pupils be properly balanced against the interests of the unsatisfactory performer among the staff?

3   What are the most effective methods for identifying and dealing with unsatisfactory performance by teachers and managers?

4   What preventative measures should a head adopt to avoid teachers becoming hidebound in their approach?

5   What can be done to help teachers, and particularly heads, to cope better with the stress in their lives?

6   What is it about well-run organisations that enables them to get essential work (for example, maintenance) done efficiently, promptly, unobtrusively and without constant badgering? How can such conditions be brought about in schools?

7   What structural and attitudinal changes should be made to encourage more cost-effective expenditure in schools (including more investment that will pay for itself)?

8   What is the single most important initiative that heads can take to improve the effectiveness of the relationship between their Education Committees, LEA officials and schools?

9   Should outstanding performance by teachers be rewarded? If so, how can this be done when promotion opportunities are declining?

10   What assumptions about human behaviour underlie the school's approach to discipline? Are there alternatives? If so, how can they be tested?

11   Given that problems in schools are endemic, how can the capacity to solve them be increased?

12   What are the chief causes of policy decisions being taken which generate in schools a disproportionate number of problems? What can heads do to ensure that wiser decisions are made?

2.5 Financial management

The cost of educating a pupil in the maintained sector up to the age of 16 is over £8000 (CIPFA 1981–2). Both the capital value and the annual expenditure of a school having 500 pupils or more will normally be measured in millions of pounds, but only in the independent sector are these sums under the direct control of the head. In the state sector management of the capital assets and of the staff payroll is in the hands of the local authority, which leaves heads with budgets of only tens of thousands of pounds over which they have full control. Nevertheless, all heads are responsible for the purposeful and effective utilisation of both the capital assets and the human resources in their schools.

Increasingly, however, their responsibilities extend beyond the control of expenditure; they are involved in resourcing activities and equipment for which no (or inadequate) LEA capitation provision exists. Apart from letting income, heads administer school funds, and parent-teacher associations help to maintain them. Schools are having to run more fund-raising activities, such as school subscriptions (ranging typically from 30p per pupil to £2 per family per year), locker rentals, Christmas draws, jumble sales, school photographs, levies on club activities and on school visits. These are used, for example, to heat swimming pools, decorate the fabric, provide additional textbooks and special items of equipment, buy a minibus, subsidise the purchase of school uniform and pay for social functions. Expenditure from such funds can be well over 10 per cent of capitation allowances. Table 2.3 gives some indicative figures for a comprehensive school of 1400 pupils in 1983–4.

Table 2.3 A comprehensive school budget.

		£
	Salaries etc	900 000
	Textbooks, stationery, materials	30 800
	Furniture, fittings, equipment	22 700
Capitation	Examination expenses	18 000
allowances	Educational visits	1 500
	Cleaning	2 200
	Laundry	150
	Oil	31 000
	Electricity	12 000
	Gas	2 000
	Water	2 000
	Telephone	4 000
	Postage	1 700
	Miscellaneous	14 000
	School fund expenditure	8 000
	Total	**£1 042 050**

With the involvement of the MSC in secondary school curricula through TVEI, heads have another source of funding to tap through the LEA. In one school that was planning to collaborate with an Information

Technology Centre (ITEC) in providing a computer service to local farmers, with help from the European Social Fund, there was yet another potential source of funds, in selling a service. Likewise an independent school was selling electronic kits to its feeder prep schools. As economic stringency bites into the traditional funding for state school activities, it may be that heads will have to become entrepreneurial and exercise greater ingenuity in tapping new sources of money in order to sustain desirable levels of expenditure in their schools.

Such autonomy is being deliberately encouraged; thus some authorities, notably Cambridgeshire, are currently experimenting with major devolution of financial responsibility, giving heads powers of virement and authority to buy in services. Others delegate to heads some responsibility for minor maintenance of the buildings, while some permit only the Authority's own workmen to maintain their schools. ILEA, with its alternative use of resources scheme, is giving heads wider discretion, but not in all expenditure categories. Within schools, however, delegation of financial responsibility is normally very limited, with only the head permitted to authorise the payment of invoices. Not infrequently, heads allocate their capitation allowances without consulting departmental heads. The independent schools, and sometimes voluntary aided schools in the state sector, employ a bursar to handle the financial side of the school's affairs.

In an independent day school visited, the bursar explained that when he was managing director of a manufacturing firm he had been used to a clear management structure, with everyone having clear responsibilities, but these appeared to be less defined in schools; he did not have a formal job description, though he intended to agree one with the treasurer of the governing body who visits the school half a day a week. His first job in a school was in a newly created post, as 'administrative assistant' to the head; he was horrified by the inefficient practices in the school's 'Sunday afternoon world'. Fees lay too long in a current account and the administration was still in the quill pen era. The head, who controlled a budget of some £2 million, would not easily let things go. He meets bursars in other schools and finds many are far from businesslike, claiming that they are not running a business, though an independent school clearly is one.

In a boarding school, where the annual revenue budget might be some £3 million, of which salaries will comprise about half, the bursar is given the same kind of authority as the finance director of a business; indeed, one bursar described his role and that of the head as akin to those of joint managing directors. Major decisions, such as the level of school fees, or global adjustments to staff salaries, would be referred to a finance committee of the board of governors for ratification, but this still leaves the bursar with heavy responsibility for the financial well-being of the school. He would prepare the usual financial plans, for example long-term cash flow forecasts, five-year development plans, investment and borrowing plans and of course overall annual budgets (departments and houses having their own budgets). Clearly this implies that the bursar should have a professional knowledge of accountancy. With the introduction of electronic data-processing systems for wages and management control, a knowledge of computers is also increasingly necessary.

The bursar's role, however, does not stop at accountancy; he doubles as a personnel manager and 'works manager', insofar as he looks after the non-teaching staff, their pay and conditions; and as an estates manager. Thus he will be expected to be capable of placing major contracts with building firms, having enough civil engineering and architectural knowledge to look after the fabric of the school and plan developments; be familiar with employment legislation and the Health and Safety at Work Act, and be able to develop and administer a salary policy. The kind of experience needed to do this work derived in the case of one bursar from having been in the Colonial Service; two others had run their own businesses.

The demands on a bursar in a day school in the public sector are less formidable, but he or she must still have a head for business. It is not simply a matter of keeping the books; it is to ensure that all the staff exercise wise stewardship over resources.

One comprehensive school head, an economist, said that when first appointed he had felt keenly the responsibility for running a 'million pound operation' and exercising proper budgetary control over this expenditure, but in general heads welcomed greater devolution in financial affairs, though some thought (like Handy 1984) that this provided a good case for all large schools to have bursars. At the very least, heads should receive training in financial management, including such matters as drawing up a service contract with local firms, financial planning and budgetary control. Those heads who had been in business, or were economists, were critical of the way in which money is sometimes used in schools. They knew it was wasted, not so much as a result of thoughtless extravagance on the part of spendthrift teachers, but of a lack of awareness and experience in maximising cost-effectiveness. Several respondents were particularly bitter about the way in which local authorities frittered away money through sheer bureaucratic inefficiency – for example redecorating walls before they needed it, letting wooden window-frames rot by not painting them, buying new electronic typewriters for schools already converted to word-processing, and enforcing central purchasing procedures for goods and services that could be obtained more cheaply locally. They felt quite powerless to prevent such waste and would dearly have liked to spend the money on more important things.

Professional bursars with a business background were less critical of extravagance and waste than of over-frugal and conservative attitudes on the part of teachers; they thought that there was much scope for spending money in order to save it, for example by faster introduction of information technology such as word-processors, electronic databases and spreadsheets.

Hardly anywhere was there evidence of the use of consultants (in method study, systems analysis, office techniques, cost control etc.) to advise schools how to improve efficiency and get better value for money. Yet many a business has saved substantial sums by employing experts in this way. The exceptions were an authority that secured on secondment a management services manager from an oil company, and a school that used its head of CDT as a consultant in the zone control of the school heating system. Both initiatives were hailed as successful.

Some issues to consider

1   What measures can schools use to track the efficiency of resource utilisation and demonstrate an improvement in value for money?
2   What do teachers do which could be done more cheaply by staff on lower salaries (for example, clerical staff or unqualified assistants)?
3   What actions can heads take to inculcate among staff a greater concern for using all resources more effectively?
4   What should be done to identify unnecessary work (procedures, meetings etc.) and eliminate it where the benefits are not commensurate with the cost?
5   Can any routine work be 'automated' with the help of a computer, to save effort and money?
6   Is there a place for consultants in improving financial and resource management in schools? For example, could work study and method study techniques be applied in a school to help staff work more effectively?
7   What initiatives can schools take to reduce the ill-effects of an authority's wasteful 'bureaucratic inefficiency'?
8   Given the cost of the capital assets and the total annual expenditure in schools, are heads adequately trained in financial management?
9   Would more financial devolution from the authority to schools enhance or imperil the cost-effective use of resources?
10   Should more schools have bursars, and what should be their qualifications and powers?

2.6 Qualities needed for school management

No-one found it difficult to answer the question 'What managerial qualities do you think are most important in schools?'. From some heads and deputies a list of these came tumbling out, and they obviously judged colleagues – perhaps also themselves – on the basis of such qualities.

Sometimes they had a role model who would personify such qualities, and they would try to emulate that example.

One comprehensive school head, asked to comment on what he looked for in selecting a deputy, replied that it depended on the qualities in the rest of the team; but essentially, he looked for someone with ideas, experience both as head of year and head of department, motivation to work extremely hard and to obtain a headship, ability to communicate with children and motivate them, ability to innovate, and be someone to whom one could delegate with confidence. At one school he knew, he found that the selection criteria used to produce a short list for deputy head had been drawn up by the staff, and he did not approve. In a head of department he would look for successful teaching experience, ideas in the curriculum area, and ability to introduce them. His staff had got the idea that change comes out of staff meetings. It doesn't; it comes out of people with 'bounce'. The quality that staff most looked for in a head was probably being firm but fair; they certainly did not like decisions going by default, and they had approved his firmness compared with that of his predecessor.

The lists of qualities mentioned were a mixture of a few traits (innate aspects of the personality) and of many skills (something that could be learned). The qualities (close on 100) can be fitted into the taxonomy developed by Burgoyne in his study of management in a large manufacturing organisation (Burgoyne 1976). He correlated the qualities in a sample of managers with various measures of success and effectiveness. Table 2.4 gives both Burgoyne's category descriptions and the qualities found in this study. (Figures in brackets are the number of mentions, where there were more than one.) A few qualities could have been allocated to more than one category, so some arbitrary decisions were needed to place them.

Table 2.4 Managerial Qualities

Burgoyne's categories	School management qualities
1 Command of basic facts of situation	Knowing more than the people you work with. A good memory.
2 Relevant professional understanding	A feel for management. Capable of earning respect of staff and pupils. Cares deeply about education of children. Track record.
3 Continuing sensitivity to events	Takes the long, wide view of the future. Vision. Has clear aims (2). Ability to detect weak staff. Getting out and about. Knowing what's going on. Awareness.

4 Analytical, problem solving, decision making skills

Efficient administrator (4). Good organiser. Good at personal organisation. Ability to manage own time (2). Can determine priorities (2). Knows when to delegate up or down. Good at detailed thinking. Good devil's advocate. Good at asking questions. Decisive (3). In control. Sense of balance.

5 Social skills and abilities

Knowing when to be firm. Firmness (2). Firm but fair (2). Negotiating ability. Ability to listen. Openness to being questioned. Can accept people's ideas. Leadership (4). Ability to steer. Chairmanship. Interpersonal skills (3). Ability to handle conflict. Diplomacy, ability to handle tricky situations well (2). Ability to present a case and carry a committee. Good salesman. Good at PR. Good relationships with colleagues. Empathetic. Sensitivity. Offers support. Sincere. Kind. Inspires trust. Sense of humour. Capacity to enthuse. Ability to boost morale (2). Ability to get people to enjoy their work and care about the quality of education. Ability to relate naturally to children. Can distance himself from staff and children.

6 Emotional resilience

Motivation and ability to work long hours (3). Resilience (3). Ability to work under pressure.

7 Inclination to respond purposefully to events

Confidence. Strength to take unpopular things forward. Being up-front without a protective barrier. Ability to scare the LEA.

8 Creativity

Breadth, wide variety of interests, not dreary. Lateral thinker. Innovator, man of ideas (2). Cultivated polymath. Having bounce.

9 Mental agility

Flexible mind (2). Style flexibility.

10 Balanced learning habits and skills

Has spare, unused capacity. Has potential. Can facilitate professional development.

Two categories dominated the rest: social skills and abilities, including leadership, chairmanship of meetings, taking a firm line with people, diplomacy and sensitivity; and the administrative skills associated with analysis, problem-solving, making decisions and judgements and orga- nising one's time and one's priorities. E. Yates, in a survey of opinion on methods of professional development of school heads (Yates 1981) also used Burgoyne's taxonomy to categorise managerial qualities thought to be required and he too found that social skills and abilities came top as a group; these include exercising responsible leadership, influencing, communicating and maintaining morale. This is consistent with my observations and understanding of the nature of management in schools. However, it would be wrong to underestimate the key importance of two other qualities that got fewer mentions: emotional resilience and mental agility. The emotional demands on the teaching profession are high; there are times when robustness is needed, but if managers erect their defences so sturdily that they seem thick-skinned, then they lose out on the qualities of sensitivity and support which they are also expected to display. Yates ranked emotional resilience and self-control and the ability to work effectively under pressure without panic as fifth in his list of qualities, following social skills, staff selection, setting the school's aims and objectives and planning and controlling the use of resources.

The need for mental agility comes from the fragmented nature of the job; senior managers need to think on their feet and to adjust quickly to a new situation after being interrupted. Some people have a zest for quick thinking; others like to mull over events and consequently they come across as indecisive. Mental agility conditions how quickly a manager can develop a new skill or orientation and how far he can handle complexity.

A word Burgoyne uses to describe category 7 is 'proactivity'. There were fewer mentions of associated qualities than the managerial role normally demands, although perhaps those who mentioned 'leadership' (included under category 5) may have had it in mind. My impression is that school managers are weak in combining categories 3 and 7 – that is, the ability to sense what is going to happen and then to get ready to meet the future head-on – forward planning, in fact. Interestingly, not a single respondent mentioned 'planning' as a managerial skill, though one head who had been to Henley Management College had been more struck by the need for it (and for staff appraisal) than by anything else he had picked up on the course. Another head, who had been seconded to the planning department of a large oil company, had been equally impressed by the meticulous attention given to planning.

As one head pointed out, different managerial positions require different sets of qualities; for example, professional knowledge is more important for a head of department than a head of house. Burgoyne found the same thing; for example, emotional resilience, continuing sensitivity to events and proactivity are more important for the success of the senior manager than for the 'whizz kid', whose success stems more from analytical, problem-solving and judgement skills, mental agility and well-developed learning habits and skills. The 'backbone manager' scores plus points for professional knowledge, social abilities and trouble-shooting and problem-solving skills. A surprising contrast between Burgoyne's work and the current study is that social skills were not highly correlated with managerial success for senior managers and 'whizz kids' in industry, whereas they are the dominant category in schools. Whether they are as closely correlated with success has not been established; my subjective impression is that they are.

Some issues to consider

1   Is it fair to regard the frequency of mention of a particular quality as a rough measure of the importance that should be attached to its development?
2   Why are emotional resilience and mental agility not more frequently mentioned?
3   Why is the ability to plan not mentioned at all?
4   How far do qualities thought to be important in school management match the qualities possessed by school managers?
5   Are any of the qualities innate, and therefore incapable of being developed?

2.7 Selection

The process by which heads are selected has been the subject of a recent study (the POST report, Morgan, Hall and Mackay 1983) but is not well known to heads themselves, since their only part in the process is as applicants and interviewees. They are, however, understandably more familiar with the processes for selecting deputy heads and other senior staff, and they regard it as a key area of their jobs. In the state sector they are by no means free agents, and several complained that political considerations interfered with the process and led sometimes to the unsatisfactory appointment of someone who subsequently caused difficulties through incompetence. It is very difficult for a head when the governors overrule his choice, or when the field from which the choice is made is severely limited by the Education Committee insisting that appointments can only be made from within that Authority.

At deputy head level, the selection procedure is often laid down by the Authority and is based on a panel interview. Panel members rarely have any training in interviewing. Selection criteria are not formally agreed. In some cases questions put to the candidates are standardised, ostensibly to ensure 'fairness', thus making it impossible to follow up particular matters revealed in the curriculum vitae. Hence the selection process is little more than a lottery, according to some heads.

For appointments at head of department level, heads have more scope for imposing their own views. They are clearer about what they are looking for and can apply criteria such as a grammar school background, a proven record of personnel management, and evidence of breadth, versatility and experience outside the school setting. Some have problems in drawing up a short list of candidates if they get inundated with applications. Candidates called for interview may spend a full day at the school and be seen by the top management team as well as by the staff in the department that they may later lead. If staff are involved, they may well object to the way in which their head appoints people.

At the independent schools visited there seemed to be a very thoroughgoing approach to internal promotions, with wide, though discrete, consultation among the staff, and even among the pupils. At one school the head picked up useful clues by asking pupils, for example, 'How are you getting on with your history?'. Another, as a regular part of his monitoring, canvassed boys' views by asking 'Are you well taught?', and from the replies he pieced together a picture of staff competence and potential for promotion. He regarded the boys as 'sound judges of form' and sometimes put to them leading questions such as 'do you think Mr X would make a good housemaster?'. Outside applicants were interviewed by several senior staff independently, and checklists of questions were used. The interviewers then reviewed each candidate and came to a consensus choice – not necessarily of the candidate the head preferred.

At another independent school appointments were first discussed with the head's immediate senior colleagues, the head of department concerned, a housemaster and with the leaver. To maintain balance between the academic and pastoral sides, and between athletes and aesthetes, it was important to give housemasters' views full weight. Some appointments were especially difficult, for example that of chaplain and head of religious studies. Much of the expertise in selection was intuitive; it was risky to rely on curriculum vitae and testimonials, so the head always telephoned the heads of schools whence the applicants came, to get the *real* truth. Two important questions were: 'Who are his friends going to be in the common room?' and 'What do you see yourself doing at 60?'.

Some issues to consider

1   What can heads do to improve the selection process for senior staff (including their successors)?
2   What are the hallmarks of a reliable procedure for selecting heads of department?
3   How should the judgements of pupils be used in assessing the suitability of teachers for promotion?

4   Are there ever occasions when it is wrong to appoint the most competent candidate for the job?

2.8 School reviews

Most schools have some means of reviewing their performance, but approaches vary considerably. Some Authorities lay down a procedure for school or curriculum review, and insist on this being carried out, say, once every five years. A well-known example is ILEA's *Keeping the School under Review* (ILEA 1983), with 300 questions to be answered, culminating in: 'Would I recommend a colleague to apply for a post in this school?' and 'Would I recommend the school to friends for their children?'. In three schools the heads thought that the imposition of a review by County Hall was ineffectual; the school went through the motions of answering the questions, but did little different as a result.

The main focus of such reviews seems to be on faculties or departments, whose heads are expected to play a major part in the process. This can involve staff in over 20 evening meetings and a good deal of hard work in drafting and agreeing the report. Some school heads meticulously analyse examination results and review these each autumn with the departments concerned. Targets may be set and improvement monitored. A comprehensive school that has put a lot of effort into developing its own review procedure, which the staff call evaluation, regards target-setting and monitoring as particularly important.

There are two parts to the process: one which is confidential and unrecorded, focusing on individual teachers' performance, and one focusing mainly on curriculum development, which is recorded. The careful removal of threat, leading to willing participation, is seen as a cause of success for the process, and an important carrot for staff is access to INSET courses. The evaluation process is applied to the work of the deputy heads, but not to that of the head.

The introduction of the evaluation scheme at the outset had consisted of a letter from the head to staff asking them to write him a letter setting out their successes and failures. This had not been well-received, so it was agreed that if successes and failures were to be discussed, they would not be committed to paper. The only written record would be a report from each head of faculty about its work. Even this, however, is perceived as a threat to some senior staff. In some cases reports are bland and in others they record unresolved conflict. To supplement the evaluation discussions, the head makes a practice of visiting each teacher once or twice a year to watch a lesson, and also spends half a day each term with every faculty.

In addition, each member of staff once a year has a discussion with his head of faculty (about 12–14 staff each) and with a deputy head or his assistant. These all take place from July to October and are very difficult to fit in; indeed, the head, who sees all heads of faculty, did not complete his programme of interviews, which take about an hour each. In future, therefore, he intended to spread them over the whole year.

There are other problems. Some junior staff see the process as 'spying' and the head of faculty as an antagonist. There is no checklist of what ought to be discussed. No-one has had training in counselling interviews, but only in selection interviews (there is, in fact, no in-house training in this county; training in the management of people is not seen as sufficiently important, and there are resource constraints). There is not always discussion of work targets for the following year. Some see the discussions as a waste of time and question their purpose; others see them as 'pussyfooting'. It is known that a local firm in contact with the school conducts much more specific interviews, and the prospect of this happening at the school has caused widespread apprehension, even though the ostensible purpose is primarily professional development.

The evaluation process is not itself readily evaluated. There are intangible indications, like growth of trust and the progression of individuals, and some teachers undoubtedly see it as beneficial; for example, a newly recruited head of faculty found it an invaluable means of getting to grips with his new job. The opponents tend to be the less competent teachers for whom the county offers help with their professional difficulties.

The element that is principally missing is formal training, the provision of which is fragmented. Heads of faculties have been asked to develop formal policies for this, but in the last resort it is very difficult to shift the less competent staff. Some of these may have been unwisely appointed in the first instance, although the school has well-developed selection procedures for the junior staff. Unfortunately the governors will not delegate to the head responsibility for Scale 3 and 4 appointments, so political considerations enter into the choice of candidates.

The head himself does not have his performance formally evaluated by his staff, but he had hoped that the evaluation interviews with his deputies would be a two-way process and this is to be encouraged, perhaps at a panel discussion. He has, however, got a local industrial manager to review his work as head, and has made some changes as a result.

A head of faculty interviewed had found the evaluation procedure useful, in enabling staff to step back from their jobs and review them. Some other faculties had found it less useful, however, and had insufficient faith in the higher administration; they also said that nothing happened as a result of the reviews. It was important to keep the aim in view: helping staff to do a more professional job.

One school had introduced a system of peer evaluation; colleagues from other departments reviewed the curriculum of each department in turn and made suggestions for improvement (see 'mutual monitoring', p. 152). At another school the head convened several groups of eight staff and asked them to discuss 'What do we do well and what do we do badly?'. Two schools brought in outsiders (for example, industrial training officers) to help them in the process of school review. Another school used a Likert style questionnaire (Likert 1967), completed by staff, to assess the school's decision-making processes. One head kept putting the question to pupils: 'How can we improve the school?'. Another went round taking random samples of pupils' work and made her own judgements of what improvement was needed.

A somewhat novel and courageous approach involved the heads of two neighbouring schools; they agreed to review one another's schools. The two heads had met on a SCIP course and had decided that it would be interesting to swap places for a week, an idea supported by their education officer. One school was for boys, with a male head; the other was mixed and had a female head. The exchange was preceded by a day in which each head showed the other round the school and introduced him or her to the staff. On the occasion when the male head visited the mixed school, the receiving head was discomfited by a stink-bomb being let off in assembly, but this gave the visiting head some reassurance that it was not only in his school that such incidents occurred. This sense of relief was to be repeated during the exchange; it helped to dissolve the self-blame that untoward incidents or problems sometimes generate. The first day of the exchange gave rise to some apprehension and 'butterflies', but in fact he was well-received.

A number of things struck him on his visit to the other school, and he found these experiences of considerable interest in getting a fix on his own performance back home.

First, he was present at an event when a pupil was being disciplined. No fewer than four teachers were present, which seemed a heavy-handed and time-consuming way of handling the interview. At another interview he attended, involving some thefts from a local supermarket, the deputy head seemed to have no strategy for detecting untruthful responses from the suspect pupils, and was somewhat gauche in allowing the emotional temperature to rise by implying that a suspect had been guilty of rape. Next, at a deputy heads' meeting chaired by one of the deputies, time spent on discussing the replenishment of lavatory paper in the staff toilets, and how this was to be achieved, occupied an undue amount of valuable time. He found the children more friendly, quieter and neater than his own, and when he took some cover lessons, they took to him well.

He had far fewer interruptions (only about 25 per cent of the frequency in his own office) which surprised him, though this may have been partly due to staff saving up problems till the return of the normal head. There was a pressing problem with intruders and peeping Toms, since the school grounds abutted a park where local unemployed or truanting boys gathered at the fence to eye the girls on the other side. When the school-keeper went to send them away, he was abused, and retaliated; but the head was able to get them to go, without suffering or delivering abuse, though they still kept returning.

An embarrassing incident occurred at an assembly taken by one of the deputy heads, who read from a book on space travel. Another stink bomb went off, and she pretended not to notice the commotion that resulted. He felt he had to intervene, and by careful observation of the behaviour of the group of pupils near the incident, and subsequent questioning, he succeeded in identifying the culprit afterwards.

The heads of departments' meetings at the other school were smaller and better, though the agenda items were much the same at both schools. In both schools a serious problem is the fall-off in motivation of the children as they go up the school, with truancy, disaffection and disinterest getting worse. Other impressions gained were the seriousness of sexism, as revealed by an audit of text-books carried out in the boys' school; the courtesy of the chairperson of governors in paying a visit to the school during the exchange; the readiness of the inspector, who also paid a visit, to take undeserved credit for effecting the exchange; the feeling of intrusion at the possibility of inspecting the other head's most personal and confidential files kept in her office; and the threat implicit in the situation of being, as it were, inspected by a colleague. The reciprocity inherent in the exchange helped to allay the feeling of threat, however.

When the two heads got together after the exchange to compare notes, the female head made a number of points. There were three staff she did not like, but several she liked. The boys stared at her, and were both noisy and physical; they kept playing up to her. She liked the albums of photographs of every boy in the school, as an aid to identification, especially of miscreants. She found the (predominantly male) staff very straightforward and open; they said exactly what they meant. But the place was rife with sexism. She was impressed with the office staff, the head's secretary seeming more like a personal assistant. Lesson changes were not as slick as at her school. The staff were too militaristic, and seemed unduly anxious. The boys struck her as vulnerable and responsive at heart. The edges of the senior management were untidy. She managed to prohibit smoking in a staff meeting! One of the staff in disciplining a boy dressed him down in highly derogatory language ('You stupid boy!'), causing him to react to preserve his self-respect. The more junior staff, on the other hand, seemed to have got the relationship with the boys right. She had been impressed with her opposite number's handling of his staff meetings, and was reassured to find that both schools seemed to be facing much the same problems. An uplifting and unexpected incident occurred when some boys who had been misbehaving by talking in assembly came up afterwards and apologised to her. The boys seemed better behaved than her girls at lunchtime, were less anti-authority and did not harbour so many grudges against the staff.

Both heads felt that they had learned from their experience and must have improved their effectiveness. They felt they were each adept at summing up situations quickly, and inasmuch as they do not often get positive comments it was good to get constructive feedback for a change.

LEA advisers and HMIs were seldom mentioned as contributing much to a school review, simply because their visits were so few, short and far between. However, when they did visit, and looked in depth at the work of a particular subject department, heads valued their comments and conclusions, though in one case an oral report had been given in very stark and negative terms, which could have ruffled feathers if insensitively communicated to the department concerned.

As it happens, none of the schools visited had been subject to a full published HMI report (although one was inspected shortly afterwards), but there are clearly problems for heads in how to handle the publicity of such a report, and indeed how to manage the school's encounters with HMIs.

Some issues to consider

1   Should school review procedures be imposed, or should schools devise their own?
2   What are the pros and cons of the approaches described?
3   Should school review and staff appraisal be integrated or separated?
4   What should be the links between review policy and staff training policy?
5   What role should inspectors, advisers and people outside the education service play in a school review?
6   How should the feedback from an HMI report be handled?

2.9 Staff appraisal

The appraisal of teachers is a contentious issue. Some heads who might be described as generally competent and progressive shrank from the introduction of formal appraisal systems into their schools for fear of the opposition it would cause. They regarded appraisal as counter-cultural to the teaching profession. With one exception, all who had introduced a scheme proceeded very cautiously, with a great deal of consultation. Participation in such schemes is usually voluntary in schools, and in some cases none of the results were committed to paper. One school confined formal appraisal to a review of INSET activities, these being interpreted widely. Another used a 300-word report on staffing in each department, called for once a year, as a basis for informal discussion with staff, but with no targets set for the following year.

Heads themselves generally received no regular appraisal, though one persuaded his LEA inspector to write a report on his performance; another two got local managers from industry to help; two asked their deputies to give informal feedback. One had a set of self-evaluation questions that he put to himself.

At another school, a deputy head on her return from an industrial secondment, administered a questionnaire to elicit information about who monitored staff's progress, and this showed up the need for making the head of department the key figure in the development process. More responsibility was explicitly delegated to heads of departments to develop their staff. The head of modern languages piloted the scheme and after studying the local firm's staff appraisal scheme, he introduced appraisal for his second-in-command and for a probationary teacher. This looked at difficulties, strengths and gains in professional competence. The appraisal was not imposed; staff voluntarily carried out their own self-evaluation and discussed it with their head of department. Development appraisal forms were drawn up, and the head used these for all the heads of departments. They were felt to be useful vehicles for communication about performance. Since all forms contain a question about priorities for the coming year, they helped to establish a sense of purpose and commitment to objectives. They were also useful when the LEA carried out a professional staff review. Some resistance to the process was encountered in parts of the school. Another innovation, which helped to enhance the respect that staff had for one another, and thus build up a team, was to get heads of departments to make a presentation to their colleagues on the skills and aptitudes emphasised in their teaching.

There were three schools with formal systems that seemed to work. One of these linked staff appraisal to school review, in the way described in the previous section. In another, the head had decided to introduce it soon after his arrival, and without consultation. He operated it, however, in a very supportive fashion, aiming to discover if the staff had any difficulties in their work which he could help to resolve. Everyone took part (except his number 2) and the impression given by the staff was that the scheme was valued and successful. The head was also convinced of the usefulness and need for the scheme; how else, he wondered, could he develop and train his staff? How else can the capacity for self-delusion among teachers be overcome, save by bringing independent judgements to bear?

In a primary school visited, the head had exercised great care and patience in introducing a scheme based on mutual trust. Although voluntary, all staff took part, and her own performance was evaluated too, by the staff. The performance criteria were not easily measurable: namely, the extent to which the teachers developed in pupils qualities of self-confidence, self-reliance, motivation to work without supervision, development of positive attitudes and high aims. The scheme appeared to work well; though the older staff admitted to grave misgivings in the early days, these had been overcome, and the staff found the scheme contributed significantly to their personal development. An abridged account by the head of the introduction of the scheme follows.

Our appraisal system does not stand in isolation from day to-day happenings in the school but is inextricably linked both to *ad hoc* appraisal, which we all carry out, and to the roles of the responsibility post holders. I believe a prerequisite of a successful 'structured' appraisal system is an atmosphere amongst the staff of trust and respect for each person's strengths and weaknesses. I saw my task as showing by example that I could admit to my mistakes and weaknesses and that these 'admissions' strengthened, rather than weakened, my integrity as a person and as a headteacher. My asking the staff for help in my job had many positive benefits for myself, the staff and thus the school.

It took me 4½ years following my appointment to develop the system. It was not on my agenda to start with, because this was my first headship and I lacked skill and confidence; also the atmosphere was not right – an autocratic style was expected, there was suspicion and apprehension, and admission of mistakes was seen as condemnatory of one's professionalism and of oneself.

However, in 1981, the LEA required us to produce a curriculum review document, and this involved staff in examining practice and suggesting improvements. I initiated discussion of the link between this and teacher performance and appraisal, and we had two staff meetings about it, leading to the idea of a 'negotiated document' agreed by staff. We also discussed how to make post holders more responsible for other staff and agreed to extend their role and ask them to supplement the scheme of individual appraisals. I gave one an article on 'Effectiveness', culled from Drucker, and discussed the development of her role. The area to be covered by appraisals was discussed with staff and suggestions made at a series of meetings. A draft appraisal document was written and agreed.

The first appraisal interviews were held after school in March-April 1983, and the process later reviewed at a staff meeting. Improvements were made, and by September post holders were giving written advice to other members of staff (including the deputy head) about 'their' area of the curriculum throughout the school. I again raised the question of my own performance appraisal, and headings were agreed, covering personality factors and performance, under which it would be judged. Staff decided to meet in my absence, under the chairmanship of the deputy, to discuss my performance. I also reviewed my own performance, and we all met to share views. It was agreed that a report should be written, to minimise the risk of the deputy colouring staff's views, and that dissenting opinions would be recorded. After three 1½ hour sessions the final report of my performance was written and a further meeting held to share views and make plans for the improvement of my performance.

Staff were asked to write down their feelings about being appraised. The deputy head reported considerable apprehension and anxiety, with some sapping of confidence at first, though she thought the head handled this very well. A post holder found the appraisal interview extremely constructive, with the head inviting constructive criticism of herself, and offering extremely helpful and professional advice in a kindly way; she was looking forward to the next appraisal. A member of staff found her appraisal a rewarding experience, which instigated thoughts about attitudes towards other members of staff, about weaknesses of which she was unaware, and about strengths which were praised and consolidated; it made her feel more confident as a teacher, but less confident as a member of staff. She liked the way in which the system had been introduced. Another teacher found it helpful to have strengths and weaknesses put into words, and she liked the informal atmosphere of the interview, and the fact that it was a two-way process. A teacher who had come from a school where appraisal was already in operation found her interview relatively relaxed; she was able to express her doubts as to her capability in certain areas, and went on to discuss ways of increasing her skill and confidence. She said the experience was rewarding. Another teacher, while apprehensive at first, soon found herself at ease and able to discuss her strengths and weaknesses; her second interview, to which she had looked forward, was 'even more profitable'. She attributed the success of the scheme to the excellent relationship between the head and the staff, and the fact that it had not been imposed, but developed through staff discussion. This view was shared by another teacher, who also pointed out that the structure provided by the 'headings' for discussion were very important.

The headings used in the appraisal of the headteacher are shown in Figure 2.3. Another working example of succesful upward appraisal, this time of a head of faculty, has been described by Diffey (Diffey 1985).

Figure 2.3 Headings for headteacher's appraisal

Section 1: Personal characteristics

Confidence	Sense of humour
Appearance	Persistence
Integrity	Discretion
Adaptability	Patience
Diplomacy	Reliability
Enthusiasm	Optimism
Practicality	Consistency
Not infallible	Good memory
Warmth	Credibility
Self-discipline	Liking for people

Ability to allow members of staff to take credit where it is due

Ability to be serious in a serious situation

Section 2: Performance factors

1 *Planning*
    1 Relating present to future needs
    2 Recognising what is important and what is merely urgent
    3 Seeing ahead
    4 Anticipating future trends
    5 Analysing

2 *Creating*
    1 Having good ideas
    2 Finding original solutions to common problems
    3 Anticipating the consequences of decisions and actions

3 *Communicating*
    1 Understanding people
    2 Listening
    3 Explaining
    4 Getting others to talk
    5 Tact
    6 Tolerance of others' mistakes
    7 Giving honest praise and honest criticism
    8 Keeping everyone who needs to be informed

4 *Controlling*
    1 Comparing outcomes with plans
    2 Self-evaluation
    3 Evaluating the work of others
    4 Taking corrective action where necessary

5 *Motivating*
    1 Inspiring others
    2 Providing realistic challenges
    3 Helping others to set themselves realistic and challenging targets
    4 Helping others to value their own worth

6 *Organising*
    1 Making fair demands on people
    2 Making rapid decisions
    3 Being in front when it counts
    4 Staying calm when the going is difficult
    5 Recognising when a job is done

Some issues to consider

1   What should be regarded as the minimum practice for reviewing the performance of a school and its staff?

2   What balance should be struck between self-evaluation, evaluation by peers and evaluation by external 'experts' (HMIs, LEA advisers, industrial managers or training officers)? How, if at all, should pupils be involved?

3   What purposes would you wish appraisal to achieve in your job? Do you want the process to involve you in the judgements or to be done behind your back?

4   Which is more important – appraisal of performance with a view to improving it or appraisal of potential with a view to career development?

5   Should an appraisal scheme (a) when first introduced and (b) eventually, cover all members of the organisation (including ancillary staff) or should certain categories be excluded (for example, head, those about to leave, those who object to appraisal)? To what problems will exclusions give rise?

6   What are the relative merits of appraisal systems based on narratives of performance (achievement of targets etc.) and those based on ratings of specified qualities and skills?

7   How should the head's performance be assessed? Should heads ask their subordinates to appraise them?

2.10 Training

The picture that emerged from the research with regard to training is complex. Most respondents were asked what management training they had received, what they thought was needed and how well it was done.

It was difficult not to be disturbed by the low level of training to which the majority of those in managerial positions had been exposed – in terms of both quantity and quality. The extent to which the education service relies on chance in developing management skills in its members must be a matter for concern. If there were any underlying strategies for accomplishing this development, or sets of guidelines, these were nowhere apparent, except in one independent day school. Expectations of what training might be available, and what it could achieve by way of improved job performance, were very modest. There was little understanding of the part that training plays in developing managers and leaders in the armed services, the police service, the National Health Service, the civil service, local government outside education, or in industry and commerce, though a few who had been seconded to industry had become enthusiastic about what was done in this field and one head was using an industrial training manager to advise him on INSET courses. By no means everyone interviewed was concerned that education is a Cinderella profession as regards management development. Indeed, there were pockets of hostility not only towards management training but even to professional in-service training in teaching content and practice. From the descriptions of some of the courses teachers had attended, such attitudes were perhaps understandable, albeit difficult to endorse.

It would be helpful if this section included one case study of good all-round management training practice in a school; unfortunately none was found, although there were several good features in the school referred to on pp. 25–27. The following notes refer to a comprehensive school that had recently become alert to the inadequacy of its training provision:

The head and his deputy, in their earlier careers, had never felt the need for management training and it was only more recently that the value of this had become apparent. The head had found his Diploma in Management Studies (DMS) course valuable in giving a general appreciation of the management of people, particularly as regards group work, team effectiveness, support systems, listening, sharing, ideas discussion, hidden agendas, management styles and human relations. Apart from the DMS, the head had picked up the bulk of his management expertise by observing other heads at work. The deputy head was about to attend a management course; he did not have high expectations of it. He preferred to be *taught* subjects, not indulge in case study discussions. He had started teaching in 1965 at a time when management was not an issue.

The school carried out its own INSET courses on topics that had been identified as important through consultation; 1½ day sessions had been run over a 4-week period on curriculum analysis (a sort of productivity study); the deputy head was running a course on timetabling; pastoral care and organisation were other subjects planned. One head of department had been appointed the professional tutor, a new role intended to spearhead staff development, though not at the highest level. He was responsible for arranging INSET courses, for supervising probationary teachers and arranging teaching practice for students. He had been given latitude to build up his role, but had found it somewhat heavy going, as he did not have any guidance or training and knew of no books that could help him. He was sometimes expected to know the answers to problems and did not, which he found somewhat threatening, though it was clear that he served a useful role by simply listening actively. There was some role conflict with other heads of departments. One of them had difficulty in conceptualising things in management terms, but had been on a 2-day management course which had not made a great impression. When specific help was needed the local teachers' centre could sometimes provide it. A house activities tutor said that most problems arose on the pastoral side. Although tutor/counsellors were appointed, they had no training, but needed it.

In assessing the value of training it is, of course, important to examine the behavioural outcomes, if any. It is not enough to stimulate the mind; the question is whether performance on the job improves. It must be said that some of those questioned on this point were not conscious of any outcome (which is not to say that there was none). Others knew that they had changed, or colleagues perceived change in them. For instance, two heads of department who had been on an industrial management course were full of new words like 'prioritise' on their return; they stuck flipcharts on the walls of their rooms; and they were observed to get through meetings that they chaired more quickly – partly because they made very effective use of an overhead projector. Another participant in an industrial management course habitually set objectives for meetings on his return, and he replaced lengthy minutes by succinct action notes. He set personal priorities and planned his engagements to take place within set times. A head who had been on a DMS course felt enabled to improve the effectiveness of his senior management team: he listened more acutely; he spotted hidden agendas; and he believed that he had broadened his repertoire of management styles. A head who had attended a Brighton Polytechnic course said she had become less 'black-and-white' as a result (again probably meaning that she had increased her style flexibility); and the Grubb Institute week of a six-week course had heightened her awareness of hidden meanings, which she found useful in meetings.

At the less effective end was an LEA management course full of lectures, only about 10 per cent of which were perceived to be of any use; the simulations had not been impressive either, and the teachers on the course actively resisted all attempts to change them. The participant (a head of house) was convinced that this course had no beneficial outcome.

Insofar as respondents were able to articulate the processes by which they had learned management, it was usually something akin to osmosis; skills permeated through the membrane separating the teacher from his or her environment. The apprenticeship model, or some variation of it, was often quoted; heads tended to have modelled their behaviour on some well-respected head or heads under whom they had worked earlier in their careers. Sometimes an anti-model would be influential; the reputation of the head's predecessor in the same school often provided a stimulus for learning how not to do it.

The apprenticeship model implies that the master actively grooms his pupil and moulds him into an effective practitioner of the same craft. While one or two heads felt that they had enjoyed such a relationship when they were deputies, more often it was a case of 'sitting by Nellie' – the time-honoured way in which mill-girls learned their jobs. The deputies also gave this impression. For example, a senior master who had spent the whole of his career (19 years) at the one school said his only preparation for the number 2 role had been as a head of year; he had attended no courses. He wished he had had experience of timetabling, for which he was now responsible; the head had shown him how to do it, but had lost him on several occasions, because he did not explain his reasons for doing things.

If on-the-job training is to be fully effective, the superior or mentor does need to have coaching skills, which are subtly different from teaching skills. While six or seven heads out of the 20 undoubtedly took staff development seriously, only two came across as proficient coaches, though many stood out as teachers and had clearly developed skill in actively learning from others.

Experience of off-the-job training on courses and secondments was generally discouraging and in line with the findings of the Hughes report (Hughes, Carter and Fidler 1981); such training played a small part in the development of most heads and senior staff. Table 2.5 summarises the training records of all those respondents with whom training was discussed. Only three had professional qualifications in management. A further four had been on a course of six weeks' duration or longer. Nine had never attended a course at all.

Table 2.5 Training records of respondents

Heads

2 heads had received no management training.
1 head had had no management training except on an ICI/SCIP short course on the management of change (seen as 'very useful').

1 head had been on a DES COSMOS course ('very good') and an Industrial Society action-centred leadership course.

1 head had had no management training except a 3-day course on planning.

1 head had had no management training except one course on personnel management ('very useful for industrial relations problems').

1 head, newly appointed, had studied for an M Ed which included management skills, and had promised himself one course a year.

1 head had been on a six-week LEA course and a Brighton Polytechnic short course.

1 head had been on a one-term training opportunity course (DES 3/83) and on a week's Coverdale training course.

1 head had been on a Henley general management course ('very useful').

1 head had been on a six-week LEA management course, a Brighton Polytechnic course, an Industrial Society leadership course and two courses at Roffey Park, one on selection interviewing ('very useful') and one on counselling skills as well as having been seconded to do an MA (Ed) at Sussex University.

1 head had been on a post-graduate Diploma in Educational Administration ('useful for "bursar-type" skills').

1 head held a Diploma in Management Studies.

The training records of the remaining heads were not explored.

Deputy Heads

5 deputies had had no management training.

1 deputy had received 'little' management training – one course on 'theory', 'policy' and curriculum development.

2 deputies had been on a six-week LEA course; in addition, one had been on a three-week course involving very useful visits to other schools.

1 deputy had been on some LEA senior management courses on multi-ethnic education, under-achievement, mixed ability teaching and equal opportunities policy; but none covered implementation of policy.

1 deputy had been on a head of science course, and had been instructed to follow an Open University course on school management.

1 second master had had no management training except a three-day action-centred leadership course.

1 deputy had had no management training except a very good course on counselling.

1 deputy had attended several courses for deputy heads, but had not found them useful.

1 deputy had been on a good 'preparation for headship' course.

1 deputy was studying for a postgraduate award.

Housemasters and heads of departments

1 housemaster had had no formal management training; he said this was typical.

1 head of sixth had had no management training except for a very well-presented course on interviewing, when he worked in industry.

1 head of science (an INSET tutor) had been on 12 modules of his LEA's science heads' course, of which one day (run in industry) had been useful.
1 head of commerce had had no management training, but had twice been seconded to industry, and there had picked up some management techniques.
2 heads of department had been on a course in industry, where they had undergone psychometric tests and practised counselling skills, objective-setting, use of time and delegation.
1 post holder had been on a 'preparation for deputy headship' course, but had found that it concentrated almost entirely on how to do well at interviews for such a post.
1 head of English had been on courses on team management, interpersonal skills and counselling.
1 head of PE had been on a one-week course on counselling at Roffey Park and another at Bramley Grange.

The attitudes to training revealed in the 20 schools range from one where the head firmly believed that the most important aspect of his job was the training of his staff (yet who made practically no use of management courses), and one who frequently sent her staff on courses, to one who reflected faithfully the view of the LEA, which did not believe in management training at all. One head, who himself had had a good experience of a Henley course, found difficulty in persuading his staff to accept training. Another reported that older members of his staff were anti-training. Another, having found that his predecessor had 'gone overboard' with leadership training, had quietly dropped all management training. Another believed that some skills are unteachable. One followed an Open University course to increase his chances of promotion, rather than to become more competent.

A good deal of criticism was levelled at teacher training institutions as fountains of learning about interpersonal skills, and one probationary teacher declared that she had not found a single note she had taken on her course of any value in teaching; she had learned more of value in a few weeks in a school (which had a particularly able 'developer' as head) than in the whole of her course. Whilst this was an extreme view, many experienced teachers expressed low expectations of courses in general, and felt that initial teacher training courses in particular should include fundamentals of management (other than classroom management).

Even where there was a belief that training had something valuable to offer, difficulties in providing it were sometimes severe. Staffing ratios were felt to preclude the release of teachers for training, a situation aggravated by refusal of colleagues to provide cover (as part of the unions' protest against government policies). LEA money to pay course fees was often very tight and their attitudes cheese-paring; where teachers were prepared to pay for their own fees (as a praiseworthy number are willing to do), they were often put off by the seemingly high cost (though in fact many school management courses are very reasonably priced compared with those aimed at commerce and industry). Neither heads nor INSET tutors are properly equipped to marry horses to courses (tutors feel threatened by this); without some grounding in management and training, it is difficult to conceptualise what sort of course would suit a particular need. Thus the choice of course becomes a very hit-and-miss affair. Course descriptions often leave much to be desired.

Although many are not clear exactly what they want, they know that they want *something,* and they look to course providers to know what that something is. This is understandable in people who have very limited experience of being trained themselves, and have no language in which to talk management. Some of the needs expressed were for training in:

Understanding what management training needs cover
Communication
Interpersonal skills (especially in a pastoral setting)
Counselling
Experiential management training (for example, Grubb Institute courses)
Giving and receiving feedback
Appraisal
Selection
Coping with stress
Dealing with governors, parents and the education office
Dealing with contractors
Experience outside education
Improving systems
Curriculum analysis and timetabling
Running a discussion group
Small group work
Team-building
Developing good personal relationships
Understanding more senior people's roles
Implementation of policy
Objective-setting
Personal organisation
'Battery recharging'
Understanding what tomorrow's world will look like

Conspicuous by their absence were pleas for training in legislation, educational issues, planning, financial accounting, resource management and industrial relations. This is not to say that such training is not *needed;* it is just not *wanted* very much. The *felt* needs are predominantly in the broad category of 'dealing with other people' at a very practical level, that is, skills rather than knowledge.

For a significant minority of those interviewed, these needs were very deeply felt. At all levels, including that of head, there were respondents who clearly felt very brittle, ill-prepared and insecure. While they had learned to put on a brave front, they felt inadequate for the tasks placed upon them – threatened and even scared. The ingredients of stress were there to see. Although the more robust can survive being thrown in at the deep end of management and can respond positively to a challenge, good management consists of achieving extraordinary things with *ordinary* people. The education service places extraordinary demands on many of its ordinary staff; it is cruel to deny them the training that would help them to respond self-confidently to the challenge. The armed services know better; why should 'the Devil' have all the fun?

Some issues to consider

1   By comparison with the rest of society, the quality and quantity of management training in the education service is lamentable. Discuss.
2   How far can the apprenticeship model of on-the-job training meet the needs of senior management in schools? Can it be improved?
3   What percentage of a head's time should be devoted to off-the-job management training? Of a deputy head? Of a head of department?
4   Whose responsibility is it to manage school management training and to improve it? Whose should it be?

2.11 *Change, development and innovation*

In most of the schools visited heads declared a wish to make some changes in the status quo; they were also conscious of the need to combat inertia and get their schools moving. Their drive to innovate varied considerably, however, from one who said 'My recurring nightmare is stagnation and not moving forward' and who was highly active in initiating and encouraging change as a way of life, to one within sight of retirement who had let some previous innovations die and was content to rest on his oars.

Among the changes exercising their attention were:
Changing attitudes towards the handicapped;
Encouraging use of computer technology in administration and teaching;
Collaborating with the local rural community in promoting information technology;
Introducing job specifications for staff;
Introducing staff performance appraisal;
Building the staff into a more effective team;
Curriculum development (especially changing the knowledge/skills balance);

Developing new pedagogical skills among the staff (for example, mixed ability teaching);
Increasing liaison with industry;
Reversing the trend of falling rolls;
Becoming a community school;
Multicultural education;
Better collaboration with the youth service;
Upgrading standards of discipline, demeanour and morale.

Few heads mentioned activities aimed at changing the environment within which the school operated, yet they reported many problems whose source lay in the LEA or the Education Committee. It was as though there was passive acceptance of situations that were decided at County Hall, and a feeling not only of powerlessness in relation to these, but of acceptance of an immutable subordinate relationship of obedience ('Theirs not to reason why. . .'). Artful strategies for active management of environmental pressures outside the school were rarely encountered; a few heads went out of their way to provide the local press with copy that reflected the school in a favourable light, or to appear at public meetings. Only in one case was there mention of collective action by heads in a locality to effect change in the LEA – and that had been unsuccessful. Heads, it seems, are great respecters of authority, in the military tradition; not many have Nelson's blind eye and few appeared able to cope with a Captain Queeg. One head saw parents as a target for change:

Two of the major environmental constraints to educational development are the tyranny of the exam system and the conservatism of parents, who see the main end of education as the passing of examinations. Little can be done about the exams, but through the Parent Teacher Association and other means a gradual re-education is taking place which allows for the inclusion in the curriculum of new areas for study which are not amenable to assessment by public examination. Equally difficult has been the task of helping the parents to come to terms with the reality of the size of the school. No longer is it possible for the head to know every sixth former by name, nor can parents expect him always to be the most appropriate person with whom to discuss each and every problem of their child.

At the proactive end of the spectrum were heads who were able to articulate firmly their approach to change; some examples will capture their philosophy and understanding (I have given fuller case studies in my previous book *Effective School Management* (Everard and Morris 1985)).

1 The head's approach to the management of change was very positive. In the first place, it was important for the boys to experience a changing environment, otherwise there was an atmosphere of staleness rather than vitality. Secondly, it was for the head to lead change; this he did by writing a clear paper, which did not go into detail, and delegating to the second master the implementation phase. The second master was adept at picking up ideas and running with them. The

boys' ideas should also be worked on; he regularly asked the prefects how they thought the school could be improved. He was afraid of the school running out of momentum, and was determined to have around him people who brought ideas up. To facilitate this, he had convened groups of eight people and given them the question to discuss: 'What do we do well and what do we do badly?'; this had proved useful and productive.

Commenting on the head's style, the second master said that the head was good at introducing new things. He did not impose them despotically; indeed he positively encouraged opposition and wanted the second master to speak out against the head's views when he did not agree, even in the staff room. For example, they did not see eye to eye on questions of tenure. The head assumed full responsibility for any innovations; the second master used his 'old boy network' in the common room to try to gain the acquiescence of the unconverted.

The careers master, who had come from industry, asked to comment on how he found the management system in the school compared with Unilever's, said there *was* no management system until the present head arrived; the school was more like an unmanaged community. The new head, however, gave himself a more managerial role, by introducing objective-setting and managing the boundary with the outside world. He also introduced a managerial structure, with individual tasks being identified and assigned to particular staff; roles were clarified and assigned. He placed considerable emphasis on change, made a five-year plan, and put in a new set of people to carry it out. Objective-setting had been the key to its implementation. Unusually for a head of a school set in the classical tradition, he was very much seen as a man who took decisions.

2 The rector of this Scottish school had been a depute rector in the south-west of Scotland, before his present appointment. He was seeking, from the previous regime of consolidation, to achieve faster change. He had done an M Ed course at Stirling University six years previously on curriculum development, and had been involved with bringing about change at his previous academy; he was also very knowledgeable about school management affairs, and had had contact with industry in his previous job, including dialogue with an ICI training officer. His experience as a principal teacher (equivalent to head of department) had shown him that there were many constraints to change. He had found that the best route into the management of change was to set up working parties on 'methods of assessment', which always generated energy, and which could be steered so as to drive other changes. He also said that you had to create problems to get change. The most obstinate constraint was often the most effective lever for change, if properly set up.

The Mann and Dunning intervention had operated on a centre-periphery model, with teachers temporarily brought into the centre on working parties. This seemed to work, but there was always doubt whether agreed changes were actually implemented behind the closed doors of the classroom; it was here that many attempts at curriculum change came to grief. A similar research project to his M Ed project had been conducted by Sally Brown, a research fellow at Stirling University, who had shown that there were two reasons why curriculum development failed at the classroom level: procedural and practical. Although the end-result of the change was well specified, there was usually a shortage of practical aids (software), which took a long time for the individual teacher to produce; and there was little pedagogical guidance on how to introduce the change. This was now being improved, as it had come to be realised that it has to be spelled out to the classroom teacher in great detail what he or she should do. These findings were in tune with his own experience. He noted that there is a dearth of good literature and of courses on the management of change.

3 The culture of this school could be characterised as a hive of bubbling activity; clearly innovation was built into the system. There was an explicit use of an organisation development (OD) approach and OD values in the management style of the principal. Ideas abounded and were encouraged. The principal himself was a prolific source of them. Although many of the 130 staff had been at the school for a long time, there was a policy of exposing them to new experiences – either secondments outside the school (of which there were about six a year) or major changes in role (46 the previous year). One of the main problems the school faced was the effect of falling rolls and reduced resources on promotion opportunities for staff; one of the answers was to ensure that the school continued to be a highly developmental organisation, with plenty of innovation going on.

The deputy principal and co-ordinator of resources paid tribute to the principal's productive and creative mind; he was a man who 'fired on so many cylinders' that it was impossible to implement all his ideas. Indeed, most of the staff were unaware of how prolific these ideas were. The ideas were processed through a host of working parties. Indeed, it seemed that everything was kept under constant review by such groups. More than in most schools, the staff accepted without union opposition a high degree of flexibility and were prepared to run classes during lunch and before and after school, being given time off in lieu. But for this attitude, the school could not be run along its present lines.

The deputy principal and head of upper school, the most recent acquisition in the senior management team, said that the innovatory atmosphere had its obverse side; in practice, many of the innovations just went round and round and never got finalised. People were not disciplined to see things right through, and the lack of achievement could be frustrating.

Creating problems, assigning responsibility to task groups, seeding ideas for other staff to pick up and run with, bringing in catalysts from outside (for example, industrial managers), rewarding innovators, planting allies in obstructive committees, getting 'dead wood' teachers to retire, running weekend conferences, seconding staff to industry, manipulating the situation so that the impetus for change comes from staff, avoiding blueprints and master plans for change but proceeding stealthily a step at a time – were all part of the repertoire of skills that the more innovatory heads deployed to get things on the move.

Some issues to consider

1   Is it a mark of a healthy organisation that innovation and acceptance of change becomes a way of life?

2   What is the head's distinctive role, as the leading professional, in (a) promoting and (b) resisting change within the school?

3   Do heads get the balance right between implementing change within their schools and within the schools' environment (for example, influencing the LEA)?

4   What skills are needed to manage change? How can they best be acquired?

5   Is there a place for outsiders (consultants, catalysts, advisers) in facilitating change in schools?

2.12 Encounters with industry

'The Secretary of State sees a pressing need for head teachers and other senior teachers carrying out management functions to be better equipped for their increasingly difficult and complicated tasks. He has decided that the grants scheme will therefore include a substantial number of one-term training opportunities. . . (which) . . . will include. . . encounters with managers from other fields of education, commerce and industry' – DES Circular No. 3/83

Since the DES initiative on school management training, there has been a considerable increase in the number of dialogues about management between heads and managers in commerce and industry. My research was carried out, however, before this initiative had got very far. The way in which the 20 schools and the respondents within them were selected biased the sample towards those which had had some encounters with industry; even so, the extent of industrial influence on the way schools are managed is not negligible. Practically none of the encounters had been negative or counter-productive; mostly they were valued, and industry came out of them mainly with good repute. Even when there was no significant outcome, it was usually regarded as having offered some interesting insights and stimulation of ideas. The reaction to a secondment to ICI of one head visited can be gauged from the following excerpts from a report he wrote on his return to school:

I left my post as head of a comprehensive school with 1390 pupils and joined the Personnel function of Paints Division. . . My personal disposition towards the task of being a headmaster is that the job is that of a manager. . . Thus an attitude existed which considered experience of management, whatever the environment, to be relevant. . . Care was given to the timing, January to June, and reflection suggests that this was an appropriate incidence and span of absence from school. It was agreed that the LEA would pay my salary and that ICI would support with any out-of-pocket expenses. . . My view at the time was that ICI saw the idea as a positive move towards fostering improved links with education and was approaching it with an open and enthusiastic mind. . . The LEA's position was as positive as that of ICI. . . Part of the potential benefit was considered to be the positive repercussions to the school. . .

Adaptation to a new environment is always problematic and a permanent base for the initial phase is *essential.* . . . All of the staff with whom I came in contact responded in an exciting, encouraging and open mannner that was to be the hallmark of all of my many contacts within the Division, the Company and all external organisations. Colleagues expressed concern for my general welfare throughout and the secretarial and ancillary support was exemplary. . .

One week was spent on a Coverdale I course under the auspices of Plant Protection Division. . . Besides providing an excellent piece of in-service training it gave insights into another Division. . . Throughout the programme an impressive picture of substantial commitment to the socially desirable needs of young people in an area of high unemployment, was received. . . Within the broad framework of understanding of my tasks, I was encouraged by all colleagues to pursue lines of enquiry that became of interest as early researches led in all kinds of directions. . .

What a delight it was to meet with a range and variety of people, throughout the whole secondment, all of whom displayed an openness and awareness that quickly engaged my interest and enthusiasm. There was always present the particular stimulus of anticipated reciprocal involvement and understanding at an appropriate professional level. . . I retain a passionate feeling for the importance of education and I carried this with me into the Division. The experience of being wholly committed to education over a long period can produce an understanding that the external view is of third-rate operatives in a fourth-rate system that anybody with good sense and power can avoid. A general feeling of low status is brought about and this is reinforced by accusations of being non-productive spenders of the country's GNP who have no experience of the 'real' world. Thus there was a strong intention to see whether I could survive as a manager in the real world of ICI. The perception gained is that I could and this has given added confidence about my capacity to manage. . . Whereas previously a defensive attitude might have been taken in any dialogue with industry the future will be one of greater understanding based on this gaining of personal confidence that is matched by a confidence in what industry does. An awareness developed of the overall soundness of the operations investigated and the conclusion is that we must understand that the power of industry must be used to secure its future by participative involvement in education. . .

It is difficult to find a comparable role (to that of a secondary school head) in industry; the nearest might be Works Manager. I sense an identification with the day-to-day challenge of maintaining a complex system; analogies between kettles of chemicals and the potential for exothermic human reactions within the classroom abound. But given this, the size of operation of a large company denies its managers the opportunity to command such an operation and they must accept the management of a small part of a vast entity. Thus, a further perception is that the demands of the job of a headteacher of a secondary school are severe. . .

It was considered that the frustrations of working for a body of elected members, who knew little about the educational process, would be fully relieved in industry but parallels may be found in responding to Directors and the Board; on the other hand there is a general understanding of the Company's business whereas policy is not a universal strength of Local Authorities. I judge that in education the frustrations are similar but less subject to sensible resolution. . .

Management theory is promoted to the educational sector by suppliers of courses, texts and programmes. The general response is a sympathetic rejection because the peddlars suggest that the theories may be applied as an exact science. The reality, of course, is the sensible application of sound theory and techniques within the central issues of interpersonal relationships. I found that this operating system was one with which I could readily identify and I suggest that many educational managers would benefit from this type of experience... Perhaps a balance may be effected by recording a view on the nature of 'Headship' which can easily escape those caught up in the system. There is great job satisfaction to be gained from running your own ship and this satisfaction will be difficult to find in a large organisation. Headteachers should treasure this element of their appointments...

Having now returned it is clear to me that the change in leadership at the school has released potential that might otherwise, to the detriment of the teachers concerned and the school, have been contained. The Acting Headmaster has been able to reach parts not reached by others. My view of headship has been developed through the experience and the headship to which I have returned is not the same as the one that I left. Only a major span of time away can create that possibility and I am determined to seize the chance to move forward... The stimulus of the secondment has been up to the best possible level of anticipated consequences... A summary view is that I have gained important insights concerning myself and the workings of industry, as seen through the secondment to Paints Division. These insights have given me increased confidence about industry and about my role as a headmaster. The product of these insights and added confidence is a greatly increased incentive to act as a promoter of education and industry as co-operative enterprises which are interdependent threads of the same social fabric on which we all rely for our clothing. Pulling apart of these threads will allow chill winds to penetrate the garment of society and I shall seek to weave a closer material by pulling us together... If the end had been a conclusion the adventure would have been in vain.

The closest encounters were those in which a teacher had been seconded to a local firm for periods between three weeks and a year. A second kind was where teachers had spent part of their careers in industry before entering the teaching profession. Four had owned, or been a director of, a business. One head had been a City salesman; a head of department had been the purchasing manager of Wall's Ice Cream; another had helped to run the family hotel business. Close encounters of the third kind were those in which an industrial manager or training officer was regularly used by the school as a consultant, critic or confidant of the head; they would carry out projects on the school's organisation development, run seminars for staff and generally facilitate change. Such activity could (and did) sometimes arouse suspicion and occasionally hostility, but this usually got dissolved in respect for their professional competence and genuine helpfulness.

An initiative that one comprehensive school took with local industry was to invite two training officers to visit the school to evaluate the management work of the head and three deputies. These visits were spread over a period of six months, taking 86 hours in all. This proved rewarding, the process as much as the findings. The results were presented in three columns: findings, conclusions and recommendations. The latter included the need for more written plans, more formally monitored; establishing indicators of non-academic progress; measurement of managerial time spent on various activities to get a better balance between planning and control; clearer division of responsibilities; review of the structure and time spent (5000 hours p.a.) on meetings; deeper consideration of the staff development process.

Another practice that has been effectively introduced is an annual workshop to train the industrial trainers in relevant and topical educational issues such as the Cockcroft Report. One of these produced a checklist of questions for the use of teachers visiting industrial firms and of firms considering taking a teacher on secondment. The deputy head was convinced by her experience of industry of the pressing need to keep industry and education talking to each other so as to develop enough mutual trust 'to be rude to one another' without giving offence.

A characteristic of these close encounters was that one thing often led to another: a secondment to industry would be followed by a return visit; or the original raison d'être for the encounter would give way to another, as mutual trust grew. Not only would the school's organisation be influenced, but also the curriculum. Indeed, it seems that if industry wants to help schools to make the curriculum more relevant, a good way in is through an offer of help with management.

A village college had a good working relationship with a local telecommunications firm which had been helping with the introduction of staff appraisal procedures. The deputies now had written statements of their accountabilities and goals, and heads of departments had new responsibilities for staff development and curriculum development for which they did not all have natural aptitudes. Some training was available, however, both through internal courses and by secondment to industry either on a half-day-a-week basis or for a fortnight full-time.

As well as (and indeed consequent upon) the warden's secondment to an oil company, the latter had seconded to the LEA a management consultant who had used this college as his base. This consultant's report was concerned with the management relationships between the LEA and its schools, with particular reference to the devolution of financial responsibility by means of a pilot scheme of 'local financial management'. The report had been well-received. Both the LEA and the seven pilot schools had welcomed the comments of a third party on this major innovation and many of its recommendations had been taken on board, especially those relating to the planning function. The staff reacted very positively towards the presence of the consultant over a six-week period and, as a result of this good experience and the mitigation of personal threat when working with the industrial firms, teachers were readily seeking outside consultancy support, for example in the development of a staff appraisal scheme.

It is clear that the contacts built up with industry at this college have not only been valued by the warden and staff, but are probably now a self-sustaining feature of the college's approach to management.

At the level of insight, these are some of the things that teachers said that they learned from their encounters with industry:

In industry people (including schoolchildren on work experience) get treated like adults, whereas teachers tend to treat one another like children.
There is more inertia in schools than in industry, where faced with change.
The weakness of the feedback on job performance in schools compared with industry stands out a mile.
Staff performance appraisal and long-term planning are really useful and could be so in schools too.
Before introducing staff appraisal to a school, first look at how industry does it.
Schools are quite out of touch with tomorrow's world.
School management structures are appalling compared with industry's; heads have despotic power and patronage is rife.
Schools have a *laissez-faire* approach to organisation; industry is more aware of structures and their importance.
In commerce training is systematic, in schools random.
In commerce ideas are shared; in schools they are kept secret.
Jobs in industry are less stressful than those of teachers controlling 30 teenagers.
It is easier to plan one's job in industry.
Industry runs good courses – relevant, professional, practical and like clockwork.
Meetings are better run in industry.
Industry is far more precise and economic in its use of language; its reports are models of careful use of language.
Industrial management is sharper than schools'.
Schools pay less attention to husbandry and good stewardship of resources.
Industry is better than schools at setting objectives.
Industry has a lot to offer schools in the use of information technology; it makes impressive use of wordprocessors in particular.
Industry has unexpectedly sensible ideas about assessing schoolchildren.
Training officers really know quite a lot about getting people to learn – maybe more than teachers.

These examples, although having no statistical validity, indicate a fair amount of admiration and respect for industry, which in a number of cases had disconfirmed the stereotypes that teachers formerly held. While the balance of comment was overwhelmingly positive, there was the odd bitter comment; for example, one school that had employed as a teacher a redundant industrial scientist, found that not only was he an incompetent teacher, but he brought with him an unfavourable picture of industry and repeatedly disparaged it.

Finally, it should be remembered that in encounters with industry schools are not the only partners that need enlightenment; one school visited had run a course for local industrial managers entitled 'Comprehending the Comprehensive', which included as an aim 'to demonstrate clearly how schools are managed'; another was 'to remove misconceptions and help redress damage caused by uninformed and unbalanced media criticism'. Good management practice can cross boundaries in both directions.

Some issues to consider

1 Is there any hard evidence that encounters between school and industry introduce alien cultural values, such as materialism?
2 What are the criteria for successful and beneficial encounters with industry?
3 Are the barriers between schools and industry needlessly high?
4 Who should initiate and promote encounters with industry?

2.13 Encounters on management courses

It is a feature of some courses on school management that participants are encouraged to bring with them for mutual discussion examples of the problems they face in their schools. Indeed, as the Hughes Report showed (Hughes, Carter and Fidler 1981), teachers value the opportunity for such peer interaction as well as interaction with lecturers.

Addressing 'real' problems on management courses is often held to be more useful than working with case studies or simulations, though the way in which teachers tackle simulations also yields clues about their management practice. Hence both the real problems and the simulations on courses throw some light on the problems and practice of management in schools. I shall draw some conclusions about these later in the section.

Another source of data is from various exercises and questionnaires that are used as part of the teaching methodology. T.C. Lea of Brighton Polytechnic has been conducting a major study based on the administration of questionnaires to course participants; the purpose is to ensure that the Polytechnic's short courses on school management are kept up-to-date. The questionnaire explores the quality of senior management performance in the following areas: setting objectives, decision-making, planning, directing, co-ordinating, idea generation, communication and keeping up-to-date. It also seeks to establish how heads spent their time, what impairs staff motivation, to what extent schools have clearly defined aims and how far they achieve them.

Managing and being managed

Geoffrey Morris has been administering a 'management principles questionnaire' (Everard and Morris 1985) which has given interesting statistical information about the difference between how heads believe they manage and how they believe they themselves ought to be managed. It shows, for example, that heads believe one should ignore certain faults in others so as not to discourage them, whereas they like to be told when anyone finds fault with their own work. Or again, they think they know enough about their areas for decision-making without having to seek the views of subordinates, though if their 'boss' (in the LEA) is going to take a decision affecting them, they want to be consulted first. Although heads spend a lot of time sorting out problems that their subordinates ought to be able to deal with, they would strongly object to *their* problems being taken over and sorted out. Heads also try to tell their subordinates exactly what to do and how they want it done, whereas they themselves do not usually like being told exactly how to do their jobs. And finally, although they say they nearly always tell their staff why they are making changes, they do not appreciate the logic behind many education office decisions.

The essential point about the findings from such a questionnaire, which yields similar results in industrial settings, is that no matter at what level of management it is administered, respondents feel that they themselves are a special breed, to whom different management principles apply from those they apply to their subordinates. This is one of the problems of management; we do not do unto others that which we would have others do unto us.

Images of teachers as managers

I used another exercise with some 45 participants at the CSCS Annual Conference in 1984 when I took a session on 'Teachers as managers'. This turned out to be very revealing and to have important implications for management development and for public relations. Although the results were published in *Contributions* (Everard 1984–5), they are worth repeating here, together with the theory on which the exercise was based.

The image that we have of ourselves in any particular role is an important determinant of our self-esteem and of our behaviour. Similarly, the image that others have of us determines their attitudes and behaviour towards us. Neither of these images is necessarily an accurate reflexion of how we *really* are, since we can easily delude ourselves, and others can stereotype us from inaccurate and distorted data.

The image we hold of how we would really *like* to be, and the image that we would *like* others to have of us, represent goals to which we might aspire. The difference between the currently perceived image and the 'ideal' image can be a source of energy for development; it points the direction in which we need to grow.

Comparison of our self-image with the image that others have of us can sometimes reveal an undesirable state of ignorance in others, which we may have to dispel if we are to be treated in the way we would wish. Alternatively, it may give us clues to possible self-delusion. Thus any profession that is held in low esteem by society, when that profession believes that, in the circumstances, it serves society well, may be well-advised to attend to its public relations if the unfavourable stereotype is to be changed.

I invited two groups of comprehensive school heads and deputies, three groups of other comprehensive teachers and one group of industrialists – some 45 people in all – to construct two images: (a) of how each group thought of teachers as managers and (b) of how they would like to think of them as managers. It is instructive to examine these word-pictures, and to deduce what would have to be done to respond constructively to any unfavourable features.

First, the good points about the currently perceived image: heads saw teachers (as managers) as being concerned, loyal, hard-working, well-meaning and optimistic. The industrialists saw no good points (any more than teachers construct favourable images of industrial managers). The teachers saw themselves as good at communications, resilient survivors, opportunistic and competent at classroom management.

For all the groups, the unfavourable points far outnumbered the favourable ones, and there was considerable agreement between the groups. In Table 2.6 the letters H (head or deputy), I (industrialist) and T (teacher) are used to show the groups from which the various points emanated. The points can be clustered round eight concepts relating to disposition, job organisation and role, and job skills; two additional concepts are needed to classify the points made about how the groups would like to think of teachers as managers. Points relating to the 'ideal' image are shown in the table in *italics*.

Table 2.6 Current and *Ideal* Images of the Teacher as Manager

A Disposition

A1 Vision. Lacking in foresight, blinkered (H). Naïve (H). Unworldly (I). Idealistic (I). 'Incestuous' (I). Lacking clear objectives (I). Hand-to-mouth (T). *Having foresight (H). Imaginative (H). Visionary (T). Clear school objectives (I). Purposeful (T). Creative (H,T). Aware (H,T). Up-to-date (T). Well-informed (T).*

A2 Attitude to change. Hidebound (H). Impervious to change (H). Impervious to outside ideas (I). Non-innovative (T).
Initiators (H). Open to change (H). Proactive (H). Flexible (H,T). Experimental (H). Able to initiate change (I). Innovative (T). Optimistic (T).

A3 Management style. Authoritarian (H). Secretive (H). Anxious (H). Autocratic (I). Defensive (I). Bossy (I). Crisis management (T). *Dynamic (H,T). Enthusiastic (T). Sensitive/sympathetic (H). Affective (H). Confident (H,T). Determined (H). Set example (I). Leadership qualities (T). Inspiring (T). Charismatic (T). Goals/person-oriented (T). Humane (T). Professional developer (T).*

A4 Motivation. *Likes kids (H). Conscientious (H). Responsible (H). Loyal (H).*

A5 Personal qualities. *Sense of humour (H) Frank (H). Truthful (T). Honest (T). Congruent (T). Sense of fair play (T). Objective (T). Scholarly (T). Wary (T). Sense of proportion (T). Patient (T). Long-suffering (T). Appreciative (T). Self-aware (T).*

B Job organisation and role

B1 Contextual. Overburdened (H). Overworked (T). Harrassed (T). Stressed (T). Undersupported (T). Underresourced (T). Unaware of management role (T). Unsure of role (T). Not appreciated (T). Undervalued (T). Low status (T). Underpaid (T). Status comes from performance as a professional (T). Vulnerable (T).
In control (H). Accountable (H,I). Clear reporting relationships (I). Assessed and self-assessed (I). Empowered (T). Recognised (T). Well-paid for responsibility (T). Well-resourced through negotiation (T). Respected (T).

B2 Efficiency. Unsystematic (H). Ill-prepared (H). Ad hoc (H). Inefficient (H). Often late (H). Non-productive (H). Inattentive to detail (H). Disorganised (I). Cutting corners (T).
Well-organised (H,T). Good administrators (H). Good organisers (T). Efficient (H). Systematic (H). Cool, calm and collected (H).

B3 Isolation/collaboration. Isolated (H). Individualistic (I,T). Concern for subject (T). Belief in autonomy (T).
Responsive to colleagues (H). Collaborative (H). Co-operative (H,T). Work as a team (I).

C Job Skills

C1 Training. Untrained (I,T). Inexperienced (T). Uneasy about managing colleagues (T). Learn management role experientially (T).
Trained (T). Skilled (T). Political (T). Capable of resource decisions (T). Competent (T). Good managers of learning experiences, time, students (I).

C2 Communication. Poor communicators (H). Long-winded (I). Good at communications (T).
Good at listening (H). Communicating (H). Links with external agencies and parents (I). Empathetic (T). Communication skills (I). Articulate (T).

It is noteworthy that in both actual and ideal images, teachers' *characteristics* were mentioned more than their management *skills*. As expected, many are the opposites of those mentioned in the other image.

It may be thought from these lists that what is really needed is improved selection methods, to ensure that those teachers who succeed to positions of managerial responsibility bring the right qualities to the job. Certainly the list of desired qualities could be used in a selection process.

However, it is not difficult to translate many of the qualities into training needs; many trainers in industry and in the public service outside education are accustomed to turning data of this kind into development programmes. For instance, business school courses are often used to broaden horizons and extend the vision of managers. Secondments and projects are also used. There are specific exercises in 'future scenario building' which help to stretch the imagination. Attitudes to change can be modified similarly; people can be helped to understand the nature of change; blockages to creativity can be identified and reduced; skills in coping with change can be developed; and support systems to help those faced with change can be set up.

There are many courses concerned with management style and the development of leadership qualities; they are among the most popular of all management courses. Most are run by private sector organisations, since the affective learning that is involved sits uncomfortably in academic institutions. The motivational and personal qualities listed do not lend themselves easily to training approaches, except for the area of self-awareness and congruence, where 'sensitivity training' can be offered.

The contextual aspects of the images are only partly capable of being changed by the individual teacher; heads have some control over the context in which the teacher acts as a manager, but it is mainly the employing authorities and national government that would have to address the problems revealed under this heading.

The comments listed under 'efficiency' are, in fact, mostly basic managerial skills that can be picked up relatively easily, and which form the backbone of much of the supervisory training that goes on in industry. There are relatively few problems of transfer of this kind of training into the education sector, but academic institutions are not generally as well equipped as private agencies for mounting the courses required.

The propensity of teachers to operate in isolated subject compartments is a weakness of the school organisation; there are structural devices like working parties for breaking down some of the departmental barriers, and training in team skills can be provided to encourage collaboration and develop 'synergy' in the management team (that is, members enhancing one another's efforts, so that the whole is more than the sum of the parts). Communication skills are also readily improved through training.

To summarise, therefore, it is well within the bounds of feasibility for an individual teacher, or for a head, or for a school, to improve the image of the teacher as manager, towards the ends apparently desired by all the groups that generated the data displayed in the table. The managerial approaches and training techniques are well-established and readily available, given the necessary political will to use them.

When it was first published, one head (Evans 1985) criticised the paper for implying that teachers are a breed apart from the rest of humanity in that they find it impossible to acquire proper managerial skills. He asked whether all those who work in the classroom are born with a particular disability which inhibits their managerial powers. He suggested that the real explanation of why teachers see themselves and are seen by others to have managerial weaknesses lies in the nature of their work and the conditions under which they operate; in other words, the problem is largely contextual.

Without wanting to underestimate the effect of environmental demands and resource constraints on the difficulties of managing schools, I believe that changing the context of management is a key part of management and I shall return to this theme in Section 2.16. It would be wrong to externalise the problem of the poor self-image of the teacher as manager by blaming it on circumstances outside the teachers' control; it is the profession that owns the problem and must find ways of solving it. Heads, as leaders, are responsible for maintaining morale and low self-esteem among teachers cannot continue unchecked without jeopardising the effectiveness of the school and of the education service at large.

Psychometric tests

A feature of some industrial management courses on leadership, management style, team-building etc., is the administration of various psychometric tests on participants. According to one survey (Attwood 1979), 16 per cent of 515 UK companies approached said they utilised such tests for management development, where they are used more widely than just in training, for example in selection; and Belbin has carried out some pioneering work with such tests in analysing why management teams succeed or fail (Belbin 1981). I have found his team role tests helpful in both industrial and educational settings and have commented on their use in the latter in *Effective School Management* (Everard and Morris 1985). The Myers-Briggs Type Indicator is equally helpful as a tool in management development (Maxon 1985). Tests developed by Reddin also have a good record in industry (Reddin 1970) and also Hersey and Blanchard's *Leadership Effectiveness and Adaptability Description* (Hersey and Blanchard 1977). More recently tests on learning style have come into use (Kolb 1984; Honey and Mumford 1982).

Such tests are being applied on DES 3/83 courses, for example at the University of London Institute of Education by M. Butcher and myself and at the University College of Cardiff by C. Dimmock (Dimmock 1985). It is too early to make valid generalisations but preliminary results suggest a number of interesting factors which are worth further study. For example, it appears that some differences are emerging between primary and secondary heads which have implications for training. It seems that primary heads as a group prefer to learn management in an 'active' or 'pragmatic' mode, whereas amongst secondary heads there are more who prefer a 'reflective' or 'theoretical' mode. Since management is a practical subject, this implies that secondary heads need to develop their learning skills in the 'active' and 'pragmatic' modes.

Myers-Briggs results are suggesting that secondary heads have a preference for 'judging' rather than 'perceiving'. The implications of this in the work situation are that they may decide things too quickly, they may not notice new things that need to be done, and they like to get things settled and wrapped up, to the extent that they are not good at adapting to changing situations.

Belbin's team role tests have thrown up reasons why some of the learning groups on courses have experienced problems in team working and have suggested to participants that they may have similar problems in the senior management teams in their schools. For example, a team may lack a member who takes on the role of 'completer' or 'finisher'.

Although teachers are sometimes reluctant to undergo tests of this kind, it has been my experience, as in the industrial setting, that the vast majority who do so find them helpful in diagnosing problems and pointing the direction in which they might be tackled. They are a useful adjunct to staff appraisal for identifying specific management training needs.

Real management problems brought to courses

Since teachers who bring their current management problems for discussion on courses have understandable concerns about confidentiality, the nature of the problems known to me can only be described in general terms. The following sample brought by secondary heads on one particular course is representative of the strong bias towards 'people problems'; even those with a strong organisational flavour often turn out to be caused by the rigid attitudes of key members of staff.

1 Acting deputy head lacking in management qualities and suffering from emotional instability;
2 Mental instability of a teacher;
3 Complaints about competence of teacher suffering family and health problems;
4 Appointment of an unsatisfactory teacher in a shortage subject;
5 Misbehaviour of pupils and/or a member of staff on an away visit;
6 Caretaker with unhelpful attitudes towards both cleaners and teachers;
7 Unwillingness of a particular department to change the curriculum;
8 Obtaining compensation for accident to member of staff;
9 Amalgamation of two schools: how to organise the pastoral curriculum;

10   Damage limitation from adverse HMI report;
11   Estranged father trying to contact daughter at school.

This bias bears out the conclusion drawn from my school visits, that people problems preoccupy heads more than any other and that the specific problem of the unsatisfactory performer among the staff is one for which heads feel most in need of support and help.

Another picture can be built up from the answers given by course members to the question 'To what questions do you want answers during this course?'. Presumably a practical problem lurks at the back of each answer. A representative set of answers given on several courses from both primary and secondary heads, regrouped mainly under the categories used in section 2.4, is given below.

Staff problems

How can the head re-animate an ossified 50-year old with nowhere to go?
How can the head redirect staff who despite encouragement and positional influence exude pessimism?
How can we switch on the time-servers?
How to deal with personality problems?
How to involve unwilling staff?
How to manage failure?
How can one create a climate of trust among the staff?
How to foster a corporate spirit?

Stress

How to manage stress?
How can we avoid staff feeling threatened by change?
How to respond to the circumstances and frustrations of staff?
How can I maintain morale in the face of low pay, disparagement etc.?
How can I reconcile my ideology with reality?

Administrative problems

How do we improve record-keeping provision?
How to establish a staff appraisal (or self-appraisal) system in the school?
How can we develop an effective use of time?
What strategies are there for the management of contraction?
How do we create and use aims and objectives in school development?
What methods exist for long-term planning?
How to make effective use of new technology?
How to establish priorities?
How is the effective flow of work through the school office organised?
How can effective course teams be established across departments?
What are the basic principles of running effective meetings?
How can leadership styles be developed in internal school management?
How can the head resolve conflict in departments?

Resources and relationships with LEAs

What ways exist for influencing the LEA?
How to manage and generate money?
How do we efficiently and effectively manage resources, for example points, budgets, time, space?
How are good relations engendered between schools and LEA?

Salaries and rewards

How should a successful teacher be encouraged?
How can task rotation be reconciled with Burnham Scale points/job descriptions?

Discipline

How can we get guidance and skills in handling disciplinary procedures?
What do we do instead of caning?
What methods of pupil control are effective?

Legislation etc.

How do we manage the militant?
How should we manage the 1981 Act?
How do we cope with increased politicisation of education?

External relations

What skills are required in dealing with outside agencies?
What abilities are needed in dealing with governors?
What means are there for educating parents?
What skills are needed to improve the use of support agencies?
How can we involve the community in the school and vice versa?
To whom and for what are we accountable?
Whose interests are schools serving?
Should we be marketing schools?
How can effective links be established with primary, tertiary and careers service?
How do we develop an effective two-way communication system within and outside the school?
Should the school become the focal point of the community?
How do we engender real contacts with industry and commerce?
How can we improve the public image of education?

Change

How does one (a) encourage and (b) reject new ideas?
How does one keep the balance between stability and change?
How do you create a climate for change?
What leadership qualities are required for the head in conditions of approaching major reorganisation?
How can you involve all members of staff in management of change?

Among these particular groups of heads there were relatively fewer references to salaries and rewards and more references to external relations and to change than emerged from my school visits. Also, perhaps because of the training context, the need for improved skills on the part of the respondent was made more explicit and indeed could have become a new category.

Behaviour of heads on management courses

This is a difficult section to write, other than impressionistically, yet it strikes me as useful to record a number of my observations about heads (and other teachers) working in groups and how they reacted to management training. Having observed something like 1000 industrial managers on courses, I had some expectations of what might happen when heads were exposed to a similar experience. In many respects, the 200-odd I have encountered reacted in much the same way as their industrial counterparts, but there were some interesting differences.

Application and intensity

The typical industrial management course is a five-day residential event, starting at 9 a.m. and finishing at about 10 p.m. with perhaps two free periods during the week. Participants often 'talk shop' in unstructured time and work informally late at night. The course staff also work very late, to review the day's proceedings and plan the next. Few industrial managers or trainers have questioned this regime and there is certainly a case for arguing that an intense course is more effective. See, for example, the report of P. Allsop, a comprehensive school teacher, of a leadership course on which the working day built up to 6.30 a.m. till after midnight (Allsop 1985). It is more common for first line supervisors to object to this intensity, partly on grounds of political principle and partly because those without an academic background tend to be less resilient in an educational setting.

The typical school management course in my experience is non-residential and lasts from 10 a.m. till 4 or 4.30 p.m., particularly if participants have long distances to commute to it. This in itself makes for a much less intense experience and although some groups make plans to work outside normal hours, it does not seem to be regarded as normal even to use the evenings for reading and preparation. Nonetheless, heads sometimes complain of being drained of energy by 4.30 and the pace of the course is apt to slacken in the afternoon. An evaluation report of such a course says 'They found full lecture and seminar days too long' and elsewhere 'The days seemed long to heads used to constantly changing activity.' It is also my impression that primary heads work harder during a course than do secondary heads.

I found this difference in application and intensity very pronounced.

One conclusion is that the residential element enables a good deal more mileage to be gained and certainly there was no unwillingness of heads to work during the evening of the 24-hour residential component of the one-term courses with which I have been associated. By contrast, commuting is not a relaxing activity, though many have to get used to it.

Another possibility is that heads arrive on courses in a more emotionally drained state than industrial managers, so they tend to use the course more for 'battery recharging'. I do not think this is a major cause of difference, because the work schedules of many industrial managers are also punishing.

A further possibility is that teachers have become accustomed to thinking in terms of a 9–4 school day, even though they schedule meetings after school, take work home and arrive early. Office hours in industry are nearer 9–5.30 and most managers take work home. Yet another explanation is that industrial managers below the rank of chairman do in fact have more commitment and application to training, seeing its outcome in terms of increased possibilities of career advancement, whereas heads have got nearer the top of their profession and do not expect the same kind of reward from applying themselves to a course.

Of these explanations, I suspect that the first is nearest the truth. If so, it raises the question of whether – given that the highest cost element in training is the salary of the trainee (or, more precisely, the lost value of the normal work for which his salary is paid, and which in industrial settings should be worth more than his salary) – it would not be preferable to run more school management courses residentially and more intensively.

Leading professional/chief executive tension

Some heads are deeply conscious of a role conflict between the two parts of their job: that which is concerned with being the leading professional teacher, a *primus inter pares,* and that which is concerned with other aspects of managing their schools. Those who put the leading professional role first tend to be reluctant learners of management. In industry, similar tension is experienced by some research scientists and engineers between their professional role (and the values associated with it) and their managerial role.

However, trainers in educational management need to be a good deal more sensitive than those in industry to the risk of offending professional values. For example, one presentation on leadership, which is normally highly regarded in industry and education alike, was strongly criticised by a group of heads because it illustrated some aspects of leadership by showing a war film 'Twelve O'clock High'. It happens to be an exceedingly telling portrayal of an important aspect of leadership which is equally applicable to non-military situations; but the medium got in the way of the message.

Judgement and feedback

Although it is an essential part of the work of a manager, as of a teacher, to make judgements about people as a guide to appropriate action, for some heads this goes against the grain. Indeed one, as a matter of principle, refused to take part in an exercise that involved distributing five points among a number of her colleagues' statements of objectives to indicate which she thought were the most soundly formulated. It was, she felt, tantamount to evaluating a colleague's work. This is perhaps a rather extreme example of an underlying reluctance to give feedback. Industrial managers also sometimes express misgivings about 'taking one another apart' and some are uncomfortable in the staff appraisal role. However, the sensitivity of teachers to this issue is undoubtedly greater (as Bowden has also noted – Bowden 1985) and is perhaps associated with their reluctance to introduce staff appraisal systems.

I am in no doubt that in properly structured situations, the making of judgements about other peoples' behaviour and its effect, followed by the giving of such judgements to the people concerned, is an invaluable part of the personal development process. An objective of management should be to obtain willing consent to the giving of such judgements – which implies an atmosphere of trust in their use in the interests of the individual.

Systematic approach

The systematic approach to getting things done is a very common component, if not the core, of management training. The basic steps are:
1   Define what we are seeking to achieve in the specific situation to solve the problem;
2   Identify why we are seeking to achieve it;
3   Generate alternative means of achieving this;
4   Decide which means to adopt;
5   Act on the decision;
6   Review successes and failures in order to improve performance.

These steps are amplified by some trainers to include tuning in to the problem, setting success criteria to define what constitutes an acceptable solution, and a planning stage.

It is my impression that, as a group, heads have more difficulty than industrial managers in carrying out those steps that relate to defining the problem and what is to be achieved by solving it (including the setting of success criteria), in formulating a plan and in reviewing the process they followed to accomplish the task. They also find difficulty in managing time and fitting tasks into the time available.

While the training of industrial managers in the systematic approach is by no means always plain sailing, more of them seem to exhibit a natural readiness to think collectively and work in a team towards a commonly understood aim and then to ask themselves how they might have done better.

Heads, on the other hand, prefer to work individually and intuitively, jumping to decisions before they have properly analysed the problem. They also lose one another's good ideas in a single-minded pursuit of their own. Their listening skills are not well developed and they underestimate the value of a group thinking in silence.

This may be a reflexion of the fact that more work in industry is done by teams of people, whereas in schools most teachers work in the privacy of their classrooms. However, some teamwork is indispensible in the running of all organisations and in the management of strategic change it is particularly important. So my conclusion is that, difficult though they may find it to follow a common systematic approach, teachers would be well advised to learn how to do so.

Aims and objectives

My impression is that both in practising the systematic approach and in other ways, teachers find it particularly difficult to conceptualise terms like 'aims' and 'objectives' in the same way as industrial managers and to use them as an aid to management. They tend to perceive the work of the school as a complex set of activities of a kind that have been carried out for generations. They see their own jobs as *dealing with* things. Answers to questions such as 'What are you trying to achieve?' and 'What are your aims?' do not come naturally. This is not to say that teachers do not have aims, nor that educational aims are easy to define, but that the pursuit of aims is apparently not the mainspring of their work. They tend to define their jobs in terms of inputs rather than outcomes and seem quite happy to do tasks without being clear what they are trying to achieve or how far they have got in achieving it.

One of the exercises I use on management courses is to get the participants to formulate a personal objective on the course, a personal objective in their school after the course, and an organisational objective for their school. It takes a long time, and the results tend to be vague and unspecific, like 'To learn as much as I can', 'To apply back in school the things I have learned' and 'To improve communication in school'.

The next question is 'How will you know when you have achieved your objectives?'. In other words, what are their success criteria? Answering this question for each of the objectives takes even longer. A good deal of help has to be given before their objectives are soundly formulated; this means that they are as specific, as clear, as concise, as time-bounded and as observable or measurable as possible; they should be results-centred rather than activity-centred and realistic rather than pessimistic. Success criteria define the situation that should exist when the objective has been attained.

Managers in industry have also to be trained to think in terms of objectives; at one time 'management by objectives' (MBO) was one of the popular packages, and books have been written about it (for example, Humble 1971). It is also an integral part of Coverdale and Reddin training. Although MBO is less fashionable than it was in the 1960s, industrial managers in general seem to have become more accustomed to setting objectives and targets as a daily part of their work.

There is little doubt that objective-setting has an important part to play in organisational life. It is one of the two main methods for getting things to happen in the organisation – the other being the exercise of power and authority. Having objectives that they believe to be just within their reach motivates people to achieve them, especially if there is a reward or praise for success. Further arguments for the use of objectives and targets in managing schools have been adduced by Trethowan (Trethowan 1983a and 1985).

The following excerpts from official reports are among those that illustrate the importance attached by the DES and HMI to the setting and monitoring of aims and objectives:

HMI Mathematics: 'There was a frequent tendency among heads of departments to underestimate the need for positive leadership. . . larger schools make managerial skills essential. . . He may need to persuade his department to undertake a deeper analysis of their aims, objectives and teaching methods. . . where aims were stated they were usually in commendably liberal terms but the lessons observed with examination classes were most commonly directed much more towards the requirements of the examination than to the realisation of the stated aims. . .' (HMI 1979).

HMI Science: 'It was apparent during the survey that science departments were more likely to be well organised if there was leadership from an overall head of science. Unfortunately, not all departments were effectively led and as a result there was a noticeable lack of direction, staff cohesion and unity of purpose in the work' (HMI 1979).

HMI Modern Languages: 'The ideal head of department would have formulated, in consultation with colleagues, a programme of work which spelt out realistic objectives and indicated how these might be achieved within the limitations imposed by the ability of pupils, by school organisation and by the availability of equipment. . . It is sad to have to record that in something like 602 of the survey schools, such support (i.e. for the junior teacher) was lacking to a significant extent. . . HM Inspectors were forced to conclude that many heads of department showed little awareness of the responsibilities they bore beyond the walls of their own classroom' (HMI 1971).

The Bullock Report on the teaching of English: '"I see the role of head of department as concerned first of all with teachers. Unless he can lead his department so that it is a unit, I don't think we can progress very far". Our visits left us in no doubt how demanding a job this is, especially in large schools. . .'. In relation to a teacher who admitted that his choice of work was determined largely by impulse: "This kind of directionless drift is clearly related to questions of leadership, consultation and joint planning within the department, but the absence of a working document is an aspect of these. . ." If there is no agreed statement of purpose, every teacher is on his own' (Bullock 1975).

Paisey argues that the importance of aims and objectives arises from the need to sharpen up the inexplicit task that society gives to schools (Paisey 1981). He describes them as reference points for the efforts of the organisation, necessary for the co-ordination of effort. They define the end towards which all organisational action is directed and they are prerequisites to the determination of effective policies, procedures, strategies and rules. They are analagous to the star used for navigation.

Making plans

Another difficulty that arises in carrying out a task or solving a problem during a course is in the formulation of a plan. The word 'plan' occurs less in the common parlance of teachers than in that of industrial managers and it is sometimes confused with an 'intention' or a 'decision'.

The description of a plan contains the means of its own implementation; in other words, it specifies unmistakably who does what by when. General statements like 'The group must allocate more time to process reviews' are not plans, whereas a statement like 'At the beginning of the next task the chairman will set and work to a timetable that allows fifteen minutes at the end for a review' is a plan for achieving the group's intention.

It is an important task of management to ensure that what is decided actually gets done, hence the need for specifying a plan.

There were four people named Everybody, Somebody, Anybody and Nobody. There was an important job to be done and Everybody was asked to do it. Everybody was sure Somebody would do it. Anybody could have done it, but Nobody did it. Somebody got angry about that, because it was Everybody's job. Everybody thought Anybody could do it but Nobody realised that Everybody wouldn't do it. It ended up that Everybody blamed Somebody when Nobody did what Anybody could have done (ATM 1985).

Pedagogy

One might expect teachers to be expert in the processes by which people learn. However, as has been found by the Industrial Training Research Unit and by the Further Education Unit, this is not always the case. One of the objects of the DES 3/83 one-term courses is to equip experienced heads for training other heads on twenty-day basic courses; by no means all those who take part in one-term courses are likely to be able to fulfil this objective. Those who are steeped in traditional ways of teaching, by didactic lecturing methods, find it hard to come to terms with experiential forms of learning, that is, learning by doing. I have found an article by Josephine McHale '"Read, write and keep rabbits": a strategy for learning' (McHale 1984) helpful in making this point, but a more thorough treatment of the subject is in 'How do I learn?' (FEU 1981).

Understanding how people (especially adults) learn is an important part of a manager's job; it is sad that teachers do not seem to have a head start over industrial managers.

The self-development approach in which managers are encouraged to be responsible for their own learning, is currently fashionable (see, for example, Mumford 1980; Burgoyne, Boydell and Pedler 1978; Pedler, Burgoyne and Boydell 1978). I have not found it easy to persuade heads to take more responsibility for their own development; they seem to prefer a dependency relationship with the tutors.

Reading

Many useful books and articles have been written about management, and while they are no substitute for the practice of management skills, they can play a valuable part in the development of any manager. It has always proved difficult to get most industrial managers to read such books, because some of their study skills seem to atrophy as the years go by since leaving university or polytechnic. Unexpectedly, I have found that most heads do not read either. Despite the opportunities of a one-term course to have convenient access to libraries and to use the evenings to read, little reading is done. On the other hand, Yates in a survey of opinion about professional development of headteachers (Yates 1983) reported that heads considered personal reading likely to be by far the most acceptable and successful form of development activity, though advisers put it only fifth in the same list. In the case of award-bearing courses, the position may well be different since students are examined in what they have read.

Guided reading is an economical method of learning, so perhaps there should be stronger encouragement on one-term courses to take reading seriously and to share the perceptions and insights that follow (see section 4.10).

Presentations

One of the exercises done on a number of one-term courses is to design and deliver a presentation of some aspect of management to less experienced teachers. The artistry, imagination and flair with which some of these modules have been presented, especially by primary school heads, is admirable and in some cases surpasses that which is regarded as acceptable in industry. The use of cartoons is especially praiseworthy. Equally, heads can be very critical of unimaginative presentations to courses by visitors from industry, even though the content is relevant.

In crossing the learning bridge between industry and education, their skills in visual presentation are something that teachers could proudly carry with them.

Some issues to consider

1   How reliable are one's own perceptions of one's management style, strengths and weaknesses? Have questionnaires, psychometric tests and similar instruments a useful diagnostic part to play, (a) in selection and (b) in management development? If so, how can their use be encouraged?

2   In their management role, do teachers collectively display characteristics that differentiate them from managers in non-educational organisations? If so, what implications does this have for the profession, in terms of public image and training needs?

3   Heads appear to be highly preoccupied by people problems in managing their schools. Their counterparts in industry would often have the support of a personnel department in handling these. Should heads have a similar support system or should they learn to cope with such problems by themselves?

4   To what extent should management courses be designed as 'clinics' and address specifically the many real problems that heads are capable of bringing to such courses?

5   Would school management training be more effective if it followed the industrial pattern of a series of short intensive, residential courses?

6   Is the role conflict between leading professional and chief executive disabling enough to justify separation of the two roles (for example, head and bursar) or would schools be more effective if heads learned to resolve the conflict?

7   Making subjective judgements about people and giving them feedback is part of management, but is not a well established activity among the staff of some schools. How can it be encouraged for the benefit of both the school and the individual?

8   Does your experience confirm the judgement that teachers' ability to formulate objectives, approach problems systematically and make plans for achieving objectives is relatively underdeveloped? If so, do you consider that these skills should figure prominently in school management training courses? How can they best be developed within the school?

9   Teachers and trainers are both in the business of helping people to learn, but their pedagogical approaches are often distinctively different. What should teachers and their training counterparts in industry, the services etc., be doing at the local level to learn from one another, so that both can become more effective?

10   What can heads and management course directors do to guide and encourage the regular study of books and articles on management as a means of stimulating improvements in management practice?

2.14 Findings of other observers and commentators

The particular orientation of my studies of schools was towards characterising problems in schools and drawing parallels with management problems in industry. There have been many studies of schools by outside observers but mainly by academics rather than by industrialists or consultants working mainly in industry. Nevertheless, some observers do attempt to compare schools with industry, and I have selected a few whose findings complement my own. Some of their reports are in the form of duplicated LEA or school documents and in one case the investigator has yet to write up his interesting fieldwork.

Handy

Professor Charles Handy (formerly of Shell) made comparisons with industry when he carried out a study of school organisations for the Schools Council (Handy 1984). He adeptly captures the essence of schools as organisations and compares them with other organisations, especially those known to be effective. He concludes that criteria for organisational effectiveness in schools and industry are largely common. He contrasts primary schools, which are almost pure 'task cultures', with secondary schools which are predominantly 'role cultures' and asks if there really needs to be the difference. Role cultures are difficult to change and are bad at adapting to changes in the environment. They are alien to the disposition of teachers, who much prefer to work in organisations having a task culture or a person culture. Consequently they are difficult organisations to manage. He identifies four key differences between schools and other organisations:

1 Schools set aside practically no time for management, because it interferes with teaching;

2 They have too many purposes – educational, custodial, certificating and socialising – and too few ways of measuring success, which is itself a major management problem;

3 The teacher has to fulfil too many roles, being an adult among children, an adult among equals, a subordinate in a team and a salesperson to parents; when they have to be manager as well (a term that itself covers the conflict between 'leader' and 'administrator'), the stress becomes unreasonable;

4 The children . Although they are part of the organisation, they are not always seen to be. Their organisational role is confused; are they members collaborating in joint endeavour? Are they beneficiaries served by the endeavour? Or are they the output it shapes and develops? The way secondary schools are organised, children seem to be regarded as the *output*. In primary schools they are *members* of the organisation. In sixth form colleges they are *beneficiaries*.

Handy's findings are consistent with my own, but his emphases are different. In differentiating schools from industry, he puts more stress than I think is justified on the multi-purpose nature of schools and the multi-faceted role of the teacher. Large industrial organisations also have multiple objectives, often with tension between them, and recently the trend in their management has been away from emphasis on narrow specialist functions towards handling complete businesses. This has led managers to acquire a wider repertoire of specialisms than heretofore – public relations, personnel etc. – because such support functions have dwindled in size. Thus the separation he recommends between the role of leading professional and chief administrator (giving the latter to a bursar for example) runs counter to the current trend in industry to combine general administration with functional management. It may still be right for schools, however, if the administrator and leading professional succeed in working synergistically. In any case, as Handy says, 'The first essential in all schools must be to attend to the administrative function and staff it properly'.

Points that struck both of us from our industrial perspective were:
1   Meetings: difficult to arrange, often rushed, and relatively few in number; 'debating chamber' rather than practical problem solving style;
2   Management structure: more concentrated at the top with less discernible layers of management lower down the organisation than in industry;
3   Industrial managers more pragmatic; school managers (especially secondary) more analytical and perfectionist;
4   Children not seen as part of the organisation structure; lesson changes in secondary schools make them seem more like part of a production line than like task groups;
5   Similarity between the hallmarks of good schools, identified by HMIs in *Ten Good Schools* (HMI 1977), and those of good companies by Peters and Waterman in *In Search of Excellence* (Peters and Waterman 1982);
6   Need to have a clearer separation between policy formulation and execution; a policy structure consists of boards, councils, committees or moots, whereas an executive structure consists of individuals in roles;
7   The importance of believing that schools can change, then choosing a method of changing them.

A new book by Handy on *Understanding Schools* is being published in 1986 (Handy and Aitken 1986).

Duffett

Roger Duffett, a senior consultant in BP International Limited, was commissioned by Cambridgeshire LEA to comment impartially on aspects of the education service from an industrial manager's point of view. His report (Duffett 1982), the response to which by one head has been described in section 2.12, brings out a number of interesting points:

1 'It was a recurrent theme in the discussions that management in schools should not be compared to management in industry!'. He believes this to be based on a misconception of industrial management.

2 The education service is ill-at-ease with any hierarchial system. An industrial manager's decision, if backed by professional advice, is respected; a head does not receive similar respect.

3 Schools expect their heads to possess charisma, as a substitute for management style. In industry charisma is a bonus, not a necessity.

4 'Efficiency' is a word frequently used in schools in a pejorative sense. Pervading all considerations of efficiency and effectiveness is an excessive emphasis on scheduling rather than planning, operation rather than strategy.

5 Schools have no idea how to launch an innovation. They do not go through the processes of setting aims, preparation, education, involvement and follow-up.

6 Heads are expected to be knowledgeable teachers, to the extent that their needs to convince other teachers of their professional ability have become self-indulgent. Industrial managers are not expected to be adept at shop-floor work.

7 The gulf of responsibility between a deputy head and a head appears disproportionately large.

8 There is a yawning gap of understanding between schools, area offices and the central office of the LEA. There would be more benefit in promoting forbidden transitions between the four roles of primary and secondary head, inspectors and education officers than of secondary heads to secondment posts outside the education service.

9 Heads appear to have no difficulty with parochial identity but find it hard to define a corporate image.

10 The role relationship between the head and the school governing body is ill-developed; neither is well-equipped to discharge its responsibilities towards the other. The relationship should parallel that between a board of directors and a general manager.

11 Arrangements for the training of teachers for management and leadership are poor. Education management is seen as a discipline to be studied didactically for its own sake, with an emphasis on the understanding of theories. Industrial management training is concerned with the art or practice of management, based on participation and experience.

12 Career development should be improved by encouraging more movement across the education service, by introducing an appraisal system for all teachers and by taking action on the assessments arising from such a system.

I visited only one of the schools included in Duffett's study, but my conclusions broadly support his. There are minor exceptions, however; I could cite a few schools to which his conclusions 5 and 7 do not apply.

Jamieson

In his contacts with industrialists who have been involved with schools, Ian Jamieson, then evaluator of the Schools Council Industry Project, has noted a number of features that differentiate management in industry from that in schools (Jamieson 1981):

1   While teachers are critical of many features of industry, they admire the way in which industrialists organise themselves; management organisation and structure are given greater prominence in industry than in schools.

2   There is more management training in industry and more use of consultants. Staff development and appraisal show even bigger differences. Industrialists think that schools neglect their 'human capital'. In industry, the development of the individual is seen in the context of what the business requires to do in order to meet the company objectives; not so in schools.

3   Teachers are impressed with the human relations and interpersonal skills of senior managers in industry, for example their chairing of meetings, efficient minuting and use of time. They have much better access to data about staff, especially as regards performance on the job.

4   Industrialists say of schools that there is not enough concentration on the total product, and too much emphasis on particular sub-goals; that is, there are strong departmental barriers.

5   Industrialists also note a lack of precision in formulating aims and objectives of teaching programmes, especially at the level of the department; and there is an absence of systematic structures to review progress against goals.

6   Schools resemble pre-war family firms, with a paternalistic management style and a lack of delegation of authority and involvement in decision-making.

7   There is a pronounced lack of clerical support staff in schools compared with industry.

Again, these perceptions are congruent with my own, except that 4 is less true of primary than secondary schools.

Jenkins

Hugh Jenkins has made a direct comparison between 49 senior managers in schools and manufacturing industry and the way they each perceive their jobs (Jenkins 1985). He points out that the task/activity studies that have been carried out on school heads in Britain, the USA and Australia reveal not only a considerable similarity between continents, but when the behaviour of the heads is compared to that of non-educational managers as recorded by Mintzberg (Mintzberg 1973), again the similarity is striking. However, there are some significant differences:

1 Future planning and corporate policy making do not figure strongly in the task activities of heads; they are preoccupied with day-to-day organisational maintenance. Chief executives, on the other hand, while also involved in administration and short-term problem-solving, have a commitment to future planning and regard performance analysis and target achievement as essential components of corporate planning.

2 Heads perceive their jobs as highly people-centred but their activities are biased towards counselling staff informally and consulting them at formal meetings; they hardly mention staff development, in-service training and assessment. Pupil control and interaction with parents are also important activities. Chief executives also show a concern for people but this is linked closely to production and the more structured people-activity of industrial relations.

3 Heads' external orientation is towards the problems thrown up by the school's immediate environment. Chief executives, on the other hand, maintain links with a much wider environment, but particularly that part which deals with competition. In both cases, deputies have less developed links with the environment.

4 There is more of a harmonious balance of leadership style between chief executives and managers than between heads and deputies; in schools the roles of the top management team members appear too undifferentiated and undefined.

5 Questions of stability, control and continuity are significantly important to heads but not so to chief executives, who appear to be able to take a longer term view while immediate disturbances are resolved.

6 The range of managerial tasks carried out by heads is narrower than that of their industrial counterparts. Their over-involvement in operational issues seems to leave a vacuum in schools as far as the creation of an overall strategy or sense of direction is concerned. They do not become much involved with financial and resource planning nor with critical evaluation.

7 Heads see it as more important than do chief executives to engage in activities within the body of the organisation; they still like teaching, disciplining pupils and being the focal point of contact with parents, whereas chief executives would delegate equivalent tasks and would leave systems-maintenance tasks to middle managers while they focused on the broader picture.

8 Chief executives have real power to manage their organisations; heads have a fair degree of autonomy, but little control over resources.

All eight differences are in line with the impressions I have gained from school visits, though I would have expressed the last somewhat differently. I think it would be more accurate to say that heads have more power to manage their organisations than chief executives, but their power extends over a narrower range of activities. For instance, they have less control over the reward system, but more control over the culture of the organisation. As Torrington and Weightman say, 'The head has power in relation to staff and pupils, and status within the organisation, far exceeding that of most managers. This is not only in the legal basis of the head's appointment, but is willingly endorsed and emphasised by staff and parents. This is most clearly seen in the position of deputy heads and senior teachers, who have nothing like the range of authority and independence that is found among senior managers in business. The complexity and difficulty of running a modern secondary school – especially a comprehensive school – is far beyond the capacity of a single leader figure in the traditional role of the head, yet heads, staff and parents conspire to prevent the dispersion of power a head wields' (Torrington and Weightman 1983).

Bowden

Bowden, Head of Leftwich High School, Northwich, was seconded to the North West Educational Management Centre to study the way in which industry trains and develops managers (Bowden 1985). He has written an interesting and perceptive report which is worth summarising here, although he did not study schools as well as industry.

He found that some of his previous impressions of industry were false. He came to realise that:

1   Industrial management is not simpler and more clear-cut than school management;
2   Industrial managers too have to make do with less, cope with conflicting demands and have no easy answers to problems they share with schools;
3   They also have to cope with unworkable legislation, and have the same difficulties of getting rid of inept and ineffective staff and of suitably rewarding excellence;
4   Many companies have been reducing staff numbers for years and feel the same threat to security as schools;
5   Long hours, homework and after-hours commitments are common;
6   Deadlines, staff illness, unsuitable premises, financial cuts and unreliable suppliers are not confined to education;
7   In industrial organisations systems rule and people have to fit in;
8   The concern of some educationists about the application of industrial management techniques to education is based on a lack of understanding of management as it is practised in industry today.

As well as the similarities between the management of schools and industrial organisations, he also found differences, though I would question to what extent these are all fundamental and inherent in the nature of schools; my comments are in brackets.

1   Schools do not have generally agreed goals and priorities
2   The head has to communicate with and be accountable to more constituencies than the industrial manager and they do not all agree on the primary task of the school;
3   Teachers view teamwork, collective responsibility and autonomy differently from many commercial employees (why?);
4   Flexibility in the use of resources and operational methods is more constrained (but this is changing in the Cambridgeshire LEA);
5   The head fulfils four management functions that in industry are often carried out by different people: educational (technical), operations (plant), staff (personnel) and constituency (public relations); and sometimes also marketing and publicity;
6   Staff appraisal is underdeveloped in schools; the effectiveness of a teacher or head of department is more difficult to assess than that of a section manager [yes, but not than that of a training manager or a scientist doing long-term research];
7   The head is more open to public exposure and hence to personal stress;
8   Various *in loco parentis* duties like assembly and school meals have no counterpart in industry.
   Among his conclusions are that:
1   The jobs of industrial managers and school heads have many more common strands than differences;
2   There is in schools a potential for professional collaboration and corporate purpose which is rarely fully harnessed;
3   Industrial training experience is relevant to the needs of schools;
4   Industrial training has greater pace, intensity, directness and penetration than the typical educational course and is better at influencing attitudes;
5   Preparation and follow-up are integral parts of industrial training and are used to assess outcomes of courses;
6   It is more cost-effective to train groups of managers from fewer schools than individual heads from many schools;
7   A development structure or network is needed to provide adequate support and reinforcement;
8   Schools need to examine their administration processes to improve organisational effectiveness and diminish frenetic activity: for example, in relation to meetings, communications, jobs, tasks (problem seeking and clarification), teamwork, time management, duplication of effort and delegation, professional accountability and prevention of stagnation and burn-out.
   Bowden makes pertinent points about the stressful nature of the head's role and points out that much of the industrial training he experienced fosters the development of a coping style. In particular, it encourages learning about oneself, how one relates to others, how to develop teams,

how to clarify jobs, how to identify and separate tasks so that they are tackled logically, how to accept that not all organisational problems are the result of personal failure and how to develop a culture in which professional dialogue about performance can take place without insult or threat.

His personal reaction to the industrial management courses in which he participated has many implications for school management training. He found the content always relevant and valuable in dealing largely with real situations. Learning was by doing, not listening. In dealing with problems, it is essential to define the key issue clearly. His normal approach to problems was revealed to him as intuitive and uncontrolled. It is better to describe jobs in terms of key result areas (accountability) rather than activities. It is revealing and useful to learn how to analyse both meetings and the process of negotiation. The results of some of the psychometric tests used were 'frighteningly accurate' and were one of the most productive elements in the course. An exercise in the analysis of management activities 'provided the most practical and penetrative appraisal of performance I have encountered'.

The whole report bears strong testimony to the benefits that school heads can derive from encounters with industry at the level of a practical management course. The author's grasp of management in the industrial setting and the nature of industrial management training, strikes me as exceptionally accurate. He has picked out many of the most salient points about industry which are germane to the problems that I have encountered in schools.

Anon

Another recent study (unpublished, but described at a seminar in July 1985) has been undertaken on secondment by the headmaster of a secondary comprehensive school, who has approved my summary of his findings but wishes to remain anonymous until his report has been written up. I am indebted to him for allowing me to publish his results before he does. He interviewed 47 colleagues in England and Wales holding posts similar to his own and put to them a number of questions similar to mine. Salient conclusions were:

1 Problems
Their most prolific source of problems was some difficulty caused by a member of senior management (17 heads said this). Other problems were: staffing difficulties caused by lack of promotion prospects, lack of motivation etc. (14); performance of middle management (7); and coping with constant change in the educational scene (5). Current problems faced were: managing a declining environment (25), staff morale (18), middle management performance (9) and narrow vision of staff (7).

2 Own development
The most frequently (18) quoted source of their management ability was their previous professional experience. Twelve had had no management training since becoming head; 30 had been on a course; 16 thought they needed training in managing people, time, finance etc., and five in promoting or coping with change.

3 Weaknesses
Asked about their own weaknesses, the areas most frequently mentioned were: managing/communicating with people, not being ruthless enough, forward planning, lack of formal management training, and poor public relations.

4 Mistakes
Their main mistakes had been in: bad appointments (20), errors in relations or communications with staff (16), mistiming innovation (11), mismanagement of public relations (5) and poor industrial relations (4). Their most often quoted examples of bad management practice were: breakdown of relations with a senior member of staff (8), unsatisfactory head of department (7) and malfunctioning at middle management level (7).

5 Support
Their main sources of advice about management problems were: fellow head teachers (32) and deputies and senior colleagues (23).

6 Decisions
The dominant management style claimed by the heads was 'open', 'participative' etc. (31). Thirty-seven thought themselves good or satisfactory at delegation, and only 10 weak. Important decisions were made by the head after discussion with staff (26), by consensus, as far as possible (10), by the senior management group (7) and by 'benevolent dictatorship' (7). The decisions they found most difficult were those to do with staff – reprimanding, disciplining, hurting or disappointing. The most significant changes they had made were: adopting a more open style (10), curriculum reorganisation (9), staff–pupil relationships, usually through tutorial work (7) and community emphasis (5).

7 Job descriptions and appraisal
Twelve heads had full job descriptions for their staffs, 19 had none and 16 had a partial system or were working towards the introduction of a system. Eighteen had no formal staff appraisal system, five had, five had a partial system and 19 were working towards one or hoping to do so. It will be seen that many of the responses given echo those given in the

schools I visited, for example the dominant contribution of experience rather than training to managerial competence, difficulties with personnel management, such as the unsatisfactory performer among senior staff as a major source of concern, poor selection procedures and the lack of a professional support system (including appraisal), other than from fellow heads and senior colleagues. Although the management of change was, for some, a problem area, there were strong perceptions that a change to a more open, consultative or participative style had been a success.

Ordidge

Ordidge has studied differences in perception about delegation in educational and other institutions (Ordidge 1985). His results are not clear-cut but an interesting finding is what correlates in managers' minds between ability/willingness to delegate. For the 177 managers in education, there is a relatively low correlation with overall effectiveness; the 110 other managers thought there was a high correlation. Although for both groups of managers there was a high correlation with confidence in subordinates, staff development and motivation, only the non-education managers felt a high correlation with clear objectives, decision-making ability, firmness in dealing with others, persistency and administrative ability. In other words, it appears that education managers do not so clearly perceive the need for clarifying objectives and monitoring performance when they delegate tasks to subordinates. This supports the conclusion of a number of investigators that those to whom heads delegate tasks (mainly deputy heads) have ill-defined roles and lack measures of effective performance.

Derr and DeLong

Derr and DeLong, who have experience of both education and business, have also compared the two, albeit in the United States (Derr and DeLong 1982). They note the diffuse goals of schools compared with those of business, their propensity for making short-term, low-risk plans and their tendency, unlike business, to attract people who have high needs for autonomy and to offer a refuge for the security-oriented. They conclude that heads will have to become more expert in motivation if they are to cope adequately with all the new pressures impinging on schools.

Dwyer

John Dwyer, Head of Whitley Bay High School, North Tyneside, spent two terms on a schoolmaster fellowship at Newcastle University to study preparation for secondary headship (Dwyer 1984). He interviewed 50 heads in seven LEAs and compared management development methods in schools, industry, commerce and some professions. Among his findings were:

1 Training

The majority of heads (27) had received no formal training in management at all before their appointment. The remainder had attended mostly only one course of up to a week's duration. Of these courses, the heads said they liked the involvement of experienced heads in the training, practical rather than theoretical approaches, the value of rubbing shoulders with other course members; and every head was united in seeing it as a necessity that courses be residential. One praised the industrial management approach as it provides useful techniques.

Twelve per cent of the sample could see no significant place for training for headship. The 88 per cent who thought training desirable wanted it to take place at several stages (head of department, deputy head, head) but most favoured putting priority at deputy head level; indeed 13 thought that training at this level should be a prerequisite for appointment to a headship.

2 Support

In nearly 75 per cent of cases, heads received no help or support from anyone between selection and taking up their post. 'So far as local authorities are concerned, the picture is one of almost completely unrelieved gloom. . . Many heads clearly felt quite bitter about the negative attitude of their future authorities during this time.' All heads felt they could have benefited from more help or support during their first year; 27 were clearly dissatisfied and felt life had been more difficult than it need have been. Seven felt very lonely and exposed. Ten of the sample mentioned colleague heads as being a tremendous help to them and one specified valuable help from industry, channelled through an industrial chaplain. The vast majority (84 per cent) favoured the appointment within their LEA of a successful and experienced consultant head as an adviser.

3 Skills

Asked what skills, talents and aspects of personality they brought to headship, the most frequently mentioned (numbers in brackets) fell into the following categories:

Personnel management/personal relationships/leadership (40)

Strength of belief in philosophy and aims/commitment/determination (22)

Administrative skills/logical planning/problem solving (21)

Understanding of schools, their general aims and objectives (14)

Success as a teacher/ability to make contact with the young/counselling skills (13)

The main skills they said they needed to develop after appointment were:
Personnel management/personal relationships/leadership (22)
Administrative and organisational expertise (15)
Patience (13)
Learning to say no/taking awkward decisions (9)
Dealing with parents/outside bodies (8)
Opinions were divided as to whether there were management skills and techniques to be learned from industry, the forces and the civil service; 31 thought so, eight thought not and 11 were undecided. However, even the proponents were duly cautious and agreed that thoughtful adaptation and translation were necessary. Dwyer concluded from his discussions with industrialists that the one specific technique above all others that heads can advantageously use in schools is that of staff appraisal as part of a programme of staff development.

4 Activities
Heads were asked what were the most important things they did:
The appointment of staff (28)
Forward planning/determination of policy/overall direction (26)
External relationships (marketing the school) (24)
Availability/visibility/relationships (15)
Finance and resource allocation (7)
Staff development and INSET (7)

5 Influence
Most respondents (28, plus 14 with reservations) agreed with the proposition that the most crucial factor in the success of the school is the quality of the head.

6 Autonomy
88 per cent of heads responding wanted more autonomy in running their schools; 33 heads wanted more financial control, believing that they could use financial resources (capital and current expenditure, maintenance) more wisely and effectively than the authority does. 'There are huge amounts of waste which could be reduced' and 'I could cut down the bills fairly sharply' were two quotations illustrating this. Seventeen of the heads were unhappy with the amount of control they were allowed to exercise over staff appointments.

Here again the findings are consistent with mine and those of other observers – notably the inadequacy of the preparation heads receive for their management role, the almost non-existent support systems and the high priority attached to man-management skills. One might question, however, whether development of the quality of patience is the right inference for heads to draw from the frustration they experience in trying to effect change. The overtones of resignation and defeatism that accompany the word may be de-energising; better, perhaps, to conclude that the skill required is in learning how to stimulate, promote, facilitate and manage change more effectively.

Schofield

Jack Schofield, Head of Spurley Hey High School, Manchester, and a headmaster fellow of North West Education Management Centre from 1979–80, visited 46 schools in the north-west of England, mostly for half a day. His study (Schofield 1980) aimed to seek common features important in creating a good school over a period of 10–20 years, with particular reference to the role and abilities of the head. He found great variations between schools, often masked by the similarity of descriptions, and this made it difficult to generalise. Issues of crucial importance were thought to be (a) the creation of an effective school management structure, (b) staff appointments, (c) team building and (d) a good consultation/communication system.

In about a quarter of the schools visited, the management style was traditional, autocratic or manipulative towards staff consultation but the trend was certainly towards more consultation.

The 46 heads produced 176 different qualities, the possession of which they believed were valuable in building a school. It was found that:
1 Heads valued managerial skills (ability to administer, organise, persuade, motivate, influence, delegate, communicate).
2 The commonest quality quoted was 'accessibility', implying 'ability to get on with people, sympathy and sensitivity'. Heads valued 'tough' qualities (firmness and determination) twice as highly as 'tender' ones (humility, compassion); good health and resilience were also thought important. They placed more value on the ability to relate to people than to the job (relationship- rather than task-orientation).

A composite picture of the head of a successful school was of 'a person who values abilities as a communicator and persuader; is healthy; though sympathetic and fair, he has a tough-minded approach to work; is a participator in the educational world outside school and draws experience from this work; and while he has a competence or even a liking for school administration, he sees the best expression of his particular skills through his sensitive management of his staff'.

Weindling and Earley

Although not written from an industrial perspective, it is worth noting an NFER research project conducted by Dick Weindling and Peter Earley into the first years of headship in the secondary school (Weindling and Earley 1986). These authors visited 16 state schools on three occasions, spending nine days in each. They interviewed the head, all the deputies, the chairman of governors, senior LEA officers and a cross-section of staff. They traced career paths to headship and enquired how well heads thought they had been prepared for their jobs.

Being a deputy head or a member of the senior management team was seen as the most important preparation; a period as acting head was also valuable. Courses played an important part too, but some heads suggested preparation would be improved by short periods of second-ment to industry and commerce, and by attachments to experienced heads in other schools, which might include shadowing the head for a day. Not enough use was made of the stage between appointment and taking up post, and induction into the LEA system was not very thorough, with only 25 per cent having a programme longer than a day. The first years of headship place considerable stress on the head, and they get very little help from LEA officers or advisers. Only 14 per cent of LEAs had a 'mentor' system to link new heads with more experienced heads in other schools.

The researchers found that most change in schools takes place during the first years of a new head being appointed (and especially in the third and fourth years), as he implements his own ideas; they suggest a policy of moving heads between schools every six years or so, to stimulate change and development.

It will be interesting to compare their results with those from a follow-up study of middle management (head of department) which is planned; also with an ethnographic study into the observed activities of secondary school heads, to be published in 1986 by Hall, Mackay and Morgan.

Gray

Harry Gray has recently collated the views of a number of management trainers (including himself) who have worked with both heads and industrialists on management courses. Most of these chime well with my own impressions but he goes further in offering explanatory hypotheses. The following is a précis of his paper (Gray 1985).

Teachers steeped in the didactic tradition who receive experiential training in management sense a conceptual confusion when undergoing a training experience, whereas industrial managers find such an experience more in keeping with the process of management itself. Schools are organised around knowledge, while management development is orga-nised around experience. For heads, authority is at the very heart of their management situation and gets in the way of the group learning process, because it tends to isolate them from their colleagues rather than enabling them to work together as a team. It also influences the way they relate to management trainers, whose authority they like to question not on the grounds of their competence as trainers but on their knowledge of schools and management theory. If they come on a course expecting academic and intellectual stimulation and all they get is group tasks to do, they are apt to dismiss the experience as trivial, undemanding and inconclusive, not realising that experiential learning is a far more powerful tool for effecting behavioural change than intellectualising.

Moreover, heads are more resistant than other managers to engaging in a process of personal change, which involves learning more about oneself and one's effect on others. They see others as the prime focus for change and want to be helped to change others. But to change others you first have to learn how to change yourself! This resistance takes the form of a preference for instruction that allows them to remain outside the learning experience and to comment detachedly and judgementally on the abstract concepts that underlie the topic. Their response is cognitive rather than affective (and yet they do not take easily to the cognitive process of studying from books).

Gray picks up the sense of fear that I also noticed among teachers and heads, of losing control. Other managers, and management trainers, seem more ready to untie the boat and see what happens, perhaps because applying a problem-solving approach to a new situation comes more naturally and raises self-confidence. Indeed, to illustrate this point, when I asked one head what he had learned to do differently as a result of taking part in a course I helped to run six months previously, his most vivid and pleasurable recollection was that, instead of panicking, he had consciously applied my systematic approach to problem-solving in order successfully to recover his boat which had slipped its moorings in a gale! I would expect him also to be better able to cope with the results of unleashing ideas and people in his school.

Defensiveness is another characteristic that Gray has noticed among heads. They do not like admitting to imperfections in their school or their way of managing it, whereas industrial managers are quite ready to say what problems they are having and to ask for help in putting them right. This goes for learning too; being a teacher makes one vulnerable to one's own failures as a learner, which is very hard to endure, coming from a culture that punishes failure and induces a feeling of shame in the poor performers in a class.

Gray is at pains to point out that there are many exceptions to his generalisations and I agree that it would be wrong to stereotype all heads in these terms. Indeed, the spectrum of industrial managers certainly contains people with the characteristics he ascribes to heads. Moreover, there are differences between primary and secondary heads; it is the latter that fit best the description that Gray offers. The important point for management trainers to note is that the culture in which people do their daily work influences their responses to management learning, and it is helpful to understand, discuss and take into account the reasons for this.

These surveys help to fill in the picture of the pressing problems of management faced in schools up and down the country, which emerged from my own fieldwork, and throw further light on the present and desired state of school management practice. There are some fairly consistent patterns running through all the studies, and not a great deal of dissent between the findings of different observers, nor of the reactions of teachers in the schools I visited who had had encounters with industry (section 2.12). In the next section but one I shall try to throw some of the threads of this complex tapestry into sharper relief, so that the essential features of the school management scene can be more readily compared and contrasted with the situation to be found in industry. But first I want to draw attention to the European scene.

2.15 Comparisons with Western Europe

Under the auspices of the Council of Europe, Buckley has made an interesting comparative study of school management training in Britain, France, West Germany, Denmark, Iceland, Northern Ireland, Norway and Sweden. His book (Buckley 1985) will certainly disabuse readers of the belief that most of the problems school heads face are peculiar to the United Kingdom. Some points are worth picking out because they support my findings about problems in schools and illuminate also comparisons with industry, though this is a dimension that Buckley's survey does not explore.

1   He gained a lasting impression in a variety of European countries that heads feel lonely and are subject to increasing day-to-day pressures in a job that becomes more and more difficult. It is a role associated with considerable psychological insecurity.

2   There is a growing recognition both of the head as an agent and indeed a promoter of change, and also of the growth of understanding that the process of changing social institutions (and particularly schools) is very complex.

3   Because the pace of change is accelerating and because heads are also expected to maintain stability in the short term, they are subject to an intense 'present-future' dilemma.

4   Heads in all countries seem to have too little time for reflexion, thinking and planning; they are constantly interrupted and faced with situations that require an immediate response – just as Mintzberg found with chief executives in industry.

5   The demands on heads are increasing as a result (in the United Kingdom and several other countries) of (a) a greater need for consultation with teachers, parents and pupils, (b) more accountability to the local community, (c) problems arising from the economic recession. Fullan has noted that in USA and Canada too 'the role of the principal

has become more complex, overloaded and unclear over the past twenty years.'

A useful report of a conference on school management training in Western Europe has been compiled by Hegarty (Hegarty 1983). Some of the points made are:

1   Perhaps the greatest requirement is competence in a wide range of skills in dealing with people as individuals and in groups (p. 12). This supports my conclusions.

2   Unless training provision and professional development are embedded into the school and the LEA system, it is likely that improvement may still elude us (p. 13). I also believe that training must be integrated into a coherent set of policies on personal and organisational development.

3   It is in the area of marketing, image-building and reputation management that education may have most to learn from other sectors (p. 25). This observation, attributed to Glatter, was supported by a number of those I interviewed, who had been impressed with industrial approaches to marketing.

4   Whatever differences there may be, it appears that there is considerable similarity in work activity and managerial behaviour across the continents and that in important respects task performance is very similar to that of chief executives in other types of work organisation (p. 35). This has been a recurring theme in this book.

5   Contemporary school leaders need to be highly resourceful in coping with an increasingly turbulent environment. They need to generate initiatives and solutions which are usually not found within a standard set of techniques. Techniques have had only limited application within educational management (p. 111).

6   The school leader's role is evolving from a situation of stable definition to one of emergent definition. It is not a question of moving from being a traditional head (benevolent despot or whatever) to another well-defined role such as a leading professional. The school leader is moving rather into a situation where role definitions are to a degree continually evolving. This notion of school leadership is a challenging one. It means that school leaders cannot simply get down to doing their job – they have also constantly to be asking themselves what they should be doing (p. 134).

These last excerpts highlight the importance of helping heads to manage change and to cope with situations of uncertainty, ambiguity and turbulence. Notably in Scandinavia, though not in Germany, the focus of school management training has been moving in this direction. Outside education in the United Kingdom a similar trend has been noticed. Not only are courses on management of change growing in popularity, but those which cause managers to reflect deeply on what they ought to be doing, or could do differently, have proved very effective.

Rosemary Stewart points out that most managers are carried along by the momentum of events and fail to see the choices open to them. They exaggerate the demands on them; they tend to see the constraints as immutable; and they fail to think strategically about their work. They just pitch in and do the job in the way that comes most naturally from their previous experience (Stewart 1982).

If it is true that the role of the head is changing significantly throughout Europe, it is vital that they should regularly take stock of what they do, and how they might do it differently. Stewart gives advice in her book about how this self-questioning can be approached. One of her exercises is to ask managers to plot their jobs on a grid (Figure 2.4).

Figure 2.4 Output specification of job (vertical axis): area of operation (horizontal axis)

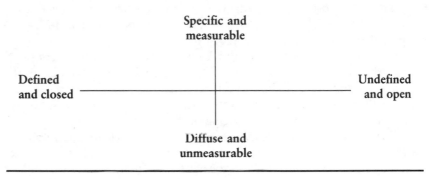

It would seem that the job of many heads would fall well into the bottom right quadrant; so it is all the more important, she would argue, to think strategically about it.

2.16 School management: salient features

Much of what I have written is the result of looking at school management through a magnifying glass. It is time now to stand back and view it from a distance, picking out the salient features of the landscape before turning round to look at industry in detail. Doubtless another observer's gaze would alight on different features; those that stand out for me are:

Change and continuity;
Need for a total systems approach;
Need for a personnel management support system;
Need for leadership;
Need to understand management.

Change and continuity

It is widely accepted that managing a school has become a much more demanding job than it was. Secondary schools in particular have got larger and mostly cater for a wider cross-section of pupils less ready to accept the old norms. Schools' boundaries have become more permeable, as different interest groups question and challenge what they do. Politicisation and the growth of union activity destabilise the status quo. Contraction – demographic and economic – heaps more problems on to the management of the whole education service. One change after another engenders the feeling that schools are lurching from crisis to crisis. The turbulent society, the 'age of discontinuity' and 'future shock' are beginning to be mirrored in the life of the school.

But continuity and settled order are also characteristics of the educational world; not for nothing has the Department of Education and Science been dubbed 'a vehicle with the engine of a lawnmower and the brakes of a juggernaut'. Likewise with school life, teaching goes on at the heart of it all, sometimes little changed; timetables bring structure to the day, exams to the year; the same old problems arise which teachers have faced since schools began as they 'clean up the sour pastures of youth' (Plato's view of education).

The young people of today think of nothing but themselves. They have no reverence for parents or old age. They are impatient of all restraint. They talk as though they alone know everything and what passes for wisdom with us is foolishness to them. As for the girls, they are foolish, immodest and unwomanly in speech, behaviour and dress (Peter the Hermit, AD 1050).

The balance between continuity and change may have tilted only a little, but that brings disproportionate growth in the complexity of management. And so with other institutions: it does not take much of a shift in balance to test the competence of management, even to destruction. Where survival depends starkly on keeping the balance sheet in the black, there is heavy reliance on good management to preserve employees' livelihoods. Independent schools can face a similar threat if management is wanting, but with state schools there is more of a cushion between inadequate management and organisational failure, for the organisations have a durability independent of those in charge of them.

Perhaps this gives rise to a false sense of security; it is possible for an LEA's own management systems to stay deficient and for it to ignore the growing gap between the managerial demands made on heads and senior staff and their ability to respond to them. Hence the need for a national government initiative (DES 3/83) to upgrade the quality of management in schools. This, together with the leadership of the professional associations, has brought even to the backward authorities some awareness of the need for action. The most progressive authorities, who discerned the need a decade ago or more, are already abreast of current management development practice in most non-educational institutions, though even they have some way to go to emulate the best. But the general picture is gloomy; the school management system is not up to the demands made on it for coping with change. Today's organisation structures are monuments to yesterday's problems; until they are changed, schools are in for a rough ride.

Need for a total systems approach

What is lacking in addressing the problems of school management is a coherent total systems approach (Everard 1985a). Management within the school cannot be treated in isolation from management of the education service as a whole, because there is far too much interaction between the local government system and the school system. So instead of a strategic approach to the management of the whole organisational structure that constitutes the education service, there is a piecemeal approach in which sending heads and senior teachers on management training courses is seen as *the* way forward. This will not do. If schools are to be made more effective places for educating children whose lives will mostly be spent in 21st century society, then there is a bigger problem to be tackled than training heads to manage, vital though that is. That problem is to develop the education service of which schools are a part. Management development is but a part – albeit an essential part – of organisation development. Moreover, it is not confined to the internal management of schools; there are 'managers' in County Hall, and influential people they are, even at a comparatively lowly level in the hierarchy, where the say-so of a clerical officer working to a rule book can undermine a good management decision by a head paid two or three times his salary. Is this type of bureaucracy conducive to the effectiveness of schools?

Pervading the whole system is, of course, the influence of the political zealots at national and local level. No service, enterprise or institution in our society is proof against political intervention, but with the education service political control is tighter than most and is by no means always aimed at improving school effectiveness. The criteria (including left- and right-wing political patronage) applied to the selection of heads are a case in point; the influence of political ideologies in the teaching profession itself is another.

These are powerful forces, unlikely to weaken as the years go by, as long as Secretaries of State for Education and education committee members are party politicians. A competent management, however, has to learn how best to get to grips with them – to steer them, inform them, anticipate them, harness them, sometimes to resist them, for the good of the service or school. The necessary political skills are not well developed in those whose whole careers have been spent in the academic world. This is an aspect of management which has needed increasing attention also in industry over the last few decades. Schools ignore it at their peril.

Need for a personnel management support system

As in many an industrial firm, the education service in general and schools in particular rely heavily on the apprenticeship model for developing management, but have not introduced the structural framework needed to support it. No industrial training board would readily condone such a situation in industry. Complex organisations, as most secondary schools are, also need a maintenance support system to keep them running smoothly, but by comparison with other types of public service institutions, and with much of industry, the school management support system is primitive.

Heads who look over their shoulders to see how their non-educational counterparts cope are beginning to realise just how deficient their own support system is. Not only my study but those of other observers testify, for example, to the general inadequacy of the arrangements for inducting new heads to their job. Even if as deputies they have enjoyed the advantage of working for a head who takes his management training role seriously and even if their LEA has supported them on management training courses, the informal guidance that most people, (even senior managers) need on succeeding to a new job is often singularly lacking. It is a tribute to the resilience of the many heads who survive this baptism of fire that they cope with the demands placed on them; but it is not good management.

Another glaring deficiency of the school support system is in the area of what in industry is called personnel management, or in some American firms, human resource management. The high incidence of staff problems reported by heads is probably connected with the lack of an effective professional back-up system such as industry has come to take for granted. The role of a personnel department as a source of catalysis and advice to line managers is crucial in a complex organisation, especially one in which the key criterion for appointment to senior posts is the candidate's perceived flair for making shrewd educational, technical or commercial judgements. This quality does not always go hand in hand with a flair for managing people or organisations, so the personnel function is there to provide some kind of back-up in situations that call for professional man-management. It promotes the formulation and execution of the organisation's personnel policy and the setting up of systems and procedures that help senior management to create the conditions under which people give of their best.

Herzberg, in his theory of motivation (Herzberg 1966), distinguishes between the 'hygiene' factors which are capable of causing dissatisfaction and have to be cleaned up as a prerequisite for job satisfaction, and 'motivators' which lead to satisfaction. The latter are concerned with work content and the former with work context. It is in keeping the former under review that the personnel function performs a service to the organisation which is not well developed in schools.

A professional personnel function would also play a leading role in administering staff selection and appraisal systems, which are key areas for improvement in schools. Getting more accurate judgements and prognoses about people, especially those in line for promotion to senior management posts, would do much to prevent some of the people problems arising in the first place. Regular appraisal also helps to identify incipient problems which it may be possible to nip in the bud through counselling and training.

However, it is of no use introducing to the school management system a back-up service of this kind if the key decision-makers (who may have political axes to grind) ignore its professional advice and jib at the consequences of taking it – resource implications in particular. This presents a formidable problem in the management of strategic and political change. There is no short cut, but the best way to eat an elephant is one bite at a time.

Need for leadership

While personnel policies and support systems are important components of healthy organisations, they are no substitute for high quality management on the part of the chief executive (head) and senior management team. The exercise of personal leadership or the management of the ethos of the school is widely accepted as a crucial activity for the head, whose influence thereby on the effectiveness of the school is very great indeed. This is a matter of both selection and training – activities in which schools apparently lag well behind other institutions, and where the armed services probably have as good a record as any. In a profession that suffers from low self-esteem, and which is not as highly esteemed by the public as it deserves, it is especially important for its leaders to practise a style of management that will help to sustain morale and increase self-respect.

Whatever is true of schools about the need for leadership is also true of the education service as a whole. While many chief education officers are distinguished men of vision whose influence on the service is statesman-like and positive, even these natural leaders are hard put to it to create that ethos of self-confidence throughout their authority which makes ordinary people accomplish extraordinary things. They too are swamped by the problems of day-to-day operational management.

At the top of the educational hierarchy, there is an even greater dearth of inspired leadership, not confined to the Department of Education and Science. As William Plowden, Director General of the Royal Institute of Public Administration, cogently argued (Plowden 1985) in comparing management in the civil service to that in industry, an impoverished concept of management pervades the whole civil service – an accountant's view of management, rather than a manager's. There is low emphasis on the qualities of leadership and personality that would be critical in Marks and Spencer. There is a 'command' relationship between senior managers and their staff, which leads not only to disgruntled employees, but to an ineffective organisation, incapable of responding adequately to change. 'Many civil servants do believe that their organisation has no commitment to them. But whose job is it to express that commitment? The underlying problem is the existence of what can best be called a leadership vacuum.' One result is that the vacuum has been filled by the civil service unions and authority has drained away from the centre. Low morale is a developing problem and organisational health, standards of performance and effectiveness, are a growing concern. Plowden contrasted this situation with an industrialist's view of management, that of Sir John Harvey-Jones of ICI who suggested that management is 'about energy, about courage and determination, as well as foresight... It requires the most delicate balance of sensitivity to the feelings and reactions of others... Management is essentially about people, about the organisation of people, about obtaining their commitment to worthwhile commonly shared values and objectives...'.

All these contextual deficiencies in the way the education service is led from the top exacerbate the problems of management within the school. They sap morale to an extent that imperils the real work of the school. Although low pay may be the peg on which these ills are hung, and the Secretary of State the scapegoat for the malaise, the heart of the problem lies deeper; neither education nor teachers are held in high respect by society at large or by its representatives in the corridors of power. In this the service has something in common with trade and industry, antagonism towards which was one of the main reasons for declaring 1986 Industry Year. Both need champions, if the problems they face are to be tackled effectively.

This too is a problem for management in the collective sense: how to build the public image of education, of schools and of the teaching profession so that the environment in which their work is done may become more benign and more conducive to high endeavour. It is not just a question of weeding out the incompetents, eradicating inefficiency and remedying shortcomings in the system, important though these are; the real challenge is to inspire, esteem and energise the men and women who work in our schools, remembering that there are different kinds of leadership: 'As for the best leaders, the people do not notice their existence; the next best, the people honour and praise; the next, the people fear; and the next, the people hate. But when the best leaders' work is done, the people say, "We did it ourselves".'

Need to understand management

If most of the foregoing remarks seem to be externalising the problem of school management and blaming deficiencies on the context within which schools operate, they are not meant to absolve managers at the level of the school from responsibility. Management is not to be construed as only inward and downward looking. It involves interaction with the environment – outwards and upwards. Some heads I met seemed not to grasp this. As a collective body, locally and nationally, heads have got to 'put their act together' (Everard 1985b). They do not engage as effectively with the wider system as their situation demands or as their industrial counterparts do. The analogy is not perfect, but the CBI champions the cause of industry more effectively than the professional associations champion the cause of education.

It is true that heads have noted a growing proportion of their time having to be devoted to external affairs, but much of this activity has been reactive; what I am suggesting is a more proactive stance, not only on the part of the individual head, but more particularly in the collective sense. It is in the area of influencing the environment that some of the skills involved in the management of change have been most effectively deployed. Managers need not be imprisoned in an indominus role where they can call upon their structural authority to reinforce what they are trying to achieve; the exdominus role often affords more hope for improving effectiveness, notwithstanding their lack of coercive power when operating outside their own domain.

Because many heads have been brought up in a somewhat authoritarian school culture within an education service based on a 'command' model, the influencing skills that are needed in a more participative culture, where management is more by consent of the managed, have not always been fully developed – yet it is these that are most needed in the exdominus role.

Lacking an appreciation of management (warts and all) in other institutions, and especially in industry, managers in the education service have an impoverished and limited concept of the processes by which organisations work and by which they are managed. There is less of a common language of management in schools. This is not just a question of a limited vocabulary, although the development of management is helped by a common understanding of the words used to describe it. It is more a shortage of constructs and frameworks of thought within which to interpret the school as an organisation or the head as its manager. When teachers are operating in a managerial role, their approach tends to be intuitive rather than reasoned. Different ways of working are ill-defined and ill-articulated. The processes by which things get done are not made explicit. There is a lack of common understanding of the importance of sensing problems, of having and working towards objectives, of doing things systematically, of planning for particular results, of reviewing how work is done as well as what work is to be done and of diagnosing, describing and modifying the culture or ethos of the organisation. All these processes are crucial to organisational health and effectiveness and a manager needs to become fluent in their application.

Where 'high-level' language is used to describe managerial phenomena, it tends to be the language of administration, of structure, of traits, of power, even of ideology ('democratic management'), rather than the language of organisational behaviour with its emphasis on process, on cause and effect, on observation and on practice. But when, for the first time, a teacher begins to use the language of behaviour and to converse in it with colleagues, it is sometimes as if scales had dropped from his eyes; at last his daily experience as a member of the organisation begins to fit into a meaningful pattern and he can see why things are as they are, and how else they could be.

The same, of course, applies in industry, for few people enter organisations with foreknowledge of how they work. It is something they need to learn and, as Harry Barrington has amusingly illustrated in his book *Learning about Management* (Barrington 1984), which is about how Lever Brothers train their managers, the learning process can be vivid, dramatic and powerful. Not all of industry goes to the trouble that Unilever, Shell, Marks and Spencer, Rank Xerox and so on do to induct people into management, but it would speak pointedly to the condition of the education service if some of the management development processes from industry were to be adopted in schools.

Concluding with these few salient features of school management which I have picked out from this, the longest chapter in the book, I pass now to the other side of the divide. I shall try to set out the nature of management and some of the key management processes from the industrial setting. It would require a former head, working in the arena of industrial management development by studying problems of management and of training managers to cope with them, to produce a true counterpart of Chapter 2; I can only select the features that I think would most interest him, having encountered many of the problems at first hand, seen them discussed in the management literature and on courses, and finally noticed the self-same problems in schools.

Chapter 3

Industrial management compared

In the previous chapter I started the process of comparing school management with industrial management; now I focus more sharply on the latter and comment on features that seem particularly relevant to schools. While for simplicity I have used the term 'school management' to include the management of that part of the education service as a whole which pertains to schools, so I now use the words 'industrial' and 'industrialist' to include commerce and even those parts of the public service outside education (such as nationalised concerns) which are run by people called 'managers'.

The word 'management' must be defined and analysed if it is not to form a barrier across the learning bridge between school and industry; whatever else my contacts with education have demonstrated, it is that concepts like 'management', 'training', 'skill', 'improvement', 'appraisal', 'assessment', 'objectives' and 'planning' often mean different things to a teacher and to an industrialist. Indeed, this realisation lay at the heart of the research (see Figure 1 in Appendix 2). It is easy to talk at cross purposes if the nuances are not understood. The first and second sections of this chapter, therefore, aim at clarifying the word 'management'. However, it cannot be left in the abstract, so the third section, on good practices, exemplifies the managerial outlook by picking up for illustration some of the issues that were flagged for consideration in Chapter 2. There are especially important differences in the industrial approach to staff appraisal, management development, resource management and response to change, each of which is a key process deserving a section to itself. The scene is then set for addressing the fundamental question, 'Should schools learn from industry?' and for confronting the concerns of the hopefully diminishing number of teachers who think not. That section is followed by one that examines how schools can best learn from industry, and the final section deals with evaluation: do we really know that management training is worthwhile? First we examine the nature of management.

3.1 The nature of management

'Management' was not until recently a word in common currency in educational institutions, although it has featured in the literature on education at least as far back as 1872 (Harding 1872). Consequently there is a less clear concept of what it means and implies than there is in industry and commerce (and even here there is no agreed, precise definition). Indeed, it can have pejorative overtones, posing a threat to the autonomy and professional values of teachers by conjuring up ideas of ruthless authoritarian bosses; its use to describe a major part of the head's role may tend to distance him from the body of teachers whence virtually all heads are recruited (Everard 1982). As S. Johnson, Director of Education, Leeds wrote, 'To many teachers, the idea that they might be or could be managed is doubtless incredible and probably most distasteful' (Johnson 1983). Or as Gerald Haigh wrote under the headline 'Exterminate!', in his critical review of my previous book, *Effective School Management,* he was beginning to be convinced, against his will, that the authors' 'essentially maniacal original premiss just might be true' (Haigh 1985). The notion of management being systematically applied to education clearly raises hackles.

However, to the industrialist, management does not and should not imply the naked exercise of power, nor the subservience of anyone managed, nor insensitivity to individuals' needs, nor the renunciation of any human values. Indeed, respect for the individual and a strong sense of ethics are central values in many a successful industrial manager. There is no need for heads to fear emulating such a person; what would be totally inappropriate would be to take as a model the stereotype of the unprincipled self-seeker – any more than heads would seek to become carbon copies of their own despotic predecessors. Ends do not justify means; in well-managed organisations, the ends have to feel good and the means must allow people to take pride in their work.

Although there are no widely accepted definitions, nor clear dividing lines between manager, executive, administrator and leader, an industrialist would expect a manager to:
- know what he wants to happen and cause it to happen;
- exercise responsible stewardship over resources and turn them to purposeful account;
- promote effectiveness in work done, and a search for continual improvement;
- be accountable for the performance of the unit he is managing, of which he is a part;
- set a climate or tone conducive to enabling people to give of their best (Everard 1984).

'Administration' in industry normally signifies the running of some systems in accordance with established procedures. It implies that there is a status quo to be maintained and that disturbances that might interfere with smooth running are to be fended off. An administrator would tend to be more conservative than a manager, who would be more likely to see change and development as an inevitable concomitant of the world of business and therefore something to be steered in a dynamic and creative way.

'Leadership' qualities are indispensible to the effective manager, since he holds responsibility for inspiring the people in his charge. There are different styles of leadership – charismatic, authoritarian, participative – appropriate to different situations and individuals. Leaders can be expected to set direction, challenges, tone and patterns of behaviour and to be able to articulate a value system that provides a focal point for understanding what an organisation stands for. The word 'governance' is sometimes used to describe the collective leadership exercised by a board of directors in industry.

There is a temptation for some educationists to see management more in terms of sound administration than of imaginative leadership. Perhaps they take their cue from the civil service; in the RSA Cantor lectures of 1984 on the art of management (Bancroft 1984) there is a distinct difference between what Lord Bancroft had to say about management in Whitehall, and what Sir John Harvey-Jones said of management in the private sector. Neither speaks the last word, though each is a master of the craft as he understands it. Although there are different views and emphases, I select and summarise a private sector model to which I believe there would be widespread assent; management is not primarily about running an efficient bureaucracy, nor about the mechanical control of financial, sociological or pedagogical systems. It is not solely the exercise of a set of cognitive skills. Still less can it be broken down into a series of techniques or drills. Yet all these do have a place in the concept of management.

Management has more to do with people than with systems. It is about winning their hearts and minds – gaining their consent to be managed, their commitment to the job and their belief in its worthwhileness. It is more of a practical art than a science, though it has elements of both. It is above all about achievement and about change, usually in face of the adverse circumstances that are a common characteristic of the real world. Management is about energy, leadership, confidence and determination – not only having these attributes, but infecting others with them.

Management is also about looking ahead and the avoidance of surprise. The good manager foresees difficulties and has contingency plans for dealing with them as they arise. He is in control, rather than being controlled by unfolding events. He is constantly on the alert for incipient problems – indeed, he may even seem to be looking for trouble – because much of management consists of diagnosing and analysing problems, then solving them. More positively, he tries to turn problems into opportunities because without a problem, positively tackled, there is no scope for improvement.

Improvement is one of the lifesprings of management in industry and commerce; it is not a question of maintaining the status quo, but of being constructively dissatisfied with it. There is always a better way. Standards are always capable of being raised – either by giving a better service with the same resource, or maintaining the service with less resource, less cost and less human effort. Moreover, standards are referred to what is being achieved anywhere else in the world, not just in the UK. A number of British firms have sent small groups of employees to the USA, the Continent and Japan to raise their sights on to what is possible; and, when the British lead, these firms play host to foreign visitors.

In all this, techniques and theories have their place, like the artists' colours, but it is selection of the right one at the right time that shows the manager as an artist, and here is where intuition counts. There is no technique for choosing techniques, since every situation is different. In the face of infinite variety, there is no simple rule book, no one right answer.

Harry Barrington, who was responsible for management development in Lever Brothers, stated three truths about management (Barrington 1984):

1   Management is not a science but an art, based on observation, analysis and decision-making;

2   The nature of management varies through time, so the manager is a chameleon as well as an artist;

3   There is no such thing as 'good' or 'bad' management or 'right' or 'wrong' behaviour – but there is 'functional' and 'dysfunctional' and these behaviours have to be balanced, since managers cannot usually maintain a logically consistent portfolio of objectives.

In both industry and education, there are managers to whom this comes as a blow. In particular, those who have studied one of the physical sciences and like to construe the world in precise, rational terms find it hard to grasp that management is not a black and white subject. It cannot be reduced to simple logic, because of the dimension of intuition; managers have to use both sides of their brains. Indeed, one of the criticisms that industry levels at business schools is their over-reliance on developing analytical rationality and their seeming inability to develop intangible qualities like acumen, flair and inspiration.

To sum up, management is not a science, but it uses the observational and deductive processes of science and it can be underpinned with theory. It is more an art, and as in all art, processes of intuition are vital. It is about winning people's trust and commitment, not about coercing them. It is an ethical activity; values are central. It has far more to do with change and improvement than about defending the status quo. Problem identification, objective-setting and problem-solving are at its heart. It is predominantly a practical activity, though reflexion and anticipation have their place, especially in setting direction. As we shall see, the nature of management carries important implications for the training of managers.

3.2 Components of management

One way of understanding management is to try to analyse it into its component parts. There have been many attempts to do this. The earliest treatises on industrial management stressed concepts like decisions, command, administration, control and efficiency. Although such concepts have not been lost, nowadays there is more stress on concepts like teams, relationships, processes, systems, problem-solving, development and change. The component parts of management can be analysed through a study of skills, of management qualities, of tasks, or of roles.

For instance, analysis of the skills that are likely to be covered on a comprehensive scheme for management training in industry suggests the following groupings (Everard 1984):

1   Supervision, delegation, performance assessment, coaching and development of subordinates;
2   Interactive relationships (including communication) with all others with whom one has dealings;
3   Structuring and organising work and roles, including one's own, and one's office;
4   Problem solving and the management of change;
5   Group working, team building and selection;
6   Leadership styles, self-presentation, and climate-setting;
7   Organisational processes, structures, systems (for example, information systems) and models;
8   Financial management and control and other quantitative aspects of resource utilisation (including cost awareness);
9   Policies, strategies and planning: political and economic environment;
10   Legal matters, safety and industrial relations.

Burgoyne has developed a useful taxonomy of managerial qualities and learning goals for use in management education (Burgoyne 1976; Burgoyne and Stuart 1978). This has been used in Section 2.6 to categorise the qualities said to be needed for school management. The taxonomy was based on his studies of management in a large manufacturing organisation, but it seems equally applicable to schools, and indeed puts the 'leading professional' aspect of the head's role in perspective by suggesting that proficiency in this field is an essential part of the overall make-up of an effective manager.

Joan Dean has listed the tasks that fall to school heads, together with the corresponding skills needed to do them (Dean 1985). The skills she lists are: presentation, communication, negotiation, leading discussion, decision-making, timetabling, organisation, planning, administration, problem-solving, interviewing and evaluation. Apart from time-tabling, these would all be included among the skills of an industrial manager.

Mintzberg has studied the work of industrial managers and identified three principal roles that they play (Mintzberg 1973): interpersonal, informational and decisional. These are further subdivided and set against skills as shown in Table 3.1.

Table 3.1 Mintzberg's analysis of managerial roles

Roles		Skills
Interpersonal:	Figurehead – ceremonial	Bureaucratic and clerical skills
		Administration skills
	Leadership – formal	Resource planning and strategic
	Motivator	skills
	Control	Leadership skills
	Liaison	Counselling skills
	Personal problem	Peer skills
	resolution	Negotiating skills
Informational:	Spokesman	Decision making skills
	Consultation	Evaluatory skills
	Focus and filter	
	Monitoring	
	Dissemination	
Decisional:	Disturbance handler	
	System maintenance	
	Negotiation	
	Arbitration	
	Resource allocation	
	Organising major tasks	
	Initiate and foster	
	development projects	
	Long term planning	

In another study of the head's role, Audrey Jackson, herself a head, has analysed aspects of the role in decreasing order of perceived importance (Jackson). The first 15 listed are:

1   Producing, maintaining and developing a school philosophy (in industry the counterpart is business strategy);

2   Consultation and communication systems;
3   Upholding quality of staff (ability to teach, personality, commitment, loyalty, integrity, personal relationships, 'stickability', good manners, teamwork);
4   Maintaining one's availability (in industry this might be described as managing one's time);
5   Delegation;
6   Decision-making;
7   Pastoral care systems (in industry this would be included as part of personnel management);
8   Organisation management – translating one's philosophy into practice;
9   Staff development;
10   Careers education;
11   Contacts with the community;
12   Counselling;
13   Assessing one's effectiveness;
14   Keeping up-to-date;
15   Financial control.

There are some common threads in these different approaches to the study of management. What emerges clearly is that so many of the aspects are concerned with the skills involved in dealing with people. Another clear message is that, whether the analysis derives from a study of educational or industrial management, the same kind of component parts are found. It seems obvious that the two kinds of management have much in common, even if they are not always perceived in the same way.

One of the problems of trying to analyse management into its component parts is that significant interrelationships between various skills can be obscured. For example, a particularly important set of interrelated skills can be grouped under the heading 'management of change' which despite its obvious relevance to a major part of the head's job, is not a phrase that occurs as such in a number of analyses.

Another serious problem is that the very process of identifying separate components implies an analytical and fragmented approach to management, whereas the manager's tasks do not come to him neatly wrapped in labelled packages. Therefore, all realistic approaches to management must embody integrative components so that the totality of a manager's job is apprehended; synthesis is no less important than analysis. Analysis also implies tidiness, but most managers experience their jobs as distinctly messy, because each situation they deal with is different from the one before.

I will end this section with a personal judgement of what components of management are most in need of attention by heads, in relation to their current state of development and the nature of the problems that schools face. In my view the following are ten key areas for school management training, the importance of each of which is undervalued (relative to that attached to these areas by industrial managers) when teachers think about management:

Leadership
Setting objectives
Setting priorities
Problem finding and problem definition
Systematic approaches to solving problems and effecting change
Planning (other than timetabling)
Review processes (interpersonal, curriculum, managerial, organisational)
Staff appraisal and development
Interviewing
Running meetings

Leadership is important because it influences the ethos of the school and ethos is a strong determinant of effectiveness. It is at least as important in industry.

Setting objectives is important because it focuses attention on the outcomes of work, rather than inputs. Effort needs to be directed, not impulsive. Schools have further to go than industry in taking this skill on board.

Setting priorities is important because the work of a head is so fragmented and diffuse; the important must sometimes take precedence over the urgent.

Problem finding and problem definition are important because of the need for schools to adapt; anticipation of this need makes for planned management rather than crisis management and channels energy where it is most required.

Systematic approaches to solving problems and effecting change have proved very beneficial in industry and help to develop the effectiveness of a team. Teachers, brought up in the isolation of the classroom, are less accustomed to co-operating with others, so tend to act idiosyncratically and in disharmony rather than by a common approach.

Planning, and the monitoring that goes with it, is needed to see that the right things get done by the right time.

Reviewing (or evaluation) is an integral part of the process by which people and organisations learn to improve; it is not built into the pattern of daily life in a school to the same extent as competitive pressures have forced it into industry. It needs to become second nature.

Staff appraisal and development are an important aspect of reviewing, where the education service lags behind other parts of organised society.

Interviewing skills are important as part of the appraisal and selection process and are less highly developed than in many parts of industry.

Running meetings merits more attention because heads run many meetings, some of them large and difficult to control. Moreover, in such meetings, much work has to be done in a limited time, so improving effectiveness will pay dividends.

3.3 Good practices

Most sections in Chapter 2 ended with a list of questions for consideration. While there are no copy-book answers, it may be helpful to give a few pointers to the responses that an industrial manager (or at least a personnel or training manager) might give to some of the issues raised which are not dealt with more specifically later on. I do not wish to imply that heads would all respond differently, nor that industrial managers always behave like this. I simply quote these responses as examples of good management practice wherever it is found. They also give clues to a manager's outlook.

Structures

Organisation structures should be kept simple; avoid top-heaviness and over-specialisation; minimise the necessity for communication, but keep the parts well integrated. Group people round key result areas, for example in task forces to get something done. Specify everyone's role so that they are sufficiently clear what is expected of them. Likewise specify not so much what individuals and committees will do or consider (input), but what they will achieve (output). Record the decisions they reach, the actions they agree, and who is responsible for seeing that the action is taken, and by when.

Resist the tendency for time to become inordinately fragmented; there must be opportunity for uninterrupted thought and dialogue, whatever the pressures. Work flow and people's availability need regulating.

Ways should be sought to involve all members of an organisation in management, even if they are not called 'managers'. This helps them to empathise with those who are called 'managers' or 'heads'. Delegation, consultation and task forces are among the means for doing this. Nail the myth that only *managers* have any responsibility for managing.

Meetings

Meetings can easily degenerate into time-wasting activities. St Paul was not the only person to observe that 'meetings tend to do more harm than good' (1 Cor. 11.17). Everybody who attends meetings needs to understand why this occurs and to be able to intervene appropriately – not just the chairperson, who may indeed be the cause of the problem. See figure 3.1 for examples of interventions. Seating arrangements, availability and use of visual aids such as flipcharts and a commonly understood process for conducting a meeting all influence what happens. Training helps people to behave appropriately at meetings. Remember that meetings are costly; a two-hour staff meeting of 20 people can cost between £400 and £600. Time is precious for other reasons too; it is an inelastic resource.

Figure 3.1 Useful questions to ask at meetings

Useful questions	When to use
What do you understand to be the goals of this meeting?	Whenever they have not been stated
What order of priority should those items be in?	When the agenda looks too long
What do you understand 'X' to have just said?	When someone has not listened
Where is the discussion aiming now?	When you do not know
Where are we in the systematic approach?	When the discussion rambles formlessly
What has just been decided?	When it is not clear what has been decided
How exactly did we reach that decision?	When it was not reached systematically
Who is to do that?	When an action is not assigned
When is this to be done by?	When no time has been set
For instance?	When airy-fairy generalisations are made
What was your purpose in saying (or asking) that?	When an unhelpful contribution has been made
Have you followed your plan?	When they have not
How is the time going?	When everyone has forgotten its passage
Are we helping you?	When discussion on someone's point makes slow progress

---

Meetings and all other organisational processes and mechanisms need reviewing from time to time, to see if they are still relevant and how they can be improved. Plans are needed (who does what by when) to ensure that the improvement occurs. Since inefficiency and muddle create a negative climate and sap people's will to give of their best, it is well worth attacking these problems at source.

Ethos

The ethos or culture of an organisation has a major effect on behavioural patterns and can reduce the need for formal instructions and mechanistic communications. It is sometimes actively promulgated through internal public relations (house journals, social occasions, induction training, competitions etc.). The inculcation of safe working practices is a case in point; orientation of employees towards continual improvement is another. This results in people inwardly digesting what matters and what is the norm, and reacting accordingly.

Managers who strongly influence the ethos of their organisations are often seen around. They regularly 'walk the shop floor', listening for messages and getting known. What they do and what they say are both important, but actions speak louder than words. They promote a set of values and create a set of expectations about what is and what is not acceptable behaviour.

Whilst the person at the top of an organisation usually exerts the most influence on ethos, a well-knit 'top box' of his immediate senior associates is also influential. An even wider group of senior management who have worked together and developed a collegiate culture over time can also strongly set the tone of an organisation. Newcomers to such a team are under intense pressure to conform. If the senior people in an organisation do not offer it leadership, the ethos may well be influenced by other groups, including dissidents. This usually detracts from the effectiveness of the organisation.

If changes in the external environment call for a change in ethos (such as a move from a rich to a poor environment), this is very difficult to bring in gradually. Usually, a symbolic act is needed to register a discontinuity and mark the change in direction; this can be traumatic.

Recognition and reward

Every opportunity should be taken to recognise openly good performance by particular individuals; never should it be taken for granted and left unnoticed. Managers who wish to keep their team motivated have to demonstrate continually that they appreciate good work and are aware of people doing work of a quality above and beyond the average for the organisation, remembering that it is the outcomes of such work, rather than diligence in doing it, which benefit the organisation. Empty flattery and generalised messages of the 'Well done, chaps!' variety are no substitute for habitual, specific, personal recognition. Appraisal schemes offer a regular opportunity for taking stock of performance and contribution, but a once-a-year pat on the back is insufficient; recognition needs to be timely as well.

Some firms have rituals or procedures to mark either isolated examples of outstanding performance or a sustained contribution of a high order.

One of IBM's rituals is called 'dinner for two'; the company invites an employee to take his wife (or her husband) out to dinner and send the bill to the company. ICI has a performance bonus system for making one-off payments additional to salaries. It also has for its research staff a 'scientific ladder', conferring the titles of 'research associate' and 'senior research associate' (with appropriate salary increments and other perquisites attached) on those whose record of innovation is outstanding. This enables professionals to be promoted without having to take on the additional administrative duties that go with promotion up the managerial ladder; one wonders whether a similar promotional ladder could not be devised for exceptionally gifted teachers, not all of whom would necessarily make good managers. A further device used in ICI for giving tangible recognition to excellence is the Fleck Award, which is given to young people under 21, irrespective of academic attainment, whose all-round performance (including service to the community) is judged by a panel of managers and trade unionists to be exceptionally meritorious.

These examples illustrate ways in which excellence is celebrated and affirmed in industry. They are not, of course, without their critics; there are problems in achieving scrupulous fairness without an inordinately complicated system and in mitigating the ill-effects of discrimination. Nevertheless, it is an observed fact that people do respond positively to praise and tangible recognition; they also respond negatively to its absence when it is due. While teachers readily understand this when dealing with children, they do not always remember that it is applicable also to adults.

Unsatisfactory performance

Prevention of unsatisfactory performance is always better than cure. Good selection procedures are essential. Early experience in a new job strongly shapes subsequent behaviour, so it pays to coach new recruits carefully and point them in the right direction. Early diagnosis of unsatisfactory performance and its possible causes is also vital, so that bad habits do not become ingrained. The manager needs to spell out his expectations with unmistakable clarity. Target setting and regular reviews are helpful. Sometimes remedial training is useful, but firm management on the job is better. If unsatisfactory performance persists, it is important to keep written records of progress or lack of it, partly as an earnest of one's determination to manage the situation and partly to provide a formal basis for subsequent redeployment if all else fails.

Hidebound behaviour is also preventable by establishing a climate in which innovation is the norm. People need to be given new experiences so that they can become more confident in coping with innovation. Recognition and reward should support those who do try to keep up with the times.

Stress is to some extent preventable by inculcating good habits of personal work organisation ('the hurrieder I become, the behinder I get') and by devising a support system that enables help to be obtained when needed. It is when people try to soldier on alone that stress builds up. Good managers keep close enough to those for whom they are responsible to notice signs of undue stress.

Repeated failure to meet deadlines, to fulfil promises to supply a service etc., should be recorded and incidents discussed *en masse*. An attempt should be made to negotiate not perfection but agreement for a continual improvement, which will be monitored and periodically reviewed. Instances showing improvement should be recognised and praised.

Performance improvement

Striving for performance improvement is very much a way of life in industry, supported by all kinds of initiatives and internal propaganda. Management and training together try to inculcate habitual constructive dissatisfaction with the status quo and a belief in the possibility of doing better. As L. Peter observed, 'Bureaucracy defends the status quo long past the time when the quo has lost its status.' This tendency needs counteracting.

Industry is driven by competition, in much the same way as an athlete pits himself against all opposition. The main focus for improvement is the whole firm, but it spreads down to departments, groups and individuals. Improvement is accepted as 'a good thing', a worthwhile aim, a positive force. It is not automatically taken to imply that anyone is blameworthy because performance needs to be improved. 'How are we going to make this company do better?' is not a question necessarily suggesting that it is doing badly at the moment. The corresponding question asked in a school or in a group of teachers, however, usually seems to evoke a defensive reaction.

Performance improvement is linked to organisational learning. It consists of regularly reviewing experience in order to do better. It begins when two things have happened: (a) there is an *appreciation* or conceptual understanding of *present performance* and (b) there is a *sense of direction* along which it is *desired* to change performance. The sense of direction can be either vague, such as 'Make better use of resources' or quantified, such as 'Increase the return on capital to 20 per cent.' Specific targets are more motivational. The desire to move along the direction of improvement may spring both from an unease with present performance and from anticipation of a better tomorrow (sense of future achievement, reward or recognition). The actions that managers take to strengthen motivation to improve are:

1   Clarify understanding of present performance ('O wad some pow'r the giftie gie us, to see oursels as others see us!' – Burns);

2 Increase discomfort, dissatisfaction or frustration with present performance ('The greatest of faults is to be conscious of none' – Carlyle);
3 Sharpen the sense of direction by providing a clearer vision of where we want to be ('Where there is no vision, the people perish' – Proverbs 29.18);
4 Make the goal seem more attainable ('possunt quia posse videntur: They can because they think they can' – Virgil).

Note that performance improvement does not follow from an increase of understanding alone ('The belief that enhanced understanding will necessarily stir a nation or an organisation to action is one of mankind's oldest illusions' – Andrew Hacker). It necessitates working on people's attitudes also ('The greatest discovery of our generation is that human beings, by changing the inner attitudes of their minds, can change the outer aspects of their lives' – William James). Failure to understand that recognition of a problem (that is, being in a situation different from the one we would rather be in) does not naturally lead to improvement is common; some people behave as though once a problem is stated, they expect it to be solved, and if it is not then people are fools or villains. Sometimes a problem is not tackled because others take priority, or because people have conflicting objectives or because they think that tackling one problem will create others; but frequently it is because they do not have the confidence or skill to make a move. That is why a systematic approach to problem-solving is so valuable; it is effective, it is widely applicable and it leads in a logical and disciplined way to a plan for action.

To bring about complex improvements, the systematic approach will have to be used repeatedly, as progress in the required direction is made in stages, with a review at the end of each stage. This review is vital, because it shows where people were successful or unsuccessful, so that they can continuously learn from their experience and thus adopt a more successful strategy for tackling the next stage of the route to improvement; moreover, their increased knowledge, properly reviewed, may enable them to redefine their goal more appropriately.

The process of performance improvement can perhaps best be understood in terms of acquiring a skill. With respect to any particular skill, the population can be (simplistically) divided into four quadrants (Figure 3.2).

Nothing can be done with the 'unconscious incompetents' until they are moved to the right. This can only be done by giving them feedback till it dawns on them that they have a problem. The 'conscious incompetent' quadrant is uncomfortable to be in, and people can lose self-esteem if they stay there too long. They need therefore to acquire both a sense of direction (to the quadrant above) in which they want to move and a means of getting there (a systematic approach). People who are already there (that is, who not only are competent but know how and why they

Figure 3.2 Quadrants of competence (after Dubin)

Unconscious Competent	Conscious Competent
Unconscious Incompetent	Conscious Incompetent

became competent) can help to haul others up, by explanation, example and coaching.

People in the top left quadrant can be a menace. Not understanding why they are competent, they are apt to attribute it to their inherent superiority and to think everyone below the line is congenitally inferior. They are frequently mistaken; most skills are learned, not hereditary. Most can still be learned in adulthood. However, there is a difficulty, as Saul Gellerman pointed out: 'For training purposes, an adult can be defined as someone who has overlearned what he or she already knows and does. All adult training is an unequal competition with pre-existing habits, especially those which are supported by simply conforming to whatever one's colleagues are doing and to what one's superiors presumably expect. This is formidable competition, and the sheer mathematics of the situation militate against effectiveness of unsupported training.'

Learning is helped not only by support but also by experience of success. Success is a spur to further learning and it reinforces the desire to improve. Hence an initial learning objective should preferably be closed down to what is just achievable, and be followed if necessary by more challenging ones, after the learner has got reassuring feedback that he *is* learning.

The example of an individual learning process can be extended to group learning. This begins with a conceptual understanding of the work of the group and its quality, a sense of direction towards improved effectiveness, and the opportunity of practice in new group skills, which is always reviewed. The learning goal is effective group performance. To get there, individuals have to modify their behaviour so as to mesh in with and enhance the contributions of other members of the group, until they act like a real team, such as a winning football team, whose capacity for achievement exceeds the sum of the individual members' capacities.

Going further along the 'organisational dimension', we realise that if a total organisation is to improve its performance, it must go through the same learning process, whereby its constituent groups (or departments or management levels) study the interfaces between them to understand how they work together, review successes and difficulties, define what has to be done to work more effectively together, and then practise doing it. They also have to believe in both the possibility and value of learning in this way, aiming at a situation in which the different groups use one another's skills and enhance one another's contributions, until they attain the ultimate organisation goal, effective organisational performance.

Unfortunately, no situation is static; changes in the environment in which the organisation operates erode its effectiveness, so the learning process must be continuous to maintain, let alone improve, performance. The organisation must adapt to changing situations. Hence every individual should appreciate the need for more rapid organisational development, in response to the accelerating rate of change in the environment. What improving performance amounts to is developing a whole learning system.

Management development

By far the most important way in which managers learn is by doing a variety of real management jobs and getting feedback as to how well they were done. An individual's own manager normally sets up the feedback loop; he may also use that provided by the organisation (staff appraisal, for instance) or he may set up his own (as part of self-development). In all cases feedback is conscious and systematic.

Job rotation is a valuable part of management development, because it gets people accustomed to change, it widens experience and it leads to 'cruciform stimulation'; in other words, not only does the individual learn from the process of fitting into his new job, but his arrival stimulates his colleagues to learn, above, below and on each side.

The apprenticeship model of learning management is commonly used and is effective, but it needs to be supported by a structure of job descriptions, job objectives and targets, guided practice, coaching, training and personal study. The learning process is not left to chance; it is managed. Most opportunities for learning management occur not in formal training but on the job; but many are not recognised or, if recognised, badly used.

Not all managers want their subordinates to become more effective; well-trained managers are more aware of their boss's shortcomings. A manager should take responsibility for his own learning; it is too important a process to leave to the organisation. Self-development occurs most easily when his own manager creates an expectation that it will occur, supports the process, monitors progress and displays an evident interest in it. Managers in charge of their own learning processes usually learn more than those who are taught.

Training courses have their place, but other opportunities for developing management skills should be examined first. Self-directed learning on the job is usually cheaper, easier to apply and can be more relevant, though as Ben Jonson said, 'Very few are wise by their own counsel or learned by their own teaching. For he that was only taught by himself had a fool for his master'. Hence the need for someone to act as mentor, coach or facilitator of learning.

Reflective observation is the most under-used, and abstract conceptualisation the most over-used of the various learning techniques.

Training and managing are about changing behaviour, and if you want to change other people's behaviour, you must first learn to change your own.

Do not assume that when managers express a particular need for training for themselves or their subordinates, the need exists. Some problems that present as training problems have their roots in organisational structure, reward systems, poor selection etc.

Do not assume that managers who need training want it, or will benefit from it if they receive it; the motivation to improve one's performance in a job by analysing how one does it can be outweighed by apprehension at the outcome and at what changes in oneself this will call for.

The centipede was happy quite
Until the toad in fun
Asked 'Pray which leg goes after which?'
This queered her mind to such a pitch
She lay distracted in a ditch,
Considering how to run.

Time spent in systematically analysing training needs often brings better dividends than time spent in training, because it helps to ensure that the training is really relevant. To be effective, all management training should relate to what the manager actually does in his job – not to what managers generally are supposed to do; there is often a world of difference between espoused theory and theory in use.

Since self-esteem is at risk when experienced managers submit to training, Pope's dictum should be observed: 'Men should be taught as though we taught them not, and things unknown proposed as things forgot.'

3.4 *Appraisal*

One of the obvious differences between the management of schools and most other institutions is that in schools systematic appraisal of staff is uncommon. It is seen all too often as a negative process aimed, like exams, at failing people. In the forces, the civil service and most of commerce and industry (at least for the large firms), staff appraisal is such a well-established process that many non-educationists cannot comprehend how educational institutions can be properly managed and developed without it. It is one of the principal means by which staff get considered answers (which, it is thought, they are entitled to receive) to some very natural questions like:

What is expected of me?

How am I judged?

How am I getting on?

How can I do better?

How can I further my career?

Indeed, responding to these questions in an appraisal process has been part of good management practice for so long that the problems of introducing it are no longer as fresh in the memory as they once were.

Of course, however, there are some firms that do not operate a formal system of appraisal, and some managers in firms that do who opt out of it. There are also appraisees who are critical of the appraisal system. But those who object to appraisal in industry and the public service (outside education) are evidently in the minority. For example, as long ago as 1973 the Civil Service Department conducted a major research study in a government department taken as representative of the service as a whole, which showed that only 3 per cent of the appraisees were actually against job appraisal reviews (Fletcher 1973). Yet while in the education service there may be a majority in favour of staff appraisal, there is certainly a vocal minority against. Clearly, therefore, heads and LEAs face a more difficult task in introducing appraisal schemes than their counterparts outside education had 10, 20, 30 or 40 years ago.

Appraisal in industry has been the subject of Institute of Personnel Management surveys of practice during the 1970s and trends expected till 1987 (Gill 1977). At the time of the last survey (1977) 82 per cent of companies had appraisal schemes; it was mainly small companies that did not. These schemes covered 80 per cent of senior management and 90–91 per cent of middle/junior management. The most frequently mentioned purpose of appraisal was to assess training and development needs (96 per cent). Other purposes were: to help improve current performance (92 per cent); to assess future potential/promotability (87 per cent); and to assess new levels of salary (only 39 per cent). The trends were to concentrate even more on performance appraisal and less on potential, though there was a revival in the use of personality trait ratings.

The immediate superior was responsible for carrying out an individual's appraisal in 86 per cent of the companies surveyed; only in 7 per cent was the superior's manager (i.e. the 'grandfather') responsible. The immediate superior also usually conducted the appraisal interview (84 per cent).

Evidently belief in the value of appraisal in these firms was overwhelming. However, some problems were encountered, the main ones (which may have a message for schools) being:

1   Over-elaborate paperwork;
2   Failure to consult about the introduction of a scheme;
3   Lack of commitment at the top of an organisation;
4   Lack of follow-up on agreed actions after an appraisal;
5   Unequal standards of judgment, skewed ratings and leniency;
6   Ossification of the system, due to absence of any review of its operation;
7   Lack of training for appraisal (indeed, 67 per cent of companies believed that appraisal would be of no value unless accompanied by formal training in interviewing).

Although the survey is now a little out of date, it probably still gives an accurate picture of the wide acceptance and main objectives of appraisal in industry, and of the causes of success and failure. In the rest of this section, I shall not attempt to offer a blueprint for an appraisal scheme or a plan for its introduction (see Everard and Morris 1985; Warwick 1983 and Randall, Packard and Slater 1984 for more practical guidance); I shall discuss a number of points from industrial and civil service experience which seem particularly germane to decisions about appraisal in schools.

Purpose

It is essential to be clear what appraisal is for. Since teachers tend to be uncomfortable about specifying aims and defining how they will recognise success in achieving them, it is especially important, before introducing formal appraisal, to decide exactly what it is hoped to achieve and to judge whether this is a realistic objective.

For instance, if a scheme were to be used for making judgements about merit increments in teachers' salaries, it would have to achieve a level of fairness and defensibility that would make it largely unworkable; otherwise it would risk creating more dissension and demotivation than motivation. Industrial appraisal systems are not, as a rule, closely coupled to salary schemes; they are usually operated at a different time of year from that in which salary revision takes place and insofar as they influence decisions, the influence is such as to make the decisions fairer and better informed than they would otherwise be.

Attempts have been made in some firms to quantify judgements about staff performance and relate these judgements closely to salary decisions; while some success has been claimed, this is an unpromising avenue for the education service to explore. Nevertheless, it is a problem for some heads to know how best to reward outstanding performance, which could well be characterised and documented by means of an appraisal scheme. A respected appraisal scheme, and a well conducted interview, can serve to reinforce the informal messages that people get which tell them that they are doing well; and this in itself is a form of reward and a source of further motivation.

Having dismissed merit payments as a primary purpose of staff appraisal, what should it aim to achieve? The most important purpose is probably to *balance the needs of the organisation against the contributions of the people in it,* that is, to explore what the organisation expects of an employee, and how far his contribution meets that expectation. Insofar as there is not a good fit between the expectation and the contribution, what adjustments are necessary and how can they be made? This needs looking at against a time-scale; not only should appraisal take stock of past performance to see what lessons can be drawn about improvements, but it needs to match the future needs of the organisation against the aspirations of the individual. It can assess the *potential* of the individual to meet the future needs, perhaps in a more senior job or a similar job elsewhere, as well as the *performance targets* he needs to strive towards in doing his present job more effectively over the coming year (or term etc.). Thus appraisal should be constructive, developmental and forward-looking – not threatening or punishing. Teachers generally see the objectives more as judging than counselling them, though they regard the appraisal interview as the most valuable aspect of the process (Lusty 1983).

It is important to be clear about whether the purpose of appraisal is to assess performance or potential or both, because the ways in which each is explored and recorded are different. In assessing potential, one needs to know what qualities the individual displays in the performance of the job – the sort of qualities that are important in giving references, career planning, succession planning, selecting staff and keeping records of the stock of human resources in the organisation, to balance against future requirements, as part of the manpower planning system. Manpower planning is not as highly developed in the education service as in industry, so until more progress is made here, the emphasis in appraisal in schools is much more likely to be in the improvement of performance. Nevertheless, careful assessment of potential is important to individual teachers with career aspirations, and this aspect of appraisal cannot be ignored altogether. The question is whether it is to be covert and intuitive or open and systematic.

Of course, performance and contribution are not determined solely by the person himself; there are always mitigating circumstances over which he has little or no control. For this reason, it is a vital part of performance appraisal to examine those features of the organisation and the environment which are helping him or could help him, and those features that are hindering him, or might hinder him, from achieving the objectives of his job and the outcome that he and the organisation seek. It is unhelpful to visit the sins of the 'father' (manager, head, LEA) on the 'son' (subordinate, teacher) or to blame an individual for shortcomings in the system. The true causes of success or failure have to be carefully diagnosed and agreed.

The key agent in the organisation for helping people to do a better job is their immediate manager. Hence one of the outcomes of a formal appraisal of performance and the planning of improvements is likely to be a list of actions for the manager, as well as for the individual. Changes in the description or shape of a job, opportunities for training, changes in the working system, provision of new resources and delegation of work are examples of the kind of actions that might follow a joint review of performance. The appraiser and the appraisee should always be on the look-out for obstacles and constraints to the release of talents that could be harnessed to the aims and needs of the organisation and provide for the individual a deeper sense of self-fulfilment. Such a search lies at the heart of staff appraisal.

Inevitably, however, as well as the strengths, overt and latent, that make people successful in their jobs – strengths that need celebrating and exploiting – there are weaknesses that limit their success and sometimes lead to failure. Just as important are the weaknesses that detract from peoples' potential for career advancement. If these can be identified and remedied, not only will the organisation gain, but the individual stands to gain.

For some teachers, it goes against the grain to point out weakness and failure in others. Indeed, this is the case with some managers outside education. The Civil Service study already cited (Fletcher 1973) commented on the reluctance of interviewers to talk about weaknesses, for fear of eliciting hostile, defensive reactions; the result was that appraisees gained an erroneously favourable impression of how the organisation regarded them overall and were disillusioned when they did not advance within it. In fact, the appraisees themselves valued appraisers' judgements on their weaknesses; asked to pick the three functions of appraisal (out of a list of seven provided) which were most important and useful to them personally, they put at the top of the list 'getting to know your strengths and weaknesses'.

I suspect that most aspiring deputy heads and newly appointed heads would regard insight into their weaknesses as a beneficial outcome of their own appraisal, even if they preferred to concentrate on the strengths of others when appraising them. The appraisee may well have a different view from the appraiser of what would be most helpful to him. This should be explored.

This raises the question of whether appraisal is as useful for older and more senior members of an organisation as it is for the young and junior. In general at least in industry, older people find it less acceptable, partly because their powers of self-appraisal have probably grown with experience and partly because aspirations for personal development usually tail off as one gets older. Nevertheless, appraisal can be effective even in the closing years of one's career, because the organisation's environment places changing demands on it, for which senior people also need to develop new skills. Although at the very top of an organisation such as ICI, the chairman is unlikely to conform to an appraisal system designed for the middle and lower ranks, even at board level there are ways and means of identifying strengths and weaknesses and providing training to overcome weaknesses. Public speaking, television interviewing and management of change are examples of training undertaken by managers at the very top. A particular advantage of senior managers undergoing appraisal is that the experience of being appraised is very helpful in developing competence as an appraiser.

Focus

In the last page or two, a number of words were considered in pairs: individual and organisation; past and future; strengths and weaknesses; top and bottom of the organisation. These can be regarded as defining different dimensions of appraisal (Figure 3.3).

Where should appraisals focus? Should we concentrate on the top management team because they have such an influential effect on organisational performance, or on young trainees because they are more malleable? Should we focus on appraising organisational or team performance first and foremost (for example, school review) or should we concentrate on the individual? Should we devote most of our attention to work done over the past year, or look forward to the future and use appraisal to assess and develop potential? And should we identify, recognise and build on strengths or seek to eradicate weaknesses?

Industrial experience suggests that it is better not to bias appraisal towards one end of any dimension but to seek a balance somewhere in the middle. There need to be explicit links between individual performance and organisational performance and this is usually best achieved by defining aims and targets for each, seeing that the aims are aligned and that individual performance targets are relevant to what the organisation

Figure 3.3 Dimensions of appraisal

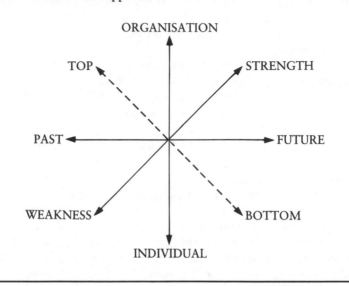

as a whole is trying to achieve (for advice on target setting in schools, see Trethowan 1983a). Likewise, although performance and potential are different concepts, the assessment of future potential rests partly on a consistent and sustained track record of past performance. With success and failure (or strength and weakness) it is psychologically better to recognise and build on strengths, as a number of management thinkers like Drucker and Coverdale have pointed out; but this is no reason to turn a blind eye on weakness and failure, for unless it is dealt with, the effectiveness of the organisation is impaired. The secret of tackling weakness and failure constructively is to do so within a supportive environment and to avoid apportioning blame.

Appraisal is likely to be less effective in an organisation that cannot cope with the necessary actions that appraisal throws up; if a training need is identified and there are no resources for training, it only causes disillusionment and cynicism – unless it helps people to help themselves more and to come to terms with working in an impoverished environment. The belief that appraisal is irrelevant in a contracting organisation, because there is no opportunity for career advancement, is totally misguided, because as we have seen, that is not the only (or necessarily the main) purpose of appraisal.

Systems

An appraisal system is always a compromise between conflicting desiderata. It should be workable, easy to administer and not unduly time-consuming; yet it should be fair and reliable; it should be sufficiently standardised to enable it to be used across the organisation, yet flexible enough to cope with the needs of a particular department or level; it should be systematic without being bureaucratic; it should lead to analytical, objective thinking and disciplined judgements but not come across as inhumane or mechanistic.

There is thus no perfect system, but there are degrees of imperfection. The balance should be struck at a point that provides the best fit with the particular organisation's culture, state of development, size and needs at a particular point in time. A small business (or junior school) might be better off with a relatively informal system depending heavily on good personal relationships, while a larger business (or secondary school) with several departments and a more defined structure, may require a more structured system for appraisal. On the whole, it is better to err on the side of simplicity and to tolerate a little rough justice than to devise a system with so many checks and balances in the interests of scrupulous fairness that no-one has time to operate it. I know of one system devised by a staff consultative committee rather than by managers; it was so complicated as to be almost unworkable.

Some appraisal systems use forms with a few brief headings or questions to which the appraiser responds with a narrative answer (for example, how well has the appraisee done his job? What would help him to do it more effectively?). Others specify the qualities that have to be assessed and may provide a semantic differential or numerical scale against which to mark a response and to add brief explanatory comments. Typical qualities are, from one form used in industry, initiative, attitude to change, orientation, motivation, relationships, expertise, routine administration, communication skills and leadership; from another, mental capacity, versatility, acceptability, reliability, imaginativeness, initiative, organising ability, integrity, literacy, numeracy and persuasiveness; from another (used for senior ICI managers), analytical ability, judgement/initiative/innovation, breadth of vision and foresight, communication, leadership and resilience – each of which is defined; and from another, leadership, depth of knowledge, breadth of competence, soundness of judgement, application, originality, written word, integrity, management of time, perseverance, behaviour to supervisor, working with others. Some forms are provided with 'anchored scales', that is, phrases that describe typical performance at various graduations of the scale are given to provide a common standard for comparison.

Provided there are not too many qualities to assess which are difficult to differentiate, there is some value in defining a common framework for appraisal, especially of potential. It certainly helps in the process of selection for future appointments. On the other hand, if appraisal is focused more on improving performance, it is better to relate it more closely to assessment of specific contributions to furthering the aims of the organisation and an analysis of how these could be enhanced. Emphasis on skills which are capable of development through training and teaching is usually more constructive than comments on qualities like 'judgement', 'integrity' and 'resilience', which are more difficult to unravel and improve.

The design of a suitable form for recording an appraisal is probably something best done within the organisation where it is to be used, building on any transferable ideas from the forms used in other organisations. A prerequisite of any form is that there must be a space for recording agreed action plans or targets, which will be reviewed the next time an appraisal is carried out. Needless to say, an action plan must state who does what by when.

In interpreting appraisals that embody a rating procedure, it is important to bear in mind the strong tendency of appraisers to 'mark high'. Even if the intention is to secure a normal distribution around the 'average' or 'satisfactory' mark, in fact the distribution is likely to be skewed towards the 'good'. This is a reflexion of the fact that appraisers are more reluctant to record weaknesses than strengths. It is also important to be aware of the fact that the reliability of appraisals is never perfect. The adventitious fluctuations of performance and the capriciousness of appraisers' judgements result in only perhaps about 70–80 per cent of the perceived performance being connected with the true performance. Increasing this reliability is costly and time-consuming, and appraisees have to understand that in the nature of the appraisal process, there will be some years when they get a rough deal. Over a career, the rough and the smooth will probably balance, especially if the appraisers change.

Training for appraisal

Before an appraisal scheme is introduced, and to equip new managers to operate a scheme already in place, training is essential. Not only is the process of judging performance and qualities a skill that has to be learned (or at least improved), but the proper conduct of appraisal interviews does not seem to come naturally to appraisers.

Interviewers should leave the appraisee with: self-esteem maintained and enhanced; a feeling of having been listened to and responded to with empathy; a feeling of joint endeavour with the appraiser to solve the problems or difficulties that have been identified; and a clearer sense of direction into the future.

There is even need for training of appraisees, so that they understand the process and how to get the most benefit from it. Two mistakes are commonly made: first, appraisers often spend far too much time doing the talking. The object should be to get the appraisees to talk. Secondly, there is far more to be gained from a joint 'problem-solving' approach in reviewing performance than in trying to 'tell and sell' to the appraisee what he must do.

The most useful training provides role-playing practice in interviewing skills, possibly with the help of closed-circuit television, but in any case with an observer to report back on the process. Even experienced appraisers can learn to improve on the job by carrying out a review with the appraisee at the end of an appraisal interview ('Let us think how we can make this appraisal process work better next time. What went well and what went badly?').

A very effective and professional one-day course on appraisal was designed by a group of primary heads as part of a one term DES 3/83 course on which I was a tutor at the University of London Institute of Education. It is currently available in course manual form from the NDCSMT at Bristol. Also Harris has adapted a commercial course for use in school management (Harris 1985).

Ideally, appraisal should be seen as a joint process in which the appraisee's perception of his performance and potential under various agreed headings are taken into full account and compared with the appraiser's. It does not matter if the perceptions differ, but if they do, the reasons need exploring. In many appraisal schemes, there are separate forms (or parts of forms) for the appraisee to complete independently of the appraiser. There is also a section in which the agreed conclusions and actions arising from the discussion of the two appraisals are recorded, and often signed by both parties. Such conclusions could embody remarks about the appraiser's style of management or degree of day-to-day support he provides. After all, many managers work very closely with subordinates (for example, head and deputy head) and the focus of the appraisal may well be on the partnership's performance (or the team's). Actions arising may be joint or complementary.

Contrary to what might be supposed, it has been my experience and that of others, that self-appraisals are more penetratingly critical and less favourable than those of the individual's manager, although this may depend on the degree of trust that exists between the two. I have found that even very defensive subordinates, who resented being judged by me because they thought I knew insufficient about their work, can pour out self-criticism of a kind that provides a very useful base for helping them to improve their performance. Some managers may be tempted to centre the appraisal so firmly on the appraisee's own self-image that they hold back from offering their own views. This is abdication of responsibility. A manager influences his subordinates' careers and his staff are entitled to know what he thinks of them, even if (in their view) he has got it wrong.

Appraisal by peers

Although it is not uncommon in industry for people to be appraised by 'uncles' (that is, managers in a more senior position but in a different department with which the appraisee deals), appraisals by 'brothers' (in the same department at the same level) or 'cousins' (in a different department) are rare. However, a form of peer group appraisal is an established process in reviewing CNAA courses and it has been used in ICI by division training managers (Everard 1974). The appraisal criteria selected were those used by the head of Sidney Stringer Comprehensive School in Coventry to judge the performance of his school – an interesting example of industry learning from a successful and innovative piece of school management. Each training manager was visited by a small group of his peers in other divisions, together with the company training manager, and a list of questions put, similar to those in a school review.

The focus of the appraisal was not so much the manager as the training function that he led; nevertheless, there were clear messages about each manager's performance, which supplemented those that he got from his immediate superior. They were also pitched at a more professional level, since peers doing a similar job often have a sharper insight into the problems than managers do one level up the hierarchy.

Because of the difficulty that heads face in getting themselves appraised, a group of them may find it useful to experiment with a similar process of peer group appraisal. The nearest equivalent to this which I have encountered was the exchange of places by two heads for a week, followed by a review (Section 2.8).

Appraisal by subordinates

It may be thought even more revolutionary to consider the possibility of upward appraisal. Indeed, when it is suggested to teachers that their client population, the pupils, should be in any way involved, the idea meets with incredulity and almost total rejection; yet it has been demonstrated that pupils are capable of being very effective judges of teaching and that their assessment corresponds closely with that of professional assessors such as HMIs (Lusty 1983).

The need to consider upward appraisal seriously is a particular problem for those like heads at the pinnacle of their organisations; who appraises them? In a large firm there are also senior managers, such as chairmen of division boards, responding to a distant main board, aspects of whose performance cannot be as closely assessed by their superiors as is possible when appraiser and appraisee are in adjoining offices. Where there is a well-established company personnel department, it may be possible for its general manager or a personnel director to perform at least some of the functions of appraisal, and certainly in ICI they provided a service to the main board in senior appointments. The equivalent function in LEAs, however, is not well developed. Chairmen of governors may be called upon to appraise heads, but are unlikely to see more than a fraction of their work, and therefore may not have a sound enough database on which to write a comprehensive appraisal.

Although bottom-up appraisal is not widely practised in industry, the possibility of making it a two-way process was encouraged in ICI in 1969 when the 'staff development programme' (SDP) was launched as a company-wide initiative for organisational change. This led to experiments in upward appraisal which were highly counter-cultural at the time, which have some relevance to the appraisal of heads and which can be compared with the bottom-up appraisal scheme developed in the school mentioned in Section 2.9.

The two objectives of SDP were:

1   In the short term, the achievement of an exceptional and demonstrable improvement in organisational effectiveness;

2   In the longer term, the development of an environment in which major improvements occur naturally and continuously without being enforced or imposed.

The participative management philosophy that lay behind the second objective is worth a passing thought and is illustrated in this excerpt from the guidelines to managers which accompanied the launch of the programme (author's italics):

The process of collaborative examination of work is initiated at the top and spreads downwards to involve each member of staff in every department and location. The need for every piece of work, and the best method of doing it, should be examined both from above *and from below;* and wherever possible, staff should be encouraged to take on more responsible and challenging work, with the minimum of direct supervision and checking.

The idea of their work and the way they did it being open to inspection and comment by their subordinates did not greatly appeal to those managers whose style was authoritarian, and the change of organisational culture which this implied was experienced as threatening. Many managers, therefore, resisted the change, but as Pettigrew chronicles in his study of ICI (Pettigrew 1985) some change did occur as early adopters of the new philosophy felt their way into the unknown.

At the time, I managed a department of 21 staff (mostly graduates, but including clerical staff), two of whom asked me to agree to be assessed by my subordinates. If the experiment was successful, they envisaged that it could be spread to other departments as a complement to conventional appraisal methods. I agreed to the experiment and afterwards put the proposal to a departmental meeting and got everyone's assent, including that of the more senior staff who were also to be assessed from below.

One person (a sociologist by background) was put in charge of the experiment and interviewed everyone separately to establish whether they really wanted to participate. He also devised forms and guidance notes for assessors (Figures 3.4 and 3.5). Subsequently, he interviewed all participants to find out their reactions to the experiment.

Figure 3.4. Form for subordinates to assess a manager

Staff assessment by subordinates

Who are you assessing?

As a manager, what things does he do that you find most helpful?

What things does he do that you find least helpful?

How do you think these latter things might be improved?

Your Name: Date:

Figure 3.5. Guidance notes for assessors of managers

Notes for assessors of bosses

This is designed in response to points made by participants, and is intended as an aide-memoire when completing the form.

What's the point of assessment?

To give your boss feedback on how he manages. To point out his strengths – because being human he is likely to respond to encouragement – and his weaknesses – so he knows what is impeding his management and so he can do something about it.

Completing the form

Since the point of the form is to enable you to give feedback, please do not let the particular wording of the questions impede this.

As a check list to help you answer the second question, some possible helpful things might be:

Giving you encouragement and support
Passing on information
Not interfering – giving you a job and letting you get on with it
Sticking to decisions
Judging fairly
Helping you develop your job or your personal skills
Listening to what you have to say
Being open-minded to new ideas or new information, etc.

A similar embryo check list on things he might do to make your job difficult is:

Interfering in your work
Being aloof/too busy
Giving decisions without explaining the reasons behind them
Changing his mind frequently
Being insensitive to people's feelings
Giving too much or too little information
Criticising you destructively
Having strong opinions or a closed mind – jumping to premature conclusions, etc.

Discussing the assessment with the boss

Can we talk about this when you have done the assessment, so we can decide which is the best way to play it?

Of the 21 who could have participated (including seven assessees with some sort of managerial responsibility, all of whom agreed), 13 declined to assess any of their superiors and another six declined to assess at least one of them. They gave their reasons as follows (figures in brackets are the numbers giving the reason):

'There is no point. The things I would criticise he cannot change, so it would do no good' (7).
'He might be upset by the criticism, might hold it against me and it could damage our working relationship' (6).
'I think all written assessments are wrong in principle' (5).
'If I have to criticise, I criticise at the time, on the job – not on a form several months later' (5).
'I cannot assess him fairly because I do not see him often enough' [two staff worked on a site 200 miles away] or 'I have not been here long enough' (4).
'I have no criticism to make of him; he is a good boss' (4).
'The issues are already being discussed and a formal assessment would confuse things' (1).
Of the eight who agreed to assess at least one of their bosses, the reasons they gave were:
'It can help a superior to get feedback on how well he is doing and how he is seen by his subordinates' (6).
'He is fair-minded and will not hold criticisms against me' (3).
'I think assessment by subordinates is right in principle' (2).

All but one of these eight subsequently changed their minds, mostly for the reasons given by the 13 who declined in the first place, but some for lack of time, or because the momentum had died. The sociologist interpreted this *volte-face* as follows:

In a number of these cases several weeks passed between the original agreement to complete an assessment and subsequent withdrawal from the experiment. This gave a common social process time to work. Subordinate assessment of superiors is unusual, potentially very risky behaviour. It cuts straight across existing norms, and thus requires very explicit sanction from superiors that it is temporarily acceptable. As time passed, and normal departmental life continued, memories of the explicit sanctions that had been given began to fade. As uncertainty grew, people began to pick up, or imagine that they were picking up, conflicting cues, and they began to wonder just how committed their superiors really were to the experiment. Once in this frame of mind, and with no pressures on them to continue participating, the simplest solution was to quietly excuse themselves and withdraw.

So in the end, only one person actually wrote assessments, gave them to his superiors and subsequently had interviews with them to discuss what he had written. He found writing the assessments difficult and felt that he had to phrase things rather carefully because of some lingering fears that criticisms might bring recriminations. However, after the interviews, he reported that despite some unease in the initial stage of the interview both his superiors had taken the criticisms well, had been grateful for the trouble taken and had been flattered where he had praised them. Moreover, he felt the experience had given him insight which would be valuable when he subsequently came to assess subordinates.

For their part, his superiors found feedback helpful and not threatening, and respected him for his courage and for the trouble he had taken. One had agreed specific actions and asked him to monitor them. The other, however, felt that those parts of his behaviour that had been criticised were in fact necessary to do his job properly, and he could not see how he could honestly change them.

On the limited evidence of this experiment, staff assessments by subordinates are not likely to be very popular nor easy to accomplish. The reasons given for declining to take part in the experiment, or for withdrawing from the experiment after initially agreeing to participate, closely parallel the criticisms that are frequently made of conventional assessment schemes.

In this experiment, these reservations were clearly compounded by fears stemming from being asked to do something unusual and possibly rather risky, and underlying it all was the widespread assumption that only assessments which were critical could be of any value. There was little sense of the benefits that specific praise could bring in sustaining existing good managerial practice. Given this, considerable efforts would need to be made to convince subordinates that feedback was genuinely welcomed and likely to be useful before this approach to assessment could have any real chance of success.

This was but one small experiment in one small education and training department in one small part of industry; but it is indicative of the problems that may face heads who attempt to introduce bottom up appraisal. As Section 2.9 shows, one head at least seems to have overcome them, and I would not wish the difficulties that my subordinates encountered to discourage other heads from having a try. I have sensed that some heads and their deputies have a sufficiently mature relationship to enable a simple appraisal form like that in Figure 3.4 to be tried, especially after talking through some of the objections that they may share with my former subordinates and agreeing some ground rules for the process. If the experiment can be mediated by a mutually acceptable third party like my sociologist (who happened to be also a member of my department, but need not have been), it may stand a higher chance of success. Participants who (like myself at the time) have had some structured experience of giving and receiving personal feedback, for example on a training course, are also more likely to achieve a constructive outcome.

Another approach to two-way performance appraisal is a technique known as 'role negotiation'. The manager and the subordinate(s) each make lists in three columns: 'Things I would like you to do more of', 'Things I would like you to do less of' and 'Things you have got right'. The participants share and discuss the information and then strike bargains with one another. 'I will do more of this, provided you do less of that'. There is a sense in which such a complex set of bargains (sometimes unwritten or implicit) guides the development of a more effective relationship between an individual and the organisation for which he works, with the manager having the responsibility to ensure that the organisation delivers its side of the bargain.

Time spent on appraisal

One of the most persistent (and understandable) objections by managers to formal appraisal is the investment of time that is necessary to do it properly. It is difficult to do justice in under an hour to the assessment of a year's work by a colleague, especially when it is necessary to choose carefully the words to be used to convey informative feedback. Individuals taking stock of their own work may also find that they need at least an hour's careful reflexion. Such preparation for an interview is vital. The interview itself between each appraisee and the appraiser(s) may likewise take at least an hour to ensure that any judgements are (a) accurate, in the sense of being based on valid data, and (b) equitable, in the sense of being set against acceptable standards of performance. Where there is resistance to the feedback, as can happen with an unsatisfactory performer, an interview can be prolonged. If this time is multiplied for each appraiser by the number of staff he is to appraise, it will readily be seen that there are practical limits to the process.

In industry, it is unusual for a manager to attempt more than about six to ten direct appraisals, although he may have to add a few comments to full appraisals done by subordinate managers for appraisees to whom he is in a 'grandfather' relationship. In schools, with a flatter hierarchy, there may be an expectation that the head should cope with more appraisals. This would be asking for trouble in a large school. The head of department is the right level of management for assessing Scale 1–3 teachers and in general heads of large schools should not attempt to appraise staff below Scale 4 (plus key non-teaching staff such as the school secretary). By mutual agreement, time can be saved with older staff near to retirement by giving them a less thorough or a less frequent appraisal, but in general it is best not to clock-watch during an interview and not to end it until actions and targets have been agreed and responsibility assigned.

Most managers who take part in well-conceived and well-organised appraisal schemes concede that although it distracts them from operational work, the investment in time pays good dividends in terms of morale, commitment and organisational effectiveness. If experience shows the opposite, it is time to review the appraisal system to see how it can be improved; or the manager's style of interviewing to see if it is appropriate (see, for example, Warwick 1983); or the pattern of his day-to-day contact with those whom he is appraising. If early experience with a newly introduced appraisal scheme is unfavourable, it may be because its introduction was not well managed, with the result that participants are simply going through the motions of appraisal without entering into the spirit. I have come across one such situation in a school where the head imposed an over-elaborate, time-consuming appraisal system taken from industry, without any adaptation or consultation with the staff who were expected to take part in it. It was bound to fail. His next attempt (if any) will be more difficult, since he has built up resistance to appraisal in general. The importance of managing the introduction of a change as fundamental and counter-cultural as staff appraisal cannot be overemphasised (Everard and Morris 1985).

Conclusion

Despite all the difficulties and traps for the unwary, I am convinced from my industrial experience and reading (even of the distinguished critics of appraisal) that the potential benefits outweigh the acknowledged disadvantages and that this will come to be accepted in the education service and teaching profession. The introduction of regular appraisal, together with the support system to deal with some of the actions that would arise, could play an important part in reducing the incidence of the 'people problems' that seemed from Chapter 2 to preoccupy so many heads. Managed well, appraisal could go some way to restoring the self-esteem and morale of teachers. Managed badly, or introduced with the wrong motives, it could equally well undermine commitment and morale.

Although the question of appraisal has been befogged by lurid statements about weeding out bad teachers, it is worth recording that the official view of the Department of Education and Science is that it should not be seen as a threat. In the words of the Permanent Secretary (Hancock 1985) it provides:

The opportunity for the teacher to discover how his or her performance was perceived by management. For many successful and hard-working teachers this could be the only opportunity for giving praise where it was due;

The opportunity to register difficulties beyond the individual teacher's control;

The opportunity to share professional problems and seek solutions with experienced help;

The opportunity to plan ahead and consider the individual teacher's career development needs; and

The opportunity to help the school to improve standards by setting goals to which each member of staff is committed and towards which each is prepared to define his own contribution.

The Graham Report (Graham 1985) recently concluded that 'professional appraisal of all those involved in the education service will improve standards and enhance the image of the service and of the ethos of the school.' After visiting industry, other countries and UK schools that have introduced formal appraisal, and after reading the voluminous literature on appraisal, they advocated the introduction of a positive process that was constructive, honest, professional and non-threatening. It should be subject to external scrutiny so as to be capable of convincing and reassuring parents, ratepayers and taxpayers. It should aim primarily at career development and to initiate steps to deal with performance below par, though only exceptionally leading to the termination of employment. The focus should be on performance in a defined job, rather than on personality. The report warned against the compilation of worthless reports to comply with procedural instructions; rather, the process should be organic with a review mechanism to change it.

Other features they recommended also embody good industrial practice: involvement of people in their own appraisal; clear separation of appraisal from reward systems; provision of training courses in the appraisal process; reallocation of time for conducting appraisals (USA experience suggests about 8–12 hours per teacher per year); and careful attention to allaying the genuine fears and worries in the teaching profession about appraisal. They did not think that antipathy to appraisal among teachers was widespread enough to delay its introduction, and indeed they noted that there had been guarded support from some teachers' unions.

So the education service seems to be on a watershed as regards appraisal. 'There is a tide in the affairs of men which, taken at its flood, leads on to fortune.'

3.5 Developing managers

Just as there is a wide range of approaches to developing managers in education, so with industry and commerce. In this section, therefore, I give an overview derived from some recent surveys of policy and practice and exemplify approaches in two firms that have a good reputation for management development.

The context of management training

The first point to make is that management development is not synonymous with running courses for managers, though training courses are usually part of the process. Some companies recruit graduates straight on to a formal management training programme, partly on and partly off the job; others let their professional timber grow naturally in one of the various functions of the business for several years, transplant it to disparate functions to broaden experience and increase flexibility and then select the most promising candidates when they are in their thirties for more focused experience of management. In such companies, there is often no sharp dividing line between managerial and professional staff, so there can be a recognisably managerial aspect to an essentially professional job.

Because of the key role that managers play in any organisation, it is sensible to watch how the timber is growing and to tend it. This is done by setting up some process for reviewing periodically the stock of future managers, for outlining career paths and succession plans, for arranging career development moves between departments and for providing training experiences in the light of job performance. Management development is not, however, something that is 'done to' a manager by the organisation; there is a sense of joint responsibility and joint involvement in the process of growth.

It is not uncommon for senior managers to be held explicitly accountable to the board of directors for the systematic development and succession of their staff to senior positions in the organisation. A review may be held once a year of the progress of individual managers within each department and a director or personnel manager would receive an account of the departmental head's stewardship. The data collected would be fed into the company's manpower planning system to enable both strategic and tactical decisions to be made on recruitment, selection and development. A senior personnel manager would be expected to have an overview of the total stock of managers and to initiate any steps needed to overcome shortfalls or surpluses of people of the quality needed to run the business in the future. At the highest level of policy, manpower plans would be closely geared to business plans and would certainly involve long term views of the way the business would be expected to develop.

There are not many LEAs that could claim to operate such an elaborate system for ensuring that the right number of heads of the right quality and experience are developed to run the county's schools as they are expected to be in five years' time.

The use of management training courses is thus embedded in a broad approach to management development; they support the processes of development but do not play the leading part in it. The richest source of management development comes from the experience of filling a series of management jobs. There is not only a planned progression of the most able people up the organisation, but sideways or diagonal moves to broaden experience in disparate functions of the business. The equivalent process in the education service would be two-way transfers between the primary, secondary and tertiary sectors, between schools and the advisory service, and between County Hall and schools; but in education such transitions are almost forbidden or, if they occur, only one way. The armed forces make even more use than industry of transfers between 'line' and 'staff'. The effect of such moves on the coherence and quality of communication in the organisation is profound.

Training courses

A useful historical perspective of management courses has been written by Peel (Peel 1984). He traced them back to the foundation of the Harvard Graduate School of Business Administration in 1908. In the United Kingdom, Seebohm Rowntree and Colonel Urwick were pioneers in the 1920s and the Regent Street Polytechnic (now the Polytechnic of Central London) was the first academic institution to teach management.

During the Second World War a sub-committee of the ICI Board laid plans to run internal management courses for staff returning from active service; like many companies at the time, they bought a 'country house' in which to run residential courses in agreeable surroundings. In 1947 the Administrative Staff College was set up in another country house at Henley – the same year as the British Institute of Management was established. The latter acted as an examining body in management subjects until the further education sector took over this role and awarded Diplomas in Management Studies in the early 1960s.

In the early days of management training the 'harder' aspects of management received most attention; accountancy, work study, office organisation, safety, economics and legal subjects formed the bulk of the syllabuses, with the chairing of meetings, minute-taking, report writing and public speaking often thrown in for good measure. Various techniques such as 'brainstorming' (to enhance creative thinking) and 'critical path scheduling' (to improve planning) were added and 'decision-making' was treated as a subject. Methodologies such as case studies (developed especially at Harvard and the Cranfield Institute of Technology), syndicate discussions (developed at Henley) and in-tray exercises were used. The Tavistock Institute of Human Relations in the UK and the National Training Laboratories at Bethel, Maine, in the USA began to pioneer sensitivity training and group dynamics as part of management development, but it was not until the 1960s that these approaches began to take root in the UK.

The 1960s saw the growth of a number of 'packages' that have stood the test of time: Blake and Mouton's 'Managerial Grid' which attempted to illuminate and change management style, followed by the less normative and more acceptable managerial effectiveness seminars of Professor Reddin. Also from North America came Kepner-Tregoe training in problem-solving. UK pioneers were Adair, with his action-centred leadership model and Coverdale with his practice of teamwork approach.

Interestingly, these packages were seldom taken on by academic institutions except for a mere description of them. By contrast, companies used them for their internal management training, and their trainers became qualified to run their own courses based on the packages. What distinguished them most was that learning was substantially experiential, whereas the universities, business schools and polytechnics persevered with the lecture-discussion approach and became theory-dominated. There was no doubt at the time what most practical managers wanted; they much preferred the practical orientation of the 'packages' to the rather arid and unworldly theories of the academics.

Management development and organisation development

There was another important strand of development in the 1960s, usually associated with the phrase 'organisation development' or 'OD'. Again, companies pioneered this approach (ICI, Shell, Tube Investments, etc.) with their own internal training (see, for example, Pettigrew 1985); most of the academic institutions were very slow to follow (though Sheffield Polytechnic is an honourable exception). OD is a broader concept than management development and certainly broader than manager development. Manager development has as its focus the individual who has the potential to succeed to positions of significant responsibility for the resources of the organisation. It involves the identification of strengths that are worth nurturing and applying and of shortcomings that could be obstacles to progress and therefore need redressing or remedying.

Management development has as its focus the team of managers and others with managerial aspects to their professional jobs, who jointly run an organisation; while most of the activities to which it gives rise are directed towards individuals, there is a conscious effort to develop synergy in the team (that is, making the whole more than the sum of the parts), usually through careful selection of individuals who can work together and by common experience training, whilst still preserving and capitalising on the virtues of individuality and diversity. Attention is given to the needs of the total organisation, instead of just the parts of it for which each manager is responsible.

Organisation development sets the management system in the context of the total system and its raison d'être. It concerns itself with:

1 The people in the organisation and how they work together;
2 What the organisation and the community at large expect of people and how they respond;
3 The philosophy of management and how it affects the way people work;
4 The organisation as a whole in its wider setting.

Change, adaptation, effectiveness and habitual improvement of organisational processes and structures are at the very heart of OD and managers are seen as the chief agents or facilitators of change. Specifically, they will work to clarify communication, not only of facts but of views and feelings; they will seek to establish clear goals and gain their acceptance; they will uncover and resolve interpersonal and interdepartmental conflict; they will improve procedures at meetings to ensure effective outcomes; they will adopt a systematic approach to problem-solving; and they will develop a process of decision-making that leads on to action.

Although OD focuses on organisational functioning and performance, it aims simultaneously to improve the quality of working life for individuals and to maintain the balance between individuals, team and task needs. For this reason it usually involves self-study, reflexion and review, the discussion of behaviour and processes and the elicitation of the value systems prevalent in the organisation.

OD as a concept therefore embraces management development, manager development and indeed the development of all the human resources in an organisation (in the USA the initials HRD for human resource development are becoming more fashionable than OD). The approach has been widely adopted (though not without resistance and failures), especially in larger and more complex organisations in the private sector and public service, in some charitable organisations (for example, churches, YMCA) and in some North American schools.

As I have described it, and as it is seen in at least parts of industry, management development is an approach that supports, promotes and is harmoniously related to the development of the organisation. Although in the early stages of the introduction of OD concepts to an organisation with a strong tradition of manager development, tensions can arise between the more traditional management training officers and 'OD consultants', the roles are often combined and do not necessarily conflict. Indeed, I used to perform both functions, though I ran management courses before I was trained for the more exacting role of consultant.

It would appear in education, however, that the two approaches are still seen as conflicting; Buckley writes of an 'ideological divide' between an approach which originates in an in-service training tradition and one which originates in the tradition of OD (Buckley 1985). He cites France as a country where the former tradition is most obvious and Sweden as one that epitomises the latter. The Netherlands and Norway, however, combine the two. In my view he is accurately reporting a false dichotomy and as time goes by, I expect the two approaches will converge in all countries. There is already evidence that in the UK the more traditional award-bearing courses in education management are moving in the direction of the problem-based workshop activities of OD, though there are still fewer examples than in industry of consultants working within education in order to facilitate the improvement of organisational processes.

Supporting the OD approach is one commentator who has wide experience of management in both industry and education: Geoffrey Holroyde, Director of Coventry (Lanchester) Polytechnic and formerly head of Sidney Stringer Comprehensive School. He points out that there are four elements that influence effectiveness in any enterprise: (a) the managerial competence of each individual manager; (b) the level of co-operation and motivation of all members of the management team; (c) the team's commitment to the objectives and strategies of the enterprise; and (d) the environment in which the enterprise operates. He argues that the mistake made by industry in the sixties was to concentrate effort almost entirely on the first element, through the provision of manage-ment courses, and he is concerned that the education service is making the same mistake in the eighties. He recommends that a far better way of improving management performance is to work on all four elements simultaneously. This involves selecting a management team for each school and helping them as a team to improve their interpersonal relationships, communication and understanding; they then identify features (strengths, weaknesses, problems) in the school and its environ-ment on which they begin working with the express object of changing both. 'Experience in industry suggests that a management team willing to commit itself to this process, and face the issues, and manage the change in the enterprise and themselves, will be surprised at how rapidly its performance improves and the enterprise benefits therefrom' (Holroyde 1985).

One of the keys to reconciling the two approaches lies in evaluation, an aspect of management development that is remarkably backward in the education systems of most West European countries and is not well advanced in industry either. This is discussed in Section 3.10.

Surveys of management training

Industrial Society survey
The Industrial Society has recently conducted a survey of training costs in industry, commerce and the public service which gives some idea of

current expenditure levels on management training, the largest category in the training budget (Industrial Society 1985). They despatched 600 questionnaires, of which 134 were returned. Surveys of this kind have their limitations; for example, there is no agreement about what to include in training costs. Most organisations include trainees' expenses, but few their salaries during training. There are also ambiguities in what constitutes 'training'. Nevertheless, a broad picture can be painted, for comparison with the education service.

1   65 per cent of respondents (including all public service organisations) spent less than ½ per cent of their annual turnover on training their employees (as a guide, ICI's turnover in 1984 was £10bn, its salary bill was £1.3m and it had 116 000 employees worldwide);

2   23 per cent spent ½ – 1 per cent of turnover;

3   Only two companies (1½ per cent of the sample) spent more than 3 per cent;

4   More was spent on external than on internal training, especially by smaller companies;

5   Companies with smaller turnovers spent proportionately most on training; only 54 per cent spent less than ½ per cent;

6   The bulk of the budget was spent on training managerial and supervisory staff; expenditure on apprentice training came bottom;

7   Only four companies did not invest in management training;

8   97 per cent of companies trained their management and 89 per cent trained their technical and professional staff, also their secretarial and clerical staff;

BIM Survey

Another recent survey, by the British Institute of Management in 1984 (Peel 1984), also estimated current expenditure on management training as part of an overall study of current policy and practice in 194 companies, mostly in manufacturing industry.

Most firms in the survey had full-time management development and training staff who reported either to a managing director, chairman or president (53 per cent) or to a director (80 per cent). They would also administer staff appraisal in almost 70 per cent of cases. The annual budget they had for management training averaged £45 624 per trainer and varied between £31 and £67 per employee, with the smaller firms spending proportionately more. It was estimated that on average about £364 per year was spent on those employees eligible to receive management training, that is, about two days' training per year. Budgets had, in fact, increased over the previous five years for over half the companies, despite the recession, and most companies expected a continuing increase.

Regular staff appraisal was the most frequently used method of establishing training needs but requests by line managers were also of importance. About half the middle and senior managers received some form of management training at a predetermined stage in their careers.

Some of the main subject areas for training were listed in the survey questionnaire and this may have distorted the picture of what is most frequently covered, but clearly health and safety, computer appreciation, leadership, finance, employment law, selection interviewing, appraisal, industrial relations and training techniques came high on the list. The fact that 65 per cent of the sample listed training techniques is a significant pointer to the importance that is attached to the ability of managers to train others. Future priorities were seen to lie in the area of micro-computing, communications, interpersonal skills and appraisal training.

Of the common training methods, on-the-job training and internal and external courses were most frequently used, but a sizeable proportion of firms used internal team training and job rotation. 'Action learning' was not a popular method. The survey concluded that the pattern of management development and training has not altered much in 40 years, but there is a shift in emphasis towards greater flexibility, more practical involvement and more self-development.

Attwood survey

L. T. Attwood carried out a survey of management development in 515 UK companies and drew comparisons with a similar study of US companies (Attwood 1979). He concluded that management development in the UK was centred on improving the effectiveness of the organisation, whereas in the USA it was seen more in terms of the development of the individual *per se*. Its main elements were (a) improving on-the-job performance, (b) creating a pool of management talent, (c) encouraging individual development and (d) enabling vacancies to be filled quickly and effectively. It was linked to appraisal, but in some companies appraisal was not seen as very effective, namely where it had become part of the bureaucracy. A small proportion (12 per cent) of the companies studied used 'assessment centres', in which management development was linked to the process of selection; and 16 per cent linked it to the use of psychometric tests (mainly the Cattell 16PF inventory).

Harbridge House survey

Ascher studied management training practice in 80 of the 150 largest UK business organisations and found great diversity and a very wide range of internal training activities (Ascher 1983). There was no such thing as a typical in-house training programme and little agreement on the optimum content of courses at specific management levels.

Most firms tailored their training to the needs expressed in managers' annual appraisals, though banks and retail chains in particular had a series of courses, progression through which was mandatory, regardless of appraisals. The most common topics in courses, in declining order of frequency, were:

Finance;

Communication (report writing, discussion leading etc.);

People management (interpersonal skills, industrial relations);

Management principles (organisational management, management of change);

Persuasion techniques (influencing, negotiating, motivating);

Job-related skills (time management, decision-making, problem-solving);

Commercial aspects (marketing skills, sales techniques);

One-off (legislation, health and safety, computing).

A number of trends were discerned: (a) from junior towards more senior management training; (b) integration of technical and management needs (in educational terms, this would be equivalent to training heads in both a leading professional and a chief executive role simultaneously); (c) more emphasis on behavioural topics and management of change.

Expenditure on management training tended to be high and was growing, despite the recession. The big spenders were the banks, retail chains and oil companies. Just under half the companies had their own management training centres. The average size of the training function was six, but the range was 1 – 25 according to how much of the training was done in-house. Most firms thought this preferable to external training and the overwhelming majority were cynical about award-bearing courses such as MBA.

Although there was a widespread lack of serious course evaluation, belief in the value of training was signified by: (a) the training manager being senior, well respected and autonomous; (b) top management taking a genuine interest in training; and (c) a 'training ethos' being present, whereby management training was regarded as critical to one's career.

NDCSMT Survey

A smaller scale but very perceptive study, from the point of view of education, of management development outside education was carried out by Ballinger of Bristol Polytechnic for the National Development Centre for School Management Training (Ballinger 1984). She visited seven companies that were leaders in market terms or in approaches to management development or both and then synthesised an overall, albeit idealised, picture of it.

She found that the companies shared the following characteristics:

Organisational climate and structures for development
1   Strong company identity where managers felt they belonged and were valued – yet a lack of paternalism;
2   Successful ideas arose from any level;
3   Effective communication up, down and sideways;
4   Tolerance of mistakes and experiments, as part of development;
5   Trust and openness, fostered by the training function, in which the climate was compatible with that of the organisation at large;
6   Flexible response to rapid change, with 'anchor men' acting as guardians of the underlying values and providing a sense of stability;
7   The role of training changed as the company and its management function developed.

Role of managers in management development
1   Managers saw their jobs as primarily a 'people' development task;
2   Management development (defined as the process by which the management function becomes performed with increasing effectiveness) occurred through a continuous interplay between the manager, his manager and the trainer, with the focus being effective job performance;
3   This discussion was the main mechanism for identifying training needs, though it was supplemented by individual initiative and by company-wide surveys of training needs;
4   The annual appraisal interview was the other mechanism for identifying training needs – both of the appraisee and of the appraiser in the case of a genuine two-way process;
5   The manager was held responsible, as a significant part of his role, for the development of his subordinates;
6   Development mostly took place on the job, through coaching and counselling supplemented by in-company, off-the-job training in which line managers were often co-tutors – off-site training being rare.

The training process within the organisation
1   Management development policy was decided at senior management level and was integrated into a coherent overall development policy for the organisation;
2   Management training was most effective when it was trainee centred, action-based, skill-specific and with action outcomes;
3   Learning contracts were negotiated between the manager, his manager and the trainer and took account of both individual and organisational needs, the latter including succession planning;
4   Evaluation of training was done by the trainee, peer group assessment, the trainer and the trainee's manager, who was responsible for evaluating its effect on job performance;
5   A long term outcome of effective management development is role

change, notably the trend to devolve responsibility and power to semi-autonomous units.

Trainers and the credibility of training
There were four trends in companies where the training function had high credibility:
1 Young high fliers moved temporarily into training from other management functions, then got promoted;
2 Line managers were trained to acquire the skills necessary to develop their managers;
3 The value of training to the company was regularly and publicly endorsed by the highest levels of management;
4 Training managers came from management posts at the hard end of the business.

Miscellaneous
Derek Bowden, head of Leftwich High School, included in his survey of management in industry a number of observations about management development (see section 2.14).

Professor Tom Kempner, Principal of the Henley Management College, wrote of the experience of 18 heads who had joined their eight-week General Management Course mainly for managers from commerce, industry and the public service. He concluded that the management roles of a headteacher and that of any manager are very close indeed. Common needs are for an understanding of:
Personnel policies – improved selection, training, discipline, motivation and appraisal;
External relations – with a variety of the vocal pressure groups that have politicised schools;
Marketing – the need to build the 'image' of the school;
Authority, power and symbolism – the challenge to the role of the head (manager);
Planning and long term strategy – needed for survival in a world of change;
Organisation development (OD) – analysis of structure and contingency theory.

A few subjects studied by other managers have little relevance in schools – finance and investment appraisal are examples. There is much to be gained from the joint training of heads and other managers, because the other course members are not teachers, and this facilitates the transfer of knowledge between managers from a wide cross-section of society (Kempner 1984).

Chater (a head) made a direct comparison of management training provided by a private and a public sector agency (Chater 1984). He noted that on a one-week Coverdale training course, everything required for the training was available – files, papers, pencils etc., and it was held in proper surroundings. On a one-term DES 3/83 course run by a university, on the other hand, the work room and furniture were unsuitable and materials arrived late. The Coverdale course was more decisive and clear-cut in its strategies and its trainers worked on the course full-time with the group to which they were assigned; on the 3/83 course no-one ensured continuity. The Coverdale course was experiential, with no lecturing; the 3/83 course was based mainly on theory interposed with discussion and projects. The pace of the latter resembled that of much INSET work – leisurely. Both courses were effective in what they set out to achieve – the one to develop skills and the other knowledge; but of the two, he would have chosen the Coverdale course for one week rather than the university course for one term.

Examples of company approaches to management training

ICI

Management training in ICI is seen as an integral part of staff development and is closely linked to appraisal and manpower planning. It is characterised by diversity because except at senior level the task is delegated to autonomous divisions. Typically, however, the aspiring manager will first attend an induction course which helps him to understand the basic principles of personnel management and how the organisation works. Like all their internal courses, its duration is short, perhaps three days. No in-company course lasts longer than two weeks.

Perhaps five years after recruitment he will go on a one-week residential course on problem-solving and the practice of teamwork. In some divisions this is the Coverdale training package; others have developed a blend of techniques from work study, Coverdale and Adair. It has been found that the development of a common systematic approach to solving problems is one of the single most effective ways of developing management teams. These courses are highly participative, highly intensive and so structured as to provide a great deal of feedback on one's personal style and its effect on others. Success depends critically on the skill of the trainers who conduct the course.

There are courses on financial management and computers for the non-specialist managers and on business management for those in marketing and related functions. For managers who have many subordinates, there is a variety of courses on personnel policies and practice, including industrial relations, and several divisions also run a course on leadership. This is usually based on Adair's action-centred leadership model, perhaps with elements of various American approaches built in (for example, Harrison and Berlew's 'power and influence workshop' or Reddin's 'managerial effectiveness seminar'). As in the problem-solving course, there is a strong feedback element, which helps managers to become vividly aware of their personal leadership style.

The usual types of course on report writing and effective presentation of ideas are available for those managers who are in particular need of this sort of training and at the higher levels of management external agencies are used to train people in public or television presentation.

Mention should be made of a 'skills of persuasion' package which had its origin in the American Sales Administration Institute. ICI has developed this over the years and it is very effective. Qualms that teachers might have about the suitability of such an approach in the education system would not be well founded; it has a sound ethical basis and is relevant in schools. I have used it in school management training. Other approaches from the different stable of the Xerox Corporation are also used in training sales managers.

At the more senior levels of management at and beyond the equivalent of head, there is a senior international management course which is intended as a kind of induction to the higher echelons of management. It mainly deals with organisational issues – business policy, personnel policy, environmental trends and long term company strategy – and is more aimed to developing qualities of judgement than skills.

For a number of years there was a 'Directors' Conference' ('workshop' would be a more accurate description) in which invited and nominated members of division boards and their equivalents in overseas companies spent a week at the company training centre under the chairmanship of a division deputy chairman, to deal with a selected issue in depth. The mechanism was for a main board director who owned a particular problem to pose it to the conference members at the beginning of the week and to return on the Friday to hear and comment on the solution proposed. As the stage manager of this conference, I would work with the chairman to plan it and would arrange in advance for key expert 'witnesses' to make presentations on particular aspects of the problem; for example, for a problem on 'Middle East policy' I procured an oil sheikh among other people and for 'European personnel policy', one of the witnesses was an EEC Commissioner. Thursday evening and sometimes the early hours of Friday morning were spent in completing the conference report which my secretary would type ready for its presentation after breakfast. Some of these reports became quite influential documents, especially when they were presented by the director who owned the problem to the main board and after discussion and amendment became part of company policy. Sometimes key phrases emerged from a conference (for example, 'pan-European') and quickly rattled all the way down the divisions, because it was usual for the participants to report to their division boards the outcomes from the conference. Another conference left its mark on the company by proposing a 10 per cent per annum productivity improvement target and this had a visible effect on redundancy policy. Not all the problems posed were at the hard end of the business, however; one conference addressed itself to managerial stress and quality of life.

There were several advantages of this model: (a) it helped to break down barriers between division boards and the main board; (b) it helped to solve tough problems of policy and strategy; (c) it was a tangible example of participative management at the top; (d) by using outside expert witnesses it helped to combat company parochialism; and (e) it gave groups of senior managers guided practice in teamwork. The same model might well be used by directors of education or chairmen of education committees to draw on the experience of heads in solving particular problems of a strategic nature within a local education authority.

After these conferences were discontinued, a somewhat shorter event was set up, called a 'Management of Change Workshop'. The first of these was run by an American consultant, Professor Dick Beckhard of MIT, who had been a consultant to the company for a number of years. He was assisted by Professor Ed. Schein. Beckhard's work in facilitating change and the place of these workshops in achieving major reshaping of the company, has been described in Andrew Pettigrew's *The Awakening Giant* (Pettigrew 1985; see also Section 3.8). Participants in the workshop were normally nominated in pairs, for example a division chairman and one of his directors, and brought along a major problem with which they were contending, such as reorganising their division. Another pair consisted of two works managers, one of whose works was due to be closed so that production could be rationalised in the other. Latterly, most of the directors on the main board attended one of these workshops *in statu pupillarii,* bringing a strategic problem like everybody else. After the first such workshop, a small cadre of 'facilitators', including myself, was set up to take over from the two external consultants. Although the approach was very much based on real problems, with the consultants there to give process help, a number of carefully written and concise handouts were used to explain the main processes of managing strategic change and each consultant gave lectures at appropriate points in the workshop, which was flexibly structured to take account of the hour-to-hour needs of the participants. The approach to management of change which was used in these workshops and disseminated throughout ICI is described in Part 3 of my book *Effective School Management* (Everard and Morris 1985).

Again it is a model which is transferable to the education system, but it depends on participants being already familiar with basic problem-solving skills such as the 'systematic approach' or Coverdale training. ICI directors who in their earlier careers had escaped such training found the going on these workshops rather hard.

Also, it is worth mentioning a course that was specially commissioned to be run by the Oxford Centre for Management Studies (now Templeton College) by Rosemary Stewart. This was set up to deal with a problem that is also rife in schools. The division that initiated it had grown fast for many years, but had begun to plateau and was about to decline. Since promotion opportunities are highly geared to growth, a whole raft of middle managers realised that their career aspirations were likely to be thwarted and their morale and motivation began to suffer. A two-week course was designed, an input to which was a work diary which every participant kept for a few weeks before he arrived. Much time was spent in groups questioning each participant's role. Typically, they found that they viewed their own roles with tunnel vision. When they were challenged about demands, constraints and choices, they realised that they had far more scope for personal and job development than they had suspected. With a new vision of the possibilities open to them, they laid plans for expanding and enriching their jobs without having to depend on promotion opportunities to release their creative energy and sustain their motivation. This course was subsequently used by other firms; it could readily be adapted for school heads of departments who have begun to 'coast' in their jobs, to give them a new lease of life. As West-Burnham has noted (West-Burnham 1983), promotion is one of the few tangible rewards in teaching, and lack of it can lead to problems of motivation and job satisfaction. He quotes an ACSET report which forecasts that by 1995 nearly 75 per cent of teachers will be over 40 and 25 per cent over 50. The prospect of this high proportion of older teachers, turned off by lack of promotion and prospects for the future, suggests that some avoiding action should be taken now.

ICI makes negligible use of award-bearing courses such as DMS and MBA but a small number of 'high fliers' in their thirties or early forties are nominated for external business school courses of three to eight weeks' duration.

Albright and Wilson

Albright and Wilson, a subsidiary of Tenneco, mount a series of courses which managers attend over a period of 3–6 years. The first in the series is the 'staff course' which provides an understanding of the organisation and how the business works. This is followed by a pair of courses taken with a six month gap between and entitled 'Concepts and Practice of Management'. The first part develops knowledge and skills of management practice in the organisational context. It is related directly to what managers actually do and each individual has to report on his role and job description. The members also get a good grounding in the concepts developed by the leading writers on management and in the light of these ideas they develop plans for improving their performance in their jobs.

The second part called 'The Manager and his Team' is highly participative and it develops an awareness of personality as it applies to the job and working with people. Two other courses are aimed at introducing managers to financial management and safety respectively.

Then there is a course of American origin (Kepner-Tregoe) which develops a rational and systematic approach to the analysis of problems and decisions. It helps managers to identify problems, then to solve them, and to handle complex situations by setting priorities for action. This is run in two ways: either an open course for all-comers or a closed course for one or two natural work groups. The participants in the latter share the same background and the same problems, so they work together to solve these, which results in an immediate pay-off for the organisation. This common experience is particularly valuable in that it helps teams to develop a common approach to new problems; communication is improved because basic problem-solving processes are shared. During the course, participants have to think about how they think, and this is intellectually demanding.

Finally, there is a course on presentation skills which is tailored to the needs of the individual. It can deal with one-to-one situations such as interviews, small group meetings, addresses to large conferences etc. and is not confined just to the presenter's use of voice, gestures, visual aids and general stage management of a situation, but also deals with the listener's point of view and reactions. With the help of closed-circuit television and audience feedback, the participants' performance in doing a presentation is dispassionately analysed with a view to effecting improvements (Bridgwater 1980).

These examples of company training course provision are typical of the approaches adopted by a number of companies with household names. They form part of an overall policy of management development which is very much aimed at improving the way in which the business is run. Although, however, there is an underlying rationale for courses which helps to get the right people properly trained for the managerial jobs that the firm wants performed, individual managers have considerable freedom to choose how to develop their subordinates. Some will attach greater importance to giving them a variety of projects to manage, and then appraising their performance in doing these, than to nominating them for a series of formal courses. Whatever the approach preferred, management development is a conscious and deliberate activity which is seen as essential to the maintenance and prosperity of the enterprise.

3.6 Resource management

In recent years educational managers and industrial managers have had this in common: both have had to operate in an environment of contracting resources. It is difficult to manage a transition from growth to decline, but if organisations are to remain effective and indeed survive, some hard decisions have to be made about conserving resources and cutting one's coat according to one's cloth. This can strike at morale and professional values in both industry and education. Some of the suggestions in this section may therefore raise hackles, and be perceived as rather negative; they are, however, a necessary part, though only one part, of a manager's job. 'Every man should periodically be compelled to listen to opinions which are infuriating to him. To hear nothing but what is pleasing to one is to make a pillow of the mind' – St John Ervine.

Paisey defines educational management as the process of relating resources to the objectives required in organisations which explicitly exist to provide education (Paisey 1981). 'To measure the efficiency of resource allocation requires a prior specification of performance or output objectives. This is as true for schooling as for soap powder' according to Pateman (Pateman 1980). However, neither 'performance' nor the concepts of 'profitability' and 'productivity' which are used in industry as criteria for assessing the efficiency of resource utilisation, translate well into the educational scene, though some attempts have been made to do so (for example, Legon 1981). Yet some such concepts are needed in order that educational managers can give an account of their stewardship of resources to the tax-payers, rate-payers and fee-payers who put up the money for education. It is quite legitimate for these stakeholders to ask the question 'Are we getting good value for money?'. I would argue that all managers have an ethical duty to be good stewards of the resources entrusted to them, which means turning them to purposeful account. In the case of human resources, this means trying to get extraordinary results from ordinary people, by so organising their work and work environment that they are operating near the limits of their capacity. For inanimate resources, it is like the old definition of a good engineer – 'A man who can do for a shilling what any fool can do for half a crown'. Something of the same attitude of mind is revealed in Rutherford's comment on a shortage of resources in the Cavendish Laboratory: 'No money? Then we must use our brains!'.

Thus, even in a stable situation, it behoves the manager to try to improve efficiency; as resources get scarcer in a contracting economic situation, it becomes even more important to use them to full advantage. Just as the unit costs of production increase as the plant occupacity (that is, the level of operation as a percentage of full capacity) diminishes, so the unit costs of education increase as school occupacity falls. If nothing were done to close or amalgamate schools affected by falling rolls, or to reduce the staffing, the government of the day would be hard put to justify the rising costs per pupil when there are so many other causes competing for a limited sum of money.

On the other hand, while unit costs per pupil might be regarded as one measure of 'productivity' it is not helpful to consider it in isolation from the educational outcomes of incurring the costs. Similar problems arise in business, so in fact managers study a range of measures of effective resource utilisation in order to sustain and improve overall performance. The business analysts who judge international business performance in the chemical industry (and who rated ICI top of the league in 1983 and 1984) use no fewer than 40 measures (ICI 1985).

There is particularly strong resistance in the education service to a 'business efficiency' approach, yet it is hard to see how its managers can be accountable for the efficient use of resources without adapting some of the approaches that other organisations use to promote efficiency. Such approaches are used because people in organisations, and organisations themselves, characteristically behave in certain ways that undermine efficiency and these tendencies have to be counteracted.

Thus, for many people it comes more naturally to make their own money go a long way than to treat public money or institutional resources thus. There are usually more examples of waste of resources in an office, plant or laboratory than in our own homes. Managers in industry therefore have a constant struggle to learn, and to inculcate in the workforce, the kind of attitudes and habits that lead to better resource utilisation. Not only is there the general incentive of achieving a healthier balance sheet, but particular incentive schemes of various kinds are used. Many firms have suggestion schemes that reward shop-floor workers with financial bonuses if they discover ways of making savings in raw materials or services, and give wide publicity and praise to those who win such awards. Might such a scheme help to reduce heating costs, for example, in schools?

Plants are set efficiency or productivity targets to try to motivate the workforce to conserve resources and attain a higher output. Where a particular source of waste exists, for example spillage of an expensive chemical, or leaking steam valves, there may be a notice nearby to remind people just how much the wasted material costs. House journals are used for propaganda and pep talks are given to encourage the responsible and participative management of resource utilisation. Managers themselves are trained to look for sources of inefficiency and their performance in eliminating these may be monitored. Striving for efficiency becomes a way of life.

These approaches are all used to heighten the awareness of employees at all levels of the need for good husbandry as a matter of habit – like inculcating safe working practices. It is an uphill struggle which, like Sisyphus's task, never seems to end. Of course, management courts unpopularity by continued nagging about the improvements needed in resource utilisation, but experience shows that if this pressure is not continually applied, standards tail off and slipshod working practices take hold again.

Another area for management attention is work study and work measurement. This approach was very popular in the 1950s but then it became tied to bonus incentive schemes which ran counter to the newer ideas of management coming from the behavioural scientists. Yet the basic principles continue to hold good, that is, to ask what is the most labour-saving way of getting something done? By careful observation of how a fitter replaces a defective pump, or of how a waiter serves a meal, it is often possible to economise in the number of movements they each make to accomplish their tasks. It is surprising how people quite unwittingly make work for themselves by performing operations in the wrong order. The aim of work study is nowadays not to get people to work harder, but to help them to work more effectively at the same pace. The incentive to do this comes from the realisation that time is precious and costs money, so it needs using well.

How many teachers could achieve more with the same effort by planning their work better? Again, it is often possible to make much more intensive use of expensive equipment by replanning of work schedules, with resulting savings in capital costs.

Another approach is not just to improve the way work is done, but to ask if it really needs doing at all. There is an apocryphal story in ICI of a works laboratory that regularly tested the pH (acidity) of a stream running through the site. This went on for 15 years until it was realised that no-one acted on the results. On enquiry it turned out that the test was originally instituted after an ammonia tanker had started leaking, and it was necessary to monitor the resulting pollution. It had never been intended to continue testing the stream for more than a few days. The natural tendency is to exclaim that this would never happen in *my* organisation, because we are too hard-pressed to do unnecessary things. However, an outsider or new recruit is likely to find examples.

In any large organisation work is instituted to meet a particular need at the time. It is seldom that review processes are efficient enough always to detect when the need has passed, in order that this regular piece of work gets discontinued. Meetings in particular tend to become institutionalised and to go on being held long after they are really needed, at least in the same form. Since an hour's meeting of 20 teachers costs between £200 and £300, one has to judge whether a commensurate benefit ensues. Or could the meeting be smaller?

Because of this natural tendency of organisations to perpetuate activity, a number of approaches have been tried to eliminate unnecessary work. One approach is the 'overheads panel'. A task group of managers from different departments is commissioned to examine all the activities (and especially those at headquarters) that are undertaken to support the functioning of the organisation, to cost each of these activities, to ask what would happen if they were discontinued, and to assess whether the benefits outweigh the cost. Where the activity cannot be shown to be 'profitable' it is discontinued, and the effort it absorbed is redirected elsewhere to bring greater returns. Changes in work habits which such studies cause are often resented by the people affected, especially if they perceive that their jobs may be threatened; but faced with Parkinson's law that work expands to occupy the time available, how else can a healthy organisation cope with a natural tendency to 'run to seed'?

ICI tried to build an automatic corrective mechanism into its organisation in 1969, when it launched its 'staff development programme' (Section 3.4). The idea was that, as a matter of course, rather than as a one-off exercise, work would be continually examined from above and below to ascertain the continued need for doing it. However, although the initiative probably helped staff to question more regularly whether work was necessary or being done in the most effective way, there was still a need for 'productivity drives' and other sharp interventions to remind people that left to themselves organisations can easily drift into ineffectiveness.

The need to maintain effectiveness becomes acute in a declining economic environment, because firms can and do go bankrupt unless they contain their overhead costs. This usually means, in the end, cutting staff numbers, since salaries constitute the highest proportion of overhead costs. Understandably this strategy creates resistance, and managers generally cannot envisage how they can possibly operate with fewer staff. Senior management insists – or the profit and loss figures convince – and it is invariably found possible to run the business efficiently with fewer people, especially if it is mainly the 'work generators' who go. This attrition can occur again and again, despite vocal protests from managers and staff alike, yet organisations are adaptable enough to continue functioning effectively, even after they have been squeezed till the pips squeak. Some valuable activities and able people may become casualties in the process, but in a declining market the alternative to contraction is an even worse situation to contemplate. How can contraction be managed without disruption? First, managers have to win the minds of those affected, by sharing the problem with them, explaining why contraction is necessary, taking them into their confidence. Secondly, managers have to win their hearts by providing a great deal of practical help and emotional support. It is not easy; it is for many distasteful; but it is the lesser of two evils.

Pettigrew has made a study of the typical responses of organisations as they move from a relatively rich to a poor environment (Pettigrew 1983). He identifies four:

1 The organisation ignores the change;
2 It does what it always did, but more of it;
3 It perceives the hard times as transient, and does the minimum to adapt;

4 It adopts a strategy for change and allows the implications to incubate over a period of time.

The fourth response is helped by managers with a reputation as 'doers' and 'fixers', and hindered by those with a reputation as systems administrators who try to preserve the status quo.

Bone, the Principal of Jordanshill College of Education, has written about the problems of institutional management in a period of contraction, and has pointed out some of the pitfalls – for example, trying to postpone the inevitable by cutting expenditure on building maintenance, departmental expenses etc. (which never saves enough and usually requires even greater expenditure later on), or by getting rid of key non-academic staff, or by contriving to increase the number of students (Bone 1982). It is better to identify the problems of contraction of resources well in advance (and for schools the writing was on the wall demographically and economically long before the wave of cuts hit them), and plan contraction in an orderly way.

Some institutions of higher education (and independent schools) have taken on more overseas students to increase the occupacity of their plant. Others have taken on research contracts from industry to occupy their teaching staff more fully. Diversification may be easier for such institutions, but there are three examples in chapter 2 of schools doing something similar. Resource acquisition, otherwise known as fund-raising, is becoming more and more a necessity for school managers.

Industry on the whole is more ready than LEAs and schools to spend money in order to save it. The drive for productivity has led to a greater use of technology for eliminating or expediting routine jobs. There is plenty of scope in school offices, as in commercial offices, for introducing word processors and other data-processing equipment, so that secretaries and clerical staff (with whom schools are generally under-provided) can turn out more work with the same effort. As firms like BP and British Caledonian have found, considerable savings in salary costs can be made by using computer-assisted learning methods. At least some of what is taught in schools could be learned in this way, so that the teacher can tackle higher level tasks than routine instruction.

One of the biggest obstacles to improving resource utilisation can be organisation structure. The tendency in business has been to move away from a highly functional organisation, with large central research, accountancy and personnel departments, towards one in which most of the employees recognisably belong to one of a series of 'profit centres'. This has the effect of focusing management thinking on improving resource utilisation, which is more closely coupled with profit and loss than in a functional organisation. The equivalent change in LEA organisation is to devolve to the head more financial responsibility for the total operation of running the school, including building mainte-nance, cleaning, supplies etc. At the same time he is given powers of virement, that is, he can transfer expenditure from one budget heading to another, and thus apply savings made under one category to resourcing more activity under another.

The problem that arises when functional responsibility is widely dispersed is that managers always try to blame other departments for poor performance of the organisation as a whole. There is very little that a head alone can do to improve efficiency in the way that the technical services department of his authority does a job in his school. An independent school head, however, or his bursar, has direct control over his maintenance services.

3.7 Organisation problems, change and development

I have been much struck with the apparent parallels between the organisational problems currently facing schools, and indeed the education service as a whole, and the kinds of problems that faced ICI in the 1960s and 1970s. Other parts of manufacturing industry were similarly affected. It is instructive to compare the responses of the two systems to the management of the change that the problems triggered off.

During the period in question, many firms experienced the transition from a seller's to a buyer's market; international competition became fierce; trade union pressures increased; government intervention grew; the pace of social change rapidly modified the expectations of employees and of the public at large; technological change played havoc with established processes and practices, both in plant and office; and expansion gave way to economic stringency and contraction. The management of large organisations became much more difficult, and the politicians and media combined to erode the self-esteem of managers. They felt assailed, disparaged and defensive. As the balance of power changed, they came to feel emasculated and confused.

The pervading effect of all these changes in the firm's environment led a few senior managers to wonder if the way in which their organisations were structured and run had become inappropriate. They sensed the need for major strategic change within the firm to bring it back into tune with the environment.

Schools did not experience the main wave of contraction until a few years later, but it came without warning – or rather the demographic and economic warnings were largely ignored. Their ordeal of public criticism followed the Ruskin speech of 1976. Their equivalent of technological change was curricular change – new expectations, new exams, new pedagogical approaches, new educational thrusts like TVEI. It has been mainly under a right wing government that the teachers have been belaboured; for industrial managers, it was a left. Of course, change of social attitudes towards a more questioning, less deferential and more permissive society affected schools at the same time as industry, and went to the very heart of educational values. Under guises such as curriculum development and school review, leading thinkers in the education service started, like their counterparts in industry, to flag some of the areas for change in structures, outlooks and *modus operandi* of schools.

The problems that one firm, ICI, faced in responding to the significant changes in the environment which have also affected schools, have been intensively researched by Professor Andrew Pettigrew, a leading expert on organisational behaviour. His book on continuity and change in ICI over a period of 20 years is one of the most revealing exposés of organisational problems which has been published for some time (Pettigrew 1985). The fact that he studied not only the problems in the corridors of central power but also in four of the divisions makes it particularly useful, since the interaction between the autonomous divisions and the centre can be compared to that between autonomous schools and their LEAs. The same kind of inertia prevails in the two systems, but within this were some stirrings of change. Pettigrew sums it up for ICI thus:

Although the style and mode of operation of the main board and the broad corporate culture of ICI were remarkably resistant to change throughout the 1960s and 1970s, major strategic change did begin to occur in the early 1960s (page 72).

I believe there are important lessons to be learned by education from the company's experience. Failure is instructive as well as success. Regionally, some of the lessons have already been taken; the Cleveland LEA, under Harold Heller's influence, and with support from the Teesside Industrial Mission, built useful and enduring learning bridges with ICI when it was realised that schools were going to be severely affected by falling rolls. Nationally, the bridges have not yet been built.

Among the similarities between ICI and education is the sheer complexity of the two systems. The counterpart of the autonomous head is the chairman of a division – or within a division, a works manager. Teachers sometimes think that they alone operate in a political system, but political processes are also at work in organisations like ICI. No manager can manage effectively without coming to grips with them. The role of culture and climate in shaping ICI as an organisation comes through clearly in Pettigrew's book: the equivalent of *Fifteen Thousand Hours* (Rutter et al 1980).

The book also provides examples of the problems of industrial management which parallel some of those described of schools in Chapter 2, and are presented with full dramatic detail. Perhaps a few excerpts will capture some of the central problems that afflicted the company for a number of years. If you mentally substitute the nearest educational equivalents of the industrial labels, the parallels to school situations will be discerned. Thus:

For main board	read	LEA (with a little DES thrown in)
division chairman		head teacher
division board		head and deputies
senior management group		heads of departments and years
products, groups, functions		subject disciplines, pastoral systems
junior management staff		teachers

Consider first the description of one of the divisions, Plastics, at the beginning of the period of change. For various reasons it faced the most difficult problems of organisational change of all those studied and was least successful at handling them. I choose it because it seems to relate best to the education service.

The Plastics Board did not operate as a team, and there were at times rather distant relationships between the board and the group of senior managers immediately below them. The division was broken down very strongly into product groups which were very separate and the directors on the whole behaved at board level more like spokesmen for their product or function than people controlling the division as an entity (p. 269).

Key features of the pre-1964 management culture which persisted for the remainder of the 1960s and way into the 1970s were the authoritarian, distant and reactive style of management by the chairman and one or two of his senior directors, the apparent lack of cohesive working among the board itself and the at times competitive and distant relationship between the board and the senior manager group below them, and indeed between the product groups and functions. Plastics Division continued to have problems as a human system which intruded on its capacity to act as a purposive and coherent business and technical system (p. 277).

A senior director described the culture thus:

The culture of an organisation like this depends very much on the chairman. When I joined he had his own style of management. It was a curious mixture of autocracy and *laissez-faire*. Decisions tended to be made very rapidly by him if he picked it up as something he was interested in, or alternatively he would say to one of his deputies you look after that, tell me what you have done. You got what was really a rather curious culture in a sense, this curious mixture of rapid decisions made in a very autocratic and non-participative manner with a good deal of delegation (p. 277).

I have heard the behaviour of heads described in recognisably similar terms. Others described the culture as 'role bound' with very little cross-fertilisation. Handy has described the culture of secondary schools in these terms (Handy 1984). Some groups in ICI (for example, the scientists and the engineers) were formidably cohesive. Pettigrew sums up:

Of course, the conclusion should not be drawn from these statements about differentiation in Plastics Division that the culture was rent with continuing and open conflict; the management processes were a good deal more subtle than that. If anything, the management culture was characterised by the absence of confrontation. . . the chairman was taking direct action and delegating into an organisation structure where there were few co-ordinating mechanisms. . . The absence of mature policy-making and planning processes and the group and interpersonal skills to make them work had they been encouraged, meant that reaction was the order of the day. . . Not even the tremendous shock of the 1971–72 redundancies and in 1972 the death of their chairman in post, could break the pattern of caution, reactivity and independent working which by then had been primarily established in Plastics Division management culture (p. 278–9).

The number of employees in the division steadily diminished from 13 134 in 1970 to 7962 in 1981. The problems continued under a new chairman:

. . .lack of strategic perspective and team working on the board also influenced another persistent theme in the management culture, the poor integration between products and functions and between management levels (p. 282).

Similar problems in integrating the pastoral and academic systems occur in schools and long term planning and policy making are equally deficient.

A great deal of effort was put into correcting the situation that these excerpts describe. Management training and OD consultancy were both deployed over a number of years. Although some successes were achieved, the climate was as hostile to such interventions as it is to staff appraisal in education. The key disability from which those responsible for improving the managerial processes in this division suffered was the lack of political support at the very top of the organisation. If a chairman or head does not want to change, or if *force majeure* threatening the very survival of the organisation does not intervene, there is a serious constraint on what innovators can achieve in the way of fundamental change from below. In fact it was at deputy chairman level (deputy head in a school) that the most powerful resistance to change in organisational culture was found in Plastics Division during the 1970s; by the same token, even if a head is disposed to change the way things are done in a school, he may well have his intentions thwarted by his immediate colleagues, especially if they have been in post for longer than he has. Even with a deputy chairman (deputy head) who is fully alive to the need for change and who supports the change agents (as Plastics had in the second half of the '70s), if he cannot get his colleagues' support, progress is likely to be very slow.

There was certainly within the division during the whole twenty years Pettigrew studied, a realisation by a few of the managers of the need for change, but as he points out:

There is a world of difference between the development of a need for change in an organisation, people's differential awareness of such a need, their capacity to pull together an appropriate vehicle or mechanism to satisfy that need, and express it in a way and in forums where it becomes politically acceptable, and then find the political will, climate of co-operation, systems, structures and human capabilities to ensure that strategic change is successfully implanted (p. 99).

As already mentioned, not all the divisions experienced the same difficulty that Plastics Division – or the company – had in managing change. The north-east divisions were more successful and so eventually was Mond. Their approaches have been studied by the local LEAs. Among the successful attempts to initiate change were training interventions. The first of the new style courses was run in 1968:

In these training workshops the consultants worked with a small group of people in ICI to help them diagnose what lay behind this resistance to change. . . For many of these managers these training events were the first occasions they had been on a workshop as distinct from a course, where instead of being 'taught' or 'lectured to' they found their own and others' behaviour and feelings in the workshop and back at work, part of the material for learning. . . These workshops were generally viewed as helpful and successful. They brought out into the open managers' insecurities and anxieties about managing people and organisational change, about their fears of losing control. . . (p. 110–111).

Another successful training intervention was launched on the Wilton Site (shared by several divisions) in 1969. Over a thousand managers took part:

In bringing about a change on the Wilton site the director then responsible, John Harvey-Jones said 'The problem became how to get a grip of the management without the use of hierarchical power.' Of the three strands of the change strategy, one was an attempt to develop a common managerial language and set of procedures through one-week courses. These courses aimed at developing a common 'systematic approach to problem solving'. . . The emphasis was on the recurrent processes of group problem solving, such as information gathering, planning, acting and reviewing and on the need to avoid losing sight of consciously managing these processes under the weight of detailed tasks. . . The programme contributed considerably to the development of a common language and to the sharing of common problems across the site, particularly at middle management levels (p. 231–3).

However, these local successes still left plenty of problems that needed solving. After noting that his remarks about issues and improvement opportunities in organisation climate and communications should be read in the context of an organisation whose general 'health' was perhaps as good as any organisation in the world, one of ICI's consultants observed:

1   Communications between main board and divisions

There were difficulties in this linkage partly because the main board did not make clear priorities, goals and plans; partly because the board did not think through issues informally and collectively and therefore tended to communicate different messages from the centre. . .

2   Company chairman: division chairmen

There was a tendency for division leadership to play down its role as part of company management and to increase its identification as division leadership. This meant that the spirit of main board intentions was not being communicated below the top division management.

3   The lost battalions

This was a reference to unrest and moves towards collectivism on the part of junior management staff. This was partly due to compensation problems – an established annual bonus for staff at this level had recently been consolidated into a salary increment for one year – and partly due to the fact that junior management in other ways felt 'unappreciated, undervalued, helpless to influence their fate' (p. 398–9).

Similar adjectives might be used to describe teachers' feelings in 1986! And how often do heads of departments fail to convey the spirit of the school senior management's intentions?

At the same time there was formed an informal, even an illicit meeting of the division chairmen, as a defensive manoeuvre against centrally created personnel policies and practices. Its members vented their frustrations but wanted to be helpful and influential in the company, though they were beginning to be seen by the centre as a threatening combine: 'a shop stewards' committee'. The formation of this group added to the pressures for change.

The incoming company chairman at the time took the board away for two days to discuss the top structure and operation of the company. The outcome of the meeting was that three subgroups were set up, each to work on a different aspect of organisational change. To prevent a clash between the division chairmen's bottom-up initiative and the board's top-down initiative, the two groups were brought together to examine the relationship between them. It was established that no organisational change would take place without full consultation with the division chairmen.

In education, there are signs of heads exerting their influence through their professional associations, but they have not established a right to the 'full consultation' that ICI division chairmen won for themselves.

Further discussion through 1976 and 1977 highlighted afresh the main problems, which again parallel those often found in schools:

1   Not spending sufficient time discussing key strategic issues;
2   Not being able to have objective discussions on key subjects and then come to crisp decisions;
3   Not being able to handle conflicts between product, territory and function;

4   Spending too much time managing, not enough directing;
5   The management style of resistance to change, excessive consultation, insular modes of thought and behaviour and over-concern with the immediate difficulty at the expense of the longer term problem (p. 402).

However, for all the effort , the right combination of political will and environmental pressures had not yet assembled themselves in 1977, so the changes which actually occurred were mainly cosmetic.

The next move in 1978 was another training intervention: to mount a series of seminars on the management of change, to get a much greater understanding of the technology of change management, and a common language between members of the board, division chairmen and their boards. The concept was that if the top 1500 people in the company understood what technology there was for managing change, and could use a common jargon, then they would have a very much better idea of handling some of the things they had to do.

I was one of the small team that ran these workshops for several hundred of ICI's most senior managers, including members of the main board, division chairmen and directors. An essential part of their design was that participants came in pairs, bringing a change problem that they both owned and had legitimate authority to work on. The $2\frac{1}{2} - 3$ days of activity, interspersed with short inputs of concepts, ideas and techniques about management of change, focused on the real change problems that participants brought with them. Nobody Pettigrew interviewed doubted the value of these workshops; an executive director told him: 'They have given more skill, they have given more appreciation down the line and they have given more appreciation to some members of the board who never operated in that way before.' Crucially they 'helped to signal and clarify what change management was as an activity, to provide a common language for problem-solving about change and in so doing, helped to stimulate a culture for change, at the point in time when environmental pressures demanded real action and outcomes and the capability to produce these outcomes' (p. 414).

Visible structural changes and less tangible cultural changes followed and received new impetus when John Harvey-Jones was appointed chairman of the company in 1981; he also became the principal executive officer. There was more focus at board level on strategic direction; the consensual style of decision-making on the board, with the chairman as *primus inter pares,* changed; layers were removed from the management hierarchy and a clearer sense of direction emerged.

3.8 Should schools learn from industry?

Nothing is so terrifying as ignorance in motion – Goethe

The oft-repeated theme in this book is that schools should learn from industry – both from its successes and from its mistakes. However, although in recent years schools and industry have become increasingly involved with each others' affairs, there remains in the teaching profession a sizeable body of opinion voicing concern about the possible infiltration of education by commercial values and alien management practices if learning bridges are built and used. I occasionally encounter some suspicion and even hostility when I contribute to school management courses and some academic colleagues have articulated their concerns in writing. It is now time to examine their objections.

Torrington and Weightman query the point that heads should learn from managers rather than the other way round. They say that there is little evidence that the investment made by industrial and commercial companies in training managers in the last twenty years has produced impressive management performance (Torrington and Weightman 1983). To the first point I would respond that learning bridges should be crossed in both directions but, since industry has so far devoted a good deal more money and effort to developing management than has education, it is more advanced and has more experience to offer. The second point is also worth making and I shall deal with it in Section 3.10. The establishment of a causal relationship between management training investment and financial performance improvement has defied many investigators.

William Taylor expresses concern that business management concepts are antithetical to fundamental educational values and are based on naïvely conceived principles (Taylor 1976). He fears that the accomplishment of short-term managerial tasks will substitute for the achievement of longer-term educational ends. The social control processes implied by 'management' debase professional accountability and stifle personal initiative and commitment. While conceding that management concepts can help to illuminate social processes, Taylor cautions against their uncritical acceptance in case they have unforeseen and illiberal consequences in the educative task of the school. Of critical importance in headship is a superior level of judgement, and he argues that this can only come from a very much wider concept of educational administration than is encompassed in the concept of 'management'.

A more recent and vituperative critique along similar lines is in *Education plc?* (Maw et al 1984) published by the largest and most prestigious Institute of Education in the United Kingdom (that at the University of London). On the back cover of the booklet it is written:

Most of the contributors to this Bedford Way Paper are. . . critical of the industrial model, arguing from different perspectives that the *executive functions* of headteachers should be subordinate to their *professional concerns*. Several contributors argue that the correct model for this working relationship should be participatory workplace democracy rather than a manager-managed prototype.

The same kinds of arguments are heard at conferences, for example by

Michael Fielding at an Education for Industrial Society conference on 2 July 1985 and by such notable educational figures as Harry Rée and John Evans at the 1985 annual conference of the Centre for the Study of Comprehensive Schools. In the Centre's journal, *Contributions* (Rée 1985) Rée criticises the CSCS for putting over the establishment view; he writes:

CSCS worries me. . . Our tendency to bow before the philosophy of management as practised in industry and commerce and to accept some of the inhuman and easily fudgible techniques of management by objectives is another source of worry. . . It is time CSCS looked for a philosophy which transcends the aims of industry, even at the risk of losing the support of certain firms.

Three of the authors of *Education plc?* are much more trenchant in their criticism of the current encouragement of education to learn from industry. Fielding in particular, a deputy head on the Stantonbury Campus, Milton Keynes, flashes warning lights throughout his essay, *A Critique of the New Management Training Movement*. His concerns are triggered by contributions in the *Times Educational Supplement* by David Trethowan, Head of Cuckfield School, a leading advocate of the transfer to education of management practices from industry (Trethowan 1983b). Fielding contends that:

. . .the direction of David Trethowan's proposals isn't just wrongly oriented but that those approaches which provide its surface power and attraction are deeply objectionable, that these should be strenuously resisted and that our energies should be channelled towards radically different ends.

While allowing that commercial practices like target-setting and evaluation have much to recommend them, he sees:

. . . much about commercial management practice that is not only inappropriate but hostile to the kind of considerations which are crucial for headteachers and those responsible for running educational institutions.

However, he writes of 'the commercial management model' as though there were only one. His criticism of this model will attract the sympathy not only of educationists but also of the many industrialists who will not recognise this particular model as either corresponding with their experience of the commercial world or differentiating it from the world of education.

At the centre of my concern about the development of a commercially-inspired hegemony in the training of headteachers, lies the question of morality. . . The commercial imperative fits into a very different network of values and social practices to education. . . Morality. . .is seldom anywhere other than on the perimeter of the commerical arena. Quite the reverse is true of education, whose morality imbues not only the ends which are pursued but also the means by which they are attained. One of the most worrying aspects of aspiring towards the imprimatur of commercial management is that the shift will push morality from the centre to the edge of the commercial undertaking.

This 'holier-than-thou' attitude towards industry and commerce rests, in my experience, on a somewhat flimsy base; not only is one of the main themes of Peters and Waterman's account of successful firms (Peters and Waterman 1982) the emphasis placed on ethical values, but a head seconded to ICI reported that in his visits around the United Kingdom, employees behaved as though social responsibility was part of the objectives of the company, even though this was not made explicit (Buet 1985). Too many people outside industry believe that the sole objective of a company is to comply with the Companies Act, namely to act in such a way as to benefit the shareholders. There are many commercial firms in which the expression of moral values in their social behaviour is both explicit and implicit. Equally, for all the protestations of moral rectitude, I have certainly encountered unethical behaviour in the world of education. The point is not that either industry or education has a monopoly of virtue – there is an unacceptable face both of capitalism and of education – but that no institution staffed by imperfect man is a paragon of virtue. Those who seek to besmirch commercial morality often themselves infringe the first principle of morality, which according to Pascal is to work hard at thinking clearly in order to discover the truth.

Another objection that Fielding voices to his commercial model is what he pejoratively calls 'chameleon management', that is, the approach that proclaims that there is no single right or wrong style of leadership, but that the appropriate style depends on the situation. This, he argues, is tantamount to 'an elevation of manipulation into a managerial impera-tive'. However, few people would wish a consultative management style to be used to evacuate people from a burning building.

The focal position of a head, exercising a 'linchpin style' at the top of a hierarchy, also attracts Fielding's concern:

If the headteachers' training initiative is to produce fruit worth eating, the whole approach to their accountability and the evaluation of staff performance needs to be redescribed, using language and strategies which move firmly away from the enticements of commercial management, away from the linchpin conception of the head, away from hierarchical and vertical thinking, away from its atomism and towards quite different strategies resting on very different premises. . . A commercially inspired management imperative is more likely to betray rather than enhance the specifically educational nature of our schools. It is likely to do so because its network of values, its accustomed focus and its characteristic style of operation are in various ways destructive and are quite out of step with current progressive educational thinking.

The Whites add to Fielding's strictures of commercial management, quoting its theory as 'lending a spurious legitimacy to the manipulative practices of managers'. Instead, like Evans, they would prefer to dismantle the hierarchical structure of schools in favour of a workplace democracy in which each person has access to an equal share in the exercise, or control, of power. Therefore, management courses would be used to train heads to 'go back to their school and start to initiate amongst their colleagues consideration of how their particular institution might be run on more democratic lines'. I can readily concur that there are some schools whose effectiveness would almost certainly be improved if such were the outcome of management training; I am not convinced, however, that a non-hierarchical democracy is the right answer, at least in the short term.

Notwithstanding their criticism of industrial organisations and commercial management practice, and their concerns about the effect of commercial influences on schools, these authors do not shut the door to the applicability of industry-oriented management to schools. But as John White says,

It is important to establish that a case has to be made out. It is too easy just to *take it for granted* that those whose whole lives are spent grappling with the problems of industrial management or writing about them, will have valuable knowledge to pass on to heads and other senior teachers. But this should *not* be taken as read.

Such scepticism is proper; the point is worth making. There are enough examples of incompetent or inappropriate industrial management practice, and enough public criticism of the performance of British industry, to make it prudent to be circumspect in transplanting to schools management practice from industry.

What is less than fair, and indeed could be harmful, is to paint a distorted picture of industrial management practice in general, and then to argue that its transfer to schools should be strenuously resisted. There are enough barriers to much needed change already, without inciting teachers to resist what they have not experienced.

The underlying weakness of the critics' case is that some of their premises are false. One assumption they make is that there is one model of management, a model that bears a distinct resemblance to Taylorism; in fact, the most effective models in use have gone far beyond this. Another is that a hierarchical organisational structure inexorably traps managers into authoritarian management styles; in other words, there can be no place for the exercise of participative management in a hierarchy without debasing the meaning of 'participation'. In practice this is not the case. Then there is the assumption that management by objectives is inhuman; that the profit motive, coupled with the power vested in those at the top of the hierarchy, so corrupts industrial managers that morality flies out of the window; that situational management is tantamount to manipulation; and that the network of values by which commercial enterprises are managed are incompatible with those of education.

These assumptions run counter to most of my 30 years' experience in industry, during which I have been managed, have managed others, have for 15 years trained others in management, have for 2½ years been personal assistant to two ICI chairmen, have observed top management at close quarters and have thought, lectured and written about the ethics of management. Others' experiences may be different, for industry is nothing if not diverse, but I am sure that most professionals in progressive firms have a much more favourable impression of industrial management than its critics. By contrast, although my contact with education is shorter and shallower, I have encountered more examples of inhuman and downright incompetent management there than in industry.

It is therefore my belief that professional teachers in education would experience better management if their employers and managers adopted certain practices common in industry (for example, systematic staff selection, appraisal and development).

I deliberately write of the management of professionals because teachers are professionals; the appropriate industrial management model to study is therefore that used in departments or at levels predominantly staffed by professionals – research, accountancy, training, planning, marketing etc. Part of the mental blockage that teachers have in embracing the concept of industrial management is that they liken themselves, not to professional colleagues in industry, but to blue-collar production-line workers, with all the 'them-and-us' connotations that that implies. Perceiving the psychological distance between a plant manager and an assembly line worker, they naturally do not wish their role relationship with their leading professional colleague, the head, to be modelled on this (often inaccurate) perception.

It is unfortunate that some academic writers on industrial management philosophy paint what most industrial employees would see as a distorted picture. I am wary of intellectuals projecting on to employees views of the industrial world which they do not, in fact, espouse. Readers of such books as *Working for Ford* (Beynon 1984) and *Living with Capitalism* (Nichols and Beynon 1977) can easily gain the impression that all workers feel as exploited, oppressed, inhumanly managed etc., as Marxist theory would suggest. Teachers may therefore fear that the more schools adopt industrial management practices, the more they (the teachers) will feel oppressed and disadvantaged. However, so far from this being an inevitable or even probable outcome of the new school management initiative, I believe that the opposite will happen; existing wrongs will be redressed.

Nonetheless, such an outcome cannot be left to chance; education needs to discriminate between different management approaches and adopt only those that speak to the condition of education. By this token, I would commend some scepticism, so long as it does not become an excuse for procrastination, and support many (but not all) of the leads given by the authors of *Education plc?*. The following are particularly in tune with industrial management philosophy:

1   'When we face enormous changes in the social and economic substance of our way of life, it is important to have the capacity and the patience to stand back and ask fundamental questions. . .' (Fielding). Industrial managers think the same.

2   'Any training initiative should demonstrate a conspicuous awareness that the process of education rests on a bedrock of values and that management of educational institutions forms part of the hidden curriculum for staff and students. Headteachers should be people who are able to encourage that awareness. . .' (Fielding). Senior managers in successful firms do likewise; such firms are 'value-driven' (see Peters and Waterman 1982).

3   'The process of clarification, appraisal, development and application of the school's essentially educative function should involve staff and students as part of the ordinary working of the school' (Fielding). A similar process goes on regularly in industry; it is often known as 'consultation'.

4   'The spirit and mode of these processes should be part of a participatory structure in which the concept of "celebration" is centrally important' (Fielding). But this is just what is happening in industry, as another contributor to *Education plc?* found: 'On a recent visit to a firm of management consultants in the city, I was impressed by their move away from the concept of manager as leader to a more collaborative view of management' (Mitchell).

5   'Sound organisation and systematic ways of approaching problems are essential if teachers are to be freed to maximise learning' (Mitchell).

My last quotation from *Education plc?* sums it up:

What industry and commerce already practise and write about in management, is well worth an examination. There is a rich and diverse literature relating to both training activities and the theoretical frameworks which underpin such activities. . . These materials have provided the basis for training in management skills which can assist the realisation of a school's educational philosophy in a helpful and positive way' (Young).

3.9 How schools can learn from industry

In the last section we considered some of the reasons adduced for not learning from industry. The thrust of this book, however, is that learning bridges are worth building and worth crossing, because some firms are effective, ethical and successful, partly because they are well managed and organised, which is partly because their managers have developed their competence systematically. Equally, some schools are effective and successful, partly because they are well managed and organised, which is partly because their heads and senior staff have developed their competence systematically.

Moreover, there are many problems common to both schools and industry, even in schools and firms that have all the appearance of being well run; many of these problems are natural consequences of human and organisational behaviour and imply no particular blame on management for their incompetence.

In the circumstances, the sharing of ways of approaching these problems, across the learning bridge, is likely to suggest new and better ways of dealing with them, always remembering the need for circumspect discrimination in adopting practices from the other side. A number of companies have taken the lead in bringing this about. BP, for example, have pioneered the use of a workshop approach in which common management problems are discussed by participants drawn from schools and industry (CSCS/BP 1984). Five contemporary problems affecting both sides were usefully compared:

1 *Management of declining resources* and the need for deciding priorities in allocating finances to new developments;

2 *Management of a changing market* – decisions about courses and outcomes to meet the changing needs of people going into an increasingly competitive world;

3 *Management of staff development* – decisions about professional development at a time of reduced opportunities due to falling rolls and contraction;

4 *Management of conflicting viewpoints* – decisions that require heads of departments to balance their departmental needs with those of the whole school;

5 *Management of technological change* – decisions about the implications of introducing new technology and the consequent increase in efficiency and change of job opportunities.

As a result of comparing notes about case studies on these themes, teachers and industrialists alike were surprised to find how much they had in common. The realisation that others share similar problems of management can help to raise teachers' self-esteem and lead to useful links between school and industry, including the provision of consultancy help.

IBM, who have also encouraged the twinning of schools with parts of the IBM organisation, have found similar common problems (Stoner 1984); in their case the salient problems were the immobility of the labour supply (in school terms the inflexibility of staffing in relation to falling rolls), the erosion of motivation of staff faced with lack of career prospects in a declining numbers situation, and 'departmental tunnel vision'.

Just as similar management problems are to be found in industrial and in educational organisations, so are there similarities in the qualities, skills and learning needs of those in managerial positions. There seem to be differences in attainment too; certain management learning needs seem to be less well satisfied in schools than in industry and no doubt the opposite applies. Tried and tested ways of meeting these needs are available and there are increasing examples (some already quoted in this book) of teachers who have had opportunities of doing so in an industrial setting.

Heads who have been on the BP 'New Managers Development Programme' consider it to be one of the best educational experiences of their lives. They learn how they operate and how this affects others. They acquire a structured way of thinking about their dealings with other people and they even learn a good deal about their own *métier,* learning (Everard and Marsden 1985).

Of another workshop, run by Rank Xerox in conjunction with Understanding British Industry, two heads made the following comments: 'The best course I have ever been on in terms of helping us in education to know how we should be thinking and planning the future curriculum for our young people'; and 'Every headteacher should attend a course such as this.' As a result, a national course was developed for heads about the management of change (Nisbet 1982–3).

A primary school head wrote of his experience on a Trebor 'Coaching Workshop'. 'I learned much about how courses should be structured. The emphasis placed on human relationships in the workplace has much relevance to the management in schools and has, until recently, too often been neglected' (Bookman 1985). As the National Development Centre reports (NDCSMT 1984), 'it is encouraging to see the enthusiasm with which increasing numbers of people describe their interchanges with industry.' Moreover, it has been shown that these approaches are transferable from trainer to teacher, given the right conditions.

A training design I used for many years in ICI with middle managers, the 'Group Achievement Course', was adapted for use on successive OTTO courses for experienced heads at the University of London Institute of Education. One of these heads became the warden of a Primary Management Studies Centre and used the same material on his courses, not only for primary heads and their senior staff but also for his LEA staff. For most teachers, education officers and inspectors, these experiential learning techniques for developing teamwork are novel, but the results supported the approach and have led to some very appreciative comments on relevance, appropriateness and helpfulness. Some quotations from course evaluation forms will exemplify the response: 'a model for us to emulate'; 'highlighted some important elements for our work with schools'; 'emphasised that effective communication is not about lots of talking'; 'a very lovely and brave way to tutor'; 'wholly appropriate in the many group situations that exist in teaching and life'; 'the primary inspectorate would stand to gain a great deal from a similar approach'. However, participants were at pains to stress that the approach depends for its success on the skills and sensitivity of the tutor. While such skills can be learned, disposition also plays an important part in achieving competence.

A former school teacher, C.L. Marsden, has written about his experience of management training in BP. Experiential learning was unfamiliar to him and he had previously associated the word 'training' with narrow and specifically operational skills. In fact, however, this management training was:

pure open-ended 'education'. . . There is far too much made of the distinction between education and training and the different teaching techniques involved. In fact, much of the exam-based teaching in schools is far narrower in every respect than modern management training from first line supervisory level upwards. . . Much can be learned by taking part in training programmes run by a local company as these kinds of skills are common to working in all organisations of people. . . Perhaps more important, however, is the eventual knock-on effect this could have for the education of young people themselves (Marsden 1983).

Another way of crossing the learning bridge is by visits and secondments. Short visits by teachers to an industrial firm to study the problems and practice of management are of limited value and can even be counter-productive in the absence of very careful briefing and preparation on both sides. Terminological and conceptual barriers need to be overcome and mutual stereotyping must be contained. It is unsafe to leave the learning from such a visit to chance; the organisers must be quite clear what the visit is expected to achieve and narrow down the objectives to manageable proportions. General 'rubber-necking' visits (as with pupils visiting industry) are worse than useless and waste everybody's time. There is useful learning to be gained by studying the process of an encounter with industry, including the feelings engendered by entering a strange organisation. Care should be taken on both sides to be sensitive to feelings and to project a fair image of the school to industry; there is no place for self-disparagement.

Secondments for a period of a month to a year also need careful managing, but can be very fruitful to both sides. Again it is very important to decide what the objectives of the secondment should be and to plan accordingly. Giving the secondee a project to do, rather than planning a long succession of interviews, is probably the best method of enhancing learning. There ought to be a named person responsible for being mentor or counsellor to the secondee; this will not only help to open doors, but will also serve to maximise the opportunities for learning. The secondee should always be on the lookout for parallels and contrasts with his back home situation and should give continual thought to the question of how he can apply and helpfully disseminate his learning on his return. If there is a chance to attend a suitable in-company course during the secondment, this should be taken. Not only will there be value in picking up the skills that the course is designed to develop but there are usually excellent opportunities for informal and revealing discussions in the evening, when participants tend to 'let their hair down'. Companies usually appreciate some constructive feedback of the secondee's impressions; perceptive comments about what is good and what could be improved are part of the database of the company's management. An outsider who is not perceived as part of the power system is often entrusted with information not readily available to senior management and provided it is conveyed sensitively, ethically and non-attributively so that confidences are not broken, the whole organisation can benefit from the action that is taken as a result. Learning can cross the bridge in both directions.

Secondments from industry to schools are less common and less well documented but one head has described the experience of having a banker in his school for half a term (Beloe 1985). The sorts of questions that he asked made staff pursue new lines of thought. The management received a series of recommendations; valuable commercial experience was passed on. The head concluded: 'The process of secondment was a total success. . . we feel it was very worthwhile.'

Next, there is the use of consultants from industry to bring learning across the bridge. Typically these would be people who are employed to help their own managements to improve organisational effectiveness. Training managers, management services managers, personnel managers and their staff, and the rather rare breed of people called 'OD consultants' or 'process consultants', are the most likely to be able to help. Some of them will have received training in consultancy skills and will be very sensitive to the problems of coming into a strange and possibly suspicious organisation. An experienced consultant can be of enormous value in diagnosing the causes of problems and giving managers the confidence and skills to handle them effectively. Less useful and sometimes positively harmful is the consultant who comes in to find problems for which to prescribe his own pet solutions and who spends little time in diagnosing what the true needs of management are. It is also worth finding out if a consultant has useful written material; some have spent a lot of time distilling their own and other people's thoughts into succinct handouts that they use on courses and workshops. These are often far more practical and handy to use than books on management and can be stimulating documents to circulate among staff. Even well-designed forms and questionnaires can be put to good use, perhaps with a few modifications to make them suitable for the school environment.

If an industrial consultant is used, it is important for someone within the organisation to 'manage' his entry and jointly plan with him what sort of contribution he is expected to make. The process of working with an external consultant is itself a valuable learning experience and the internal contact should try actively to identify and develop the skills that the consultant deploys. The best way to do this is to review after an encounter with the school what lessons are to be learned, why the consultant acted as he did and how else he might have acted instead. The kinds of skills a good consultant uses are applicable to other management processes such as coaching, counselling and developing staff.

Finally, at a somewhat different level, there are probably many more opportunities than are usually exploited, for picking up useful advice, contacts etc. from some of the governors and parents in industry with whom the school is in contact. This can be about the wider aspects and responsibilities of management – looking after buildings, money, equipment, computers, office systems etc. Many businesses have to spend time and money before they can wisely select equipment and services and it may well be that schools could gain access to the expertise that builds up in purchasing departments and the like. Once a personal contact is made in industry, there is scope for widening the bridgehead on both sides.

3.10 Evaluation of management training

The Achilles' heel of management training is evaluation; what actually happens as a result of training managers? Is learning transferred to the work situation so that it changes behaviour? The BIM survey already mentioned (Peel 1984 p. 35) shows that almost one in three of respondents did not attempt to evaluate management training systematically.

As far as education is concerned Buckley, in his survey of school management training in Western Europe (Buckley 1985 p. 8), concluded that there is very little existing research in the field of management training for schools. The evidence from what research there is (p. 130) is that '(a) there is no one best way of training school leaders and (b) many existing courses do not change the actual behaviour of the school leader.' He went on to report (p. 153) that 'we know very little about school leadership training and its effectiveness. . . Very little progress has been made in measuring the effectiveness of school leadership training programmes.' Have those involved changed? Has their behaviour changed? Have their schools changed? Have the learning experiences of the children changed? We do not know. Not only does very little research evidence exist, but it is difficult to persuade researchers to undertake such work. Really sound evaluation, beyond the immediate reaction level, is fraught with difficulty. Consequently what evaluation does take place is largely aimed at critiquing the inputs to the course, rather than assessing the outcomes.

The nub of the difficulty is that a head's performance is often not

systematically judged, let alone measured, so any difference in performance before and after a course is a small difference between two very
vague and uncertain entities. Until appraisal becomes more systematised,
or until school reviews can be conducted with more precision, it is
unlikely to be possible to substantiate beyond doubt the claim that school
management training is worthwhile.

In industry the problem is little easier. Although it is much more
common for a manager's performance to be judged against objective and
sometimes measurable criteria, we are still looking for a small difference
between large and imprecise numbers.

Nonetheless, industrial managers, perhaps with a keen eye on the
coffers, do seem to ask themselves more frequently the question 'What
are we achieving by management development?'. They seek reasonably
hard evidence that expenditure on management training brings at least as
great a return on investment as would the same expenditure on some
other activity, such as advertising or research. This forces trainers to try
to find out if managers who have been on courses actually behave
differently – that is, more effectively – when they return to their jobs.
Does the outcome of the training show in the running of the department
and ultimately in the balance sheet? Well-documented causal relationships between management training and profit are almost as scarce
as those between school management training and examination results;
there are far too many other variables influencing each to establish such
relationships. Nevertheless, a recent survey by IFF Research for the MSC
(IFF 1985) established that at least there is a correlation, if not a causal
relationship, between business performance and training investment. Of
the 500 private sector firms studied, 93 per cent of the most profitable
run training programmes and 44 per cent of their employees received
training the previous year. Of the poor performers, only 58 per cent did
any training and only 19 per cent of their employees had training the
previous year. High-performing firms had intensified their training by 25
per cent overall in the previous five years, whereas low performers had
cut theirs by 20 per cent. The average firm spent £200 or 0.15 per cent of
turnover per employee per year on training.

At the micro level, the only reliable way of finding out if training
affects subsequent behaviour is by having some system of follow-up to
see if the manager is running his department more effectively. If this can
be combined with some consultancy, so that the manager benefits from
the trainer visiting him to follow up the course, then a link is forged
between management development and OD. This follow-up process is
one of the strengths of in-company Coverdale training.

The difficulty of acquiring hard evidence that management training
improves the way in which a business or a school is run is no valid reason
for not attempting evaluation. It is simply an admission of the fact that so
many factors affect organisational performance that it is very costly to

try to unravel them. Instead, most industrial managers make subjective judgements about the relative value of providing management training and of other ways of spending money.

If they have to salve their consciences about this, they can reflect that a manager's job consists of making countless day-to-day decisions. If, as a result of training, there is a slight tilt in the balance towards better decisions, albeit the effect on any one decision is below the level of consciousness, then training could be said to 'pay'. Another argument is based on the hypothesis that employees' performance on the job adds value to the energy and raw materials a firm buys in to convert to the finished product; and that the added value associated with any one employee's performance is roughly proportional to his salary. Then it can be shown with plausible assumptions that if the manager's performance increases by only ¼ to ½ per cent per annum as a result of his receiving a week of residential management training, the expenditure on the course will have brought a financial return. Such modest improvements in performance should be well within the capabilities of a reputable one-week course.

Another approach is to carry out spot checks in some depth on the outcomes of courses. One ICI works employed a sandwich student on a project with this aim. The student interviewed the participants on a particular course some months after the event. On one plant that dealt with an inflammable gas, maintenance often involved shutting down the whole plant, with serious loss of production, if any welding was involved. However, a safe way was discovered to cut down the loss and thereby save some hundreds of thousands of pounds. On investigation, it proved that the discovery of this alternative method of safe maintenance had come about as a direct application of problem-solving concepts learned during the course. It had led to the breakthrough in thinking. There was thus convincing evidence that one outcome of the training had had an effect on the balance sheet which far outweighed the all-in cost of the whole training programme. It only requires a few major break-throughs of this kind to justify a great deal of training, even though there are no observable outcomes with the majority of participants.

Yet another approach is to regard investment in management training as like paying an insurance premium or maintaining a fire brigade. The value of the expenditure is reflected not in what happens as a result, but in what does not happen. In another ICI works, where industrial relations were relatively militant, it was known that a strike would cost the company about £40 million per day. Contraction of the labour force because of the recession was an unwelcome necessity, which was strongly opposed by the major unions. In preparation for this contraction, managers were both trained themselves, and trained to train others, in the economic facts of life and the business position was conveyed to the workforce in terms that were unmistakably clear. This was not simply a well run communication exercise. It had a strong educational and training component. After the successful contraction of the workforce, one senior manager declared that it could never have happened in the industrial relations climate of the time without the investment of money in training. Again, the investment was negligible compared with the effects of a strike.

Although teachers will not wish to press this analogy too closely, it is indisputable that catastrophes do occasionally occur in schools, for example, William Tyndale and Stoke Poges. There are also less spectacular disasters, such as ill-judged appointments, where the prevention of the problem is less costly and less painful than the cure. Training is not, of course, the only prophylactic against disaster but, as is well known in the armed services, it helps.

Evaluation of school management courses is one of the responsibilities of the National Development Centre for School Management Training at Bristol, and their advisory paper on the subject (NDCSMT 1985) provides an excellent analysis of the problem and a set of guidelines which are worth serious consideration by all those who procure, authorise, provide or receive management training, whether in education or industry. It certainly reflects good practice, but alas not so common practice, in industry.

The report points out that there are three main reasons for evaluating courses:

1   Course improvement which is concerned with the quality of courses;
2   Course utilisation, which is concerned with the way in which courses are used by individual course members, by their schools and by their LEAs;
3   Accountability which is concerned with rendering accounts of courses and their impact to those who have provided the resources or contributed time and effort.

Of these, the second and the most significant reason is most often neglected and the first is usually dominant.

Course improvement can be pursued at two levels, that of minor modification and that of major changes in pattern and style. Unfortunately, it is often the first level that evaluation questionnaires explore – issues of popularity, interest, usefulness and even enjoyment (as though that were a basic reason for training!), as perceived by the participants. The rationale, shape and philosophy of the course can easily but wrongly be taken for granted. Questions need to be asked about the appropriateness of the course aims and priorities, the match between the choice of pedagogy and the aims and the learning outcomes of the course. All this must be considered in the context of why the participants are being trained anyway, *viz* to effect an improvement in their schools.

For this to occur, it is not simply a question of providing a well-regarded course. . . Is the selection and briefing process sound?

Have participants the aptitude and determination to learn? Are they going to have opportunities afterwards to apply what they have learned? In doing so are they going to receive support from their LEAs and colleagues? These are fundamental questions to address in deciding whether a course can be utilised. They throw into sharp relief the whole development policy of the LEA and indeed of the education service. The ultimate objective of all INSET is to get children better educated and it is not only through management development but also organisation development that this has to be achieved.

The extent to which individual members use the course depends on their attitudes, capacity to learn and skills; all these have implications for course content. Are members helped on the course to develop study skills, listening skills, teamwork skills, thinking skills, networking skills (to build their own support systems afterwards) and skills concerned with effecting the changes that will occur when the learning from the course is applied? Are they helped to cope with the re-entry problem (the 'antibody' tendency of an organisation to thwart or neutralise the injection of new ideas, either by trapping people in their old roles, by expecting the same work to be done or by more deliberate subversion)?

At the organisational level, there are contextual questions to consider: how does the LEA expect the course to be used? Have the participants been briefed about this? Is the course linked to the individual's career development and the needs of the school? Is it part of an ongoing strategy of management development? What support will be given to the participants when they return? Will they be expected to contribute to basic courses or to other INSET activities, as tutors, consultants or members of working parties? If the name of the game is to improve schools, these are among the first questions to be asked of a course, yet they often receive scant attention.

An evaluation process that covers all the areas mentioned above could prove costly to apply. Skill is needed on the part of the evaluator, who may also have to travel to course members' schools to gather the necessary data. NDC estimate that 10 per cent of the course budget may have to be set aside for evaluation.

Ballinger has analysed the evaluation reports for DES 3/83 courses up to the end of 1984 (Ballinger 1985a). While achievements within the programmes and reactions to them are fairly fully documented, the evidence for or even assertions about transfer of the learning to the school situation is almost non-existent. Even expressions of intention to apply the learning are not widely obvious. So what were the outcomes of the training? By far the most commonly recognised outcome was increased self-confidence, sometimes leading to renewed professional commitment. Action plans about reviewing current managerial practice were frequently mentioned. Most participants widened their horizons by extending their knowledge but the impact of this on behaviour and aspirations was minor. Only when knowledge and theory were closely interwoven with practice did action plans ensue from the extension of knowledge. Of all the contributors and their methods of working, the trainers from industry were welcomed not only for their effectiveness in working with the group, but because participants felt they had a better understanding of the world outside education.

The programmes where there was considerable freedom to negotiate and renegotiate content and methodology more often led to clear aspirations of changed behaviour back at school. In such programmes there was strong emphasis on seeing that the programme would have practical outcomes for the school as well as for the individual. Unless changed behaviours and practical outcomes to the job are the overriding aims of the programmes, then apparently they do not occur by chance. In other words, if personal reflexion, refreshment and growth are seen as the aims, there is no evidence that the school benefits, although the participant may well go away satisfied. Even courses based largely on lectures can be regarded as satisfactory and valuable, despite the absence of any expectation of transfer back to the job.

What comes through clearly in this analysis is that participant satisfaction and effective learning are not synonymous; it is essential to assess the outcome of the learning back in the school setting, in terms of a change of behaviour, in order to be satisfied that school management training is worthwhile.

Although the same problem undoubtedly exists in industry, there is less of a tendency to value the acquisition of knowledge for its own sake than in an educational institution, and correspondingly more pressure to get a return on investment in learning. Hence industrial management training is better aimed at producing behavioural outcomes and benefits to the organisation, even though the achievement of these outcomes is seldom subjected to measurement.

Chapter 4

School management development

In this final chapter, I shall focus on the principal agencies and systems that are supporting the development of management in schools and suggest directions in which they might move in order to emulate good practice from industry, and to avoid some of the mistakes that industry has made in the past (and indeed continues to make all too often).

As will be clear from the last chapter, I am not simply concerned with the development of professional management for its own sake; rather, as a means to an end, the end being more effective schools. This raises the question of what is an 'effective' school, which is one of the most fundamental questions for a school manager to address.

Some answers have been given in *Ten Good Schools* (HMI 1977b), in *Better Schools* (DES 1985) and in other official publications. Other answers are to be found in books on organisations – what is it that makes for an effective organisation, regardless of what the organisation is for (see, for example, Beckhard 1969)? Some answers, even for schools, can be inferred from books on effective and successful companies (for example, Peters and Waterman 1982) and useful parallels with schools have been drawn by Handy (Handy 1984; Handy and Aitken 1986). Although there may not be a commonly held concept of an effective school, it is part of the responsibility of management to build a common vision of one, and secure the commitment of all concerned to its achievement.

The principal agencies, apart from heads and other managers, which contribute to the development of management in schools are illustrated in Figure 4.1. Several of these agencies have their equivalents in the development of management in industrial firms. Business schools would be an important subsector of higher education institutions. The nearest equivalent to the NDC is the Manpower Services Commission and Industrial Training Boards. The professional associations would comprise the British Institute of Management and the Institute of Personnel Management. Instead of the DES and the LEA there would be the board of directors and a few functional departments – training, personnel and management services (at least in a large organisation) – offering in-company support. The main thrust for developing management generally comes from inside the company, whereas in schools the main stimulus currently comes from outside.

Figure 4.1 Agencies supporting development of management in schools

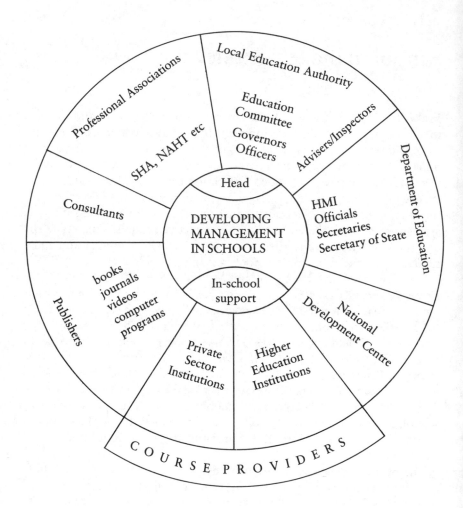

4.1 The education service hierarchy

The education service in the UK employs about a million adults, has more than 10 million full-time clients and absorbs about 11 per cent of the wealth generated (gross national product). The way in which it is managed must therefore have a major influence not only on society in general, but also on its component parts, including schools through the hidden curriculum. Unfortunately it does not provide a shining example of good management practice. The partners in the management of the hierarchy seldom work as a coherent team or even see themselves in this light. If there is an overall process of management and organisation development at work, its nature is obscure. From the point of view of a school that is consciously competent at its own management, the management structure in which it is embedded must often seem to be a shambles, giving rise to as many problems as it helps to solve. Robert Aitken, Director of Education for Coventry, puts these in a nutshell (Aitken 1985). The politicisation of local government has led at times to a virtual incapacity to govern, with the result that 'the service is showing increasingly severe signs of anomie: demoralisation, confusion, loss of belief and sense of worth.'

The DES supports management development in schools directly through HMIs (mainly in the curriculum management field and by COSMOS and other courses) but also indirectly through LEAs (mainly by the provision of funds). This hierarchical structure or 'educational sub-government', as Slater calls it (Slater 1985), is less coherent than that which influences management development in industry. While some LEAs are working with the NDC to develop a set of policies for management development, the majority have not got very far, though there may be policies on educational issues. With the help of the Local Government Training Board, other branches of local government have moved further towards systematic management development. Insofar as education committees of elected representatives influence the situation, their effect is often not to stimulate but to dampen progress, as would happen in industry when an accountancy-minded board of directors sees no point in investing money in people.

In a progressive company, the chief executive would proclaim his belief in the importance of management development and the board would match his words with supportive action. The firm's human resources would be managed with the care devoted to inanimate assets, with conscious enhancement of the stock of management talent. Statements of policy backed up by manpower planning procedures would ensure that management development indeed occurs and is monitored. There would be clear links to business policy, for it would be understood that the shaping of a business depends very much on the quality and actions of management. This would not be merely a matter of communicating to management what the business policy is, but of enabling them effectively to carry it out.

The equivalent links between educational policy, organisation development and management development are far more tenuous in the education service, giving the impression of an engine revving noisily, without being in gear. A well run business feels as if it is moving; effort under the bonnet produces progress on the road; and someone at the wheel knows where he wants it to go. I have not picked up a similar feeling in my encounters with schools, and the problem seems to be further up the hierarchy rather than in schools themselves.

To suggest that there is a need for greater co-ordination of effort and policy in the school sector of education is to invite the charge that I want more central state control. That is not the case. The sensation of being in a well run organisation is not that of subservience to higher authority; it is more akin to being a part of a team in which every member is respected and influence flows upwards and sideways as well as downwards. And upward influence is exerted very differently from the way in which teachers are currently (1985) trying to influence central government. Equally, top management is more closely in touch with the rank and file.

Policies, structures, procedures, communication, concepts of organisation and of management need a good deal of attention in the education service if they are to support and stimulate the development of more effective management in schools – and thereby of more effective schools. Today's administrative procedures were designed to deal with yesterday's problems. What is now needed is a solution for today's and tomorrow's. Yet, as Aitken points out, none of the political parties seems to have the vision, will or wherewithal to act; he suggests that educationists should look to shaping their own destiny (Aitken 1985).

How is such a solution to be found? Industry would not look first to the theorists; it would prefer to follow a problem-solving approach, of the kind in which many managers have been systematically trained. People with most knowledge of the problem and its effects might be brought together from different levels in the hierarchy to discuss in 'workshops' and task groups how the situation could be improved and then plan to bring this about. In the education service this does not happen. In the first place it is rare indeed (though not in Sweden) for heads, education officers and elected representatives to learn management skills together, so their respective approaches to problems tend to be incompatible. This makes it very difficult for task groups to be effective. Secondly, it is rare for heads to be involved co-equally with officers in addressing the issues of the day; the relationship is at arm's length.

The Institute of Local Government Studies and the Local Government Training Board, in a paper on chief officer development, suggested the introduction of training modules and workshops on emerging issues. Commenting on this, one chief education officer (Hartles 1982) stated that 'It would be an advantage for senior staff from educational institutions to join professional staff from central departments in "workshops" such as these.' He thought there would be strong support for a well-conceived programme of senior staff training in the education service hierarchy and noted the similarity of the headship training needs described in a NAHT document and those of chief education officers.

If the hierarchy is to work like a well-oiled mechanism in promoting the development of management in schools, there needs to be a good deal more contact, both in training events and workshops, between the various levels and functions.

4.2 Advisers and inspectors

My direct contacts with advisers and inspectors through my fieldwork, tutoring and the CNAA have been relatively few, so I tread here on more dangerous ground. On the one hand I see the influence of Harold Heller of Cleveland and Joan Dean of Surrey, for example, to be as positive and well-directed as that of many a good internal consultant in industry; on the other hand, I note the low regard in which many heads hold their advisers when it comes to giving them useful advice on management problems. They say that inspectors and advisers know nothing of management, never having managed themselves. The credibility of the advisory service does not stand very high, outside curriculum issues. Moreover, some seem to be overworked and accordingly difficult to contact, while others seem to be preoccupied with individual teachers to the exclusion of the more strategic aspects of their jobs.

Another criticism is that advisers and inspectors are not always very skilled in the process of giving advice, even if the diagnosis on which their advice is based is sound. I conjecture that less attention is given in the education service to training advisers in consulting skills than is the case in industry. Certainly where consultancy skills training has been provided for Schools Council Industry Project advisers by practising internal consultants in industry, its usefulness has been hailed in glowing terms (Everard 1984). The process of consultancy, and the relative merits of a prescriptive and a non-directional approach, have now become quite well understood and many consultants owe their enhanced effectiveness and acceptability to systematic training in the relevant skills.

To give advice on management, however, not only requires skill in the giving of help, but also a thorough grasp of management and organisational processes and behaviour. How many advisers in the education service have studied these aspects of their jobs, especially in an experiential mode? Unfortunately, since management is a practical subject, it is insufficient for advisers to read books about it, still less to base their advice solely on their personal experience and hypotheses. There is thus no substitute for experiential methods. Although heads may think that only people who have managed a school can give useful advice on managing schools, they are mistaken; and there is a correspondingly mistaken belief among some managers in industry. What is needed is a deeply perceptive awareness of the processes and dynamics of management rather than first hand experience of managing, although it must be said that the latter is very helpful too.

The implications of these comments are that, if the DES and LEAs wish to use advisers and inspectors for the development of management in schools, they need to be carefully selected and systematically trained for the job; the development of competence in this tricky field of process consultancy cannot be left to chance.

There is also ample evidence from industry that internal consultants (the equivalent of inspectors and advisers) can play a key role in supporting managers who are attempting change and improvements in organisational effectiveness (see, for example, Schein 1969; Pettigrew 1985). Since heads express a wish for support and advice of the right kind from someone who is competent to give it, especially in their first years of headship, it follows that there is a clear need for development of a more professional advisory service and perhaps for its expansion at least in those authorities where provision has not kept pace with the growth of demand.

Such a development will take time. Not only is there a dearth of advisers who are competent and practised process consultants, but their inspectorial role acts as a major constraint (Bolam 1978). They are widely perceived as 'task consultants' working on concrete and recognisable problems such as the teaching of reading, the evaluation of pupil performance or curriculum development. They are not perceived as people to be involved in helping the school with less obvious problems like its underlying decision-making and problem-solving procedures or in the processes of departmental and staff meetings, of communication and of the exercise of power and authority in the school. Yet these areas of organisational life are central to school effectiveness, and difficult for a school to work on unaided.

Thus, for LEA advisers and HM inspectors to become more supportive to school managers, they would not only have to extend their knowledge and skills, but also to signal a distinct change in their role and gain the acceptance and confidence of their clients in that new role. This may be too much to expect, though such transitions have occurred in industry as formerly prescriptive task consultants have changed their style towards process consultancy and gradually won the confidence of clients in their new role.

Perhaps some firm decisions within authorities and the inspectorate are needed about how advisers and inspectors can most beneficially spend their time. If their main purpose is to help schools to improve their effectiveness, what activities will lead to the most significant outcomes? This may not be so much a matter for professional judgement (which is likely to be biased towards the preservation of the status quo) as for investigation of what actually happens as a result of making different choices in the priorities they attach to different aspects of their work.

4.3 *Consultancy provision*

No organisation can hope to have internal access to all the management expertise it needs to be effective. Industrial firms, even those with a large headquarters staff of experts in various facets of management, customarily call in consultants from time to time and some retain them on a semi-permanent basis.

To use a medical metaphor, organisations have 'pathologies' and when the patient is not fit, it pays to get help. External or 'third party' consultants have a number of advantages over internal experts and managers. They are less emotionally involved with the problems of the organisation, so they can be more objective. They bring comparative knowledge of different organisations which can be very useful in identifying what is wrong. Their life work is devoted to the study of organisations, so they are more widely read on the subject than managers can ever hope to be. Their detachment and their experience of interviewing people enables a good deal more salient information to be drawn out and used to diagnose the organisational problems than would be revealed to people within the organisation. However ethical an internal consultant, LEA adviser or HM inspector might be, it is difficult for people to accept them as independent of the power system and therefore able to be trusted with possibly damaging information (Gray and Heller).

The medical metaphor referred to above should not be pressed too far, because it suggests that the consultant will prescribe a solution to the problem he finds. While there are some who act in this way, it is a risky approach; it is usually better to enter into a relationship with the client which is more like joint problem solving; ideally the manager who owns the problem should be the person to solve it and the consultant facilitates the process by judicious use of questions and observations. The process is akin to 'non-directive counselling'.

The availability and demand for consultants in educational institutions is surprisingly small, given the organisational problems that abound. One LEA (Sheffield) employs two consultants that work closely with school heads along these lines. They were set up as an independent unit by a deputy chief education officer to help heads in school management problems. It had been noticed that curriculum development simply did not occur as a result either of the publication of research studies by such bodies as the Schools Council or of sending teachers on courses. Consequently the OD team work as consultants in schools before and after courses, so that the course becomes coherent with what is happening in the school. They carry on a diagnosis of the organisation, run team-building events and become involved in the micro-politics of the school (Lavelle 1984).

The attempted provision of a general consultancy service to the education system has not proved rewarding. Those competent consultants that do offer a service* have to supplement their income from other sources, for example, publishing, business consultancy and training. It is true that some enterprising heads have acquired consultancy help by 'begging' it from industry (see Section 2.12) but this is not a very satisfactory way of dealing with the problem countrywide.

Other schools have used the staff of higher education institutions, but most academic consultants tend to purvey educational rather than organisational or process expertise. Only a few have succeeded in breaking through the stereotype of a college lecturer and have established their credibility as people who can help management in a practical way.

Altogether, there would seem to be a case for developing an independent educational consultancy service, complementing and working closely both with the providers of school management training and with the internal consultants (that is, advisers and inspectors) already in the system. It is difficult to see how it is otherwise going to be possible for management development to 'mature' into organisation development in the manner that it has done in the more progressive parts of industry. There may at first be a shortage of competent people who have knowledge not only of organisations but also of education and who have developed the necessary process consultancy skills.

Bolam, the director of the NDC, sees consultancy as an aspect of school focused INSET which can overcome the two common criticisms of traditional INSET: that it is irrelevant to the practical needs of teachers and that it ignores the characteristics of schools as social systems (Bolam 1978). He quotes Hoyle as arguing that INSET should be linked to specific school innovations, that it should focus on functioning groups (for example, a departmental team or the whole staff) and that schools should receive external support including consultancy from advisers, teachers' centres etc. Experience indicates that this approach motivates teachers to participate and maximises their potential for implementing desired changes in the school. He also agrees with Havelock's definition of a consultant: one who is a facilitator, helper or objective observer, who can diagnose needs and identify the means of meeting them and who can collaborate and encourage the client. In his experience, many

---

*For example, Deanhouse Limited, 728 London Road, Oakhill, Stoke-on-Trent, Staffs. ST4 5NP; EMAS, Marlborough Rooms, 68 High Street, Weybridge, Surrey KT13 8BL; MB Associates, 27 Forest End Road, Sandhurst, Camberley, Surrey GU17 8JT; Singleton Management Associates, 77 Grange Lane, Bromham, Bedford MK43.

teachers find this approach potentially threatening, especially when the consultant offers observations about issues of power and conflict. So it may be, but a healthy organisation does not suppress or ignore conflict; it confronts and manages it. The value of dealing with such issues has been demonstrated in industry and I share Bolam's conviction that 'We can both break out of consultancy and training models fashioned in other settings and devise models more appropriate to education. . . (paying) appropriate regard to lessons learned about intervention in these other fields.'

Murgatroyd and Reynolds, in analysing the various forms of consultancy, recommend its use for teacher education in general, pointing out that it is more likely to result in behavioural change than conventional teacher education (Murgatroyd and Reynolds 1984).

As always, there is the problem of funding; state schools have no budget for buying in consultancy help. Perhaps if the DES and LEAs come to view the development of management in schools as extending far beyond the provision of external management courses, then the important role that consultancy can play in the process will fall into its proper place and money will be found. The important question to ask is whether money spent on consultancy will have more valuable outcomes for the school than money spent on courses. In my view it will, and the balance of expenditure on courses and consultancy should move towards the latter.

4.4 Support within the school

At first sight it may be thought unlikely that the head and senior staff could turn to any agency within the school, which could support the development of management. It is true that some schools have designated a particular member of staff to be a 'professional tutor', but his role is largely to promote the pedagogical development of the more junior staff, rather than to stimulate more effective management. It is therefore left to the managers themselves to support one another – or not, as the case may be.

In Section 3.4 on appraisal, I have already suggested that subordinates can be helpful in developing better management and I am not alone in believing that pupils have a part to play; some teachers in their management role already get informal help from them.

Non-teaching staff may also help, for example the school secretary. One of my former secretaries was promoted to be a new director's secretary, and even at that exalted level she was able to play a valuable part in his induction. Both heads and industrial managers can use their secretaries to improve their personal work organisation and to help them set priorities in the planning of their work. There may not be many ex-NCOs among the ranks of caretaker, but many an industrial manager has benefited from sage advice from a warrant officer turned supervisor.

When an organisation is contracting, stress can be a problem and its management becomes important. This is true of schools as of industry (Cooper and Marshall 1978; Milsten 1985). Shell and ICI found ways of training selected employees to help management in its pastoral role to manage stress within the organisation and it was widely accepted that they played a useful role. Outcomes are not confined to building up an individual sufferer's coping skills, but also to diagnosing organisational sources of stress which managers can then work to alleviate. Shop stewards, works councillors and other employee representatives may also be pitched into this role. Managers in schools may be able to harness an informal network of sensitive and 'organisationally aware' members of staff to support their efforts to make the school a better and less tense place to work in.

Sometimes organisations fail to identify in their employees particular strengths and experiences that can be used to help in the management of the organisation and thus miss opportunities to enrich jobs. An example is given in Section 2.4 of a teacher who had once run a business and was able to use his experience outside his normal job demands, to help the school make better use of the resources on which it was spending money.

There is obviously a limit to the extent of professional support to management which can be found within a school from outside the ranks of the management team itself, but the trend towards more participative management, involving all members of staff, is likely to identify new sources. Certainly hierarchical outlooks should not obscure the value of seeking potential support from below.

4.5 Professional associations and networks

The work of the Secondary Heads Association, the National Association of Head Teachers, the Headmasters Conference, the College of Preceptors and other professional associations in seeking to promote better practice in schools is well known.

The somewhat misleadingly named Association of Teachers of Management, based on the Polytechnic of Central London, is a vigorous and growing organisation more specifically aimed at developing management, albeit not only in schools. Indeed, its influence in the primary and secondary sector is minimal, though I believe it has potentially much to offer and is more practically oriented than the British Educational Management and Administration Society (BEMAS).

Less is known about a variety of networks, some formal, others informal and mostly transient, which have sprung up usually on a local or regional basis. The Network for Organisation Development in Education (NODE) is one such national organisation which flourished for a number of years but is now largely defunct (except for its journal, *Educational Change and Development*), like the Organisation Development Network which served a wider constituency for some fifteen years.

Some DES 3/83 and other management training courses have set up networks of mutual support groups, in which members commit themselves to help one another to apply their learning back in their jobs, and to compare their experience of doing so. Reunions are held at intervals to share valuable learning and to renew commitment to achieving the ongoing aims of the course.

The building and maintenance of a network is no easy task for busy people; a lot depends on having a convener or 'spider at the centre of the web' who will supply the necessary energy to service the network. Sometimes, this role is rotated as a matter of expediency or principle but in my experience it is better if a single leader emerges who has the necessary commitment and time.

It is better still if he can procure, officially or unofficially, the administrative back-up services (secretarial, a place to meet, hospitality) which keep the network running smoothly; and there are many industrial firms that as an act of corporate citizenship have quietly supported a number of networks and associations outside their normal run of business. The experience of building a successful network and getting it serviced is itself a valuable piece of management development for an aspiring manager.

Networks of managers can be effective agents of change. Free from bureaucracy and institutionalisation, they can get things going which more rigid forms of organisation would find difficult. 'Action learning sets' are an example of networks that have proved particularly valuable aids to management learning and action. Although most management networks serve either those in business or those in education, it is likely that much would be gained by mixing industrial managers and senior staff in schools within particular localities. There are plenty of activities that would interest both.

As well as providing a vehicle for promoting management development, both networks and associations have a useful function as pressure groups. The quality of management within schools is clearly held back by some features in the schools' environment; harnessing the collective strength and ingenuity (political skills rather than naked power) of heads and their senior colleagues could well be a more fruitful outlet for their energies than managing simply within their own schools. It has already been suggested that heads have something to learn here from their industrial counterparts.

4.6 Management training provision

Management training is currently the principal agency in formally developing management in schools. Whereas education management is usually taken to imply award-bearing courses of a year or more's duration, management training courses usually last for between a day and a term and are not normally certificated. In general, education management is knowledge-oriented and management training skills-oriented, but there are certainly some award-bearing courses that are predominantly experiential and some training courses that are dominated by lectures and theory. Thus the pedagogical distinction between education and training is not very helpful; both are aimed at learning.

There are parallels between the current situation in school management training and that reported in 1962 as describing industrial management training. At that time 'not only many firms but training officers were vague about the objectives of training they offered; the universities which were involved were far too remote from industry; the teaching methods used were at best unvalidated and at worst without value; candidates for training were nominated almost at random and without any rational selection process; and training staff were often of very poor calibre' (Peel 1984).

When school management training received a fillip with DES circular 3/83, some of the courses that were offered were watered down versions of lecture-dominated award-bearing courses, with a very tenuous link to school effectiveness. Others had a strong experiential training component and a few took the form of 'fellowships' in which a tailor-made project was undertaken, leading to a specific outcome such as a survey of management practice in industry. By late 1985 a wide variety of 20-day basic courses and one-term training opportunities were being offered under the DES 3/83 banner and there had been some 1300 and 600 participants on each respectively (Bolam 1985), quite apart from the courses that had already been run by some LEAs, by the DES, by polytechnic short course units etc., and by a few private agencies.

Pre-3/83 course provision was surveyed by Jayne for ILEA (Jayne 1982). She concluded that courses were weighted too heavily on the acquisition of knowledge and not sufficiently on proficiency in using new skills. Her report identified a wide gap between what was being provided and what staff wanted: staff development, curriculum development, time planning, finance/accounting, new technology, public relations, leadership and management of change were examples of under-provision. Among the courses that were particularly highly rated on content, structure and relevance were an ILEA six-week course on authority and leadership, and courses run by ISTC (a private agency, see Section 4.9), by the Advisory Centre for Education and by the College of Preceptors. DES and university short courses were less well regarded.

Another survey of school management courses was conducted by the Secondary Heads Association in 1984 (Sayer 1984) – one of a series. This showed a considerable increase in the numbers of heads receiving training with most members reporting a good experience; 64–80 per cent of the ratings across the 55 courses were in the top two categories for appropriateness, usefulness, style, methods and achievement of aims. The unsatisfactory courses were under-powered, under-demanding, disjointed, badly planned and run by lecturers unfamiliar with the running of a school. A particular LEA course was rated as 'one of the least useful days spent in a quarter of a century of teaching'.

It is clear, therefore, that the quality of provision is patchy, reflecting the similar situation that faces industrial managers. However, the latter can be more discriminating in their choice of courses, since a consumers' guide to quality is provided by the National Training Index (see Section 4.9). DES 3/83 courses are monitored by the NDCSMT but their published survey reports, unlike NTI reports, do not identify particular institutions, so they cannot be used as a basis for advice on the quality of particular courses. Nevertheless, the reports are very illuminating about the quantity and quality of provision in general.

The first NDC survey (NDCSMT 1984) involved 18 institutions offering one-term training opportunities and in some cases 20-day basic courses. Statements of *course aims* were often ill-defined or over-cautious. Serious gaps existed in *course content*, with guidance counselling and interpersonal relations playing little or no part in well over half the basic courses. There was no common pattern in *course methodology*, except that in basic courses the lecture mode predominated and experiential learning was misconstrued as simply observation and investigation. As the report noted, 'There is ample evidence that, if the purpose of an educational enterprise is to bring about change and not merely to inform, the lecture mode, particularly a series of discrete guest lectures, is an inappropriate methodology.' The involvement of LEAs, teachers and industrialists in *course design* was very patchy, though this is understandable in the light of the tight timetable to which institutions had to work. *Course evaluation* procedures were also hastily prepared and tended to focus on interest, level, relevance and usefulness rather than on outcomes, though two good examples emerged. Only a minority of the providers had a sound understanding of the principles and practices of industrial management.

The second survey (Ballinger 1985a) showed some shift in emphasis towards a school improvement orientation, to a skills approach and to more exploration of non-education sector management, but it criticised preparation for and follow-up of programmes as an area where no progress had been made over the year. Participants were often unclear why they had been chosen and what was expected of them after the course. Links between providers, participants and LEAs needed strengthening and a better process of steering courses was needed. In other words, training courses were still seen as discrete events, the use of which was not embedded in a coherent set of policies designed to improve the effectiveness of the education service.

My own involvement with a number of DES 3/83 courses and access to several evaluation reports of other courses, corroborates these findings. Some one-term courses do not give participants nearly enough instruction and practice in the process of management training, despite their aim of equipping them to train others. Even where the 'training the trainers' component is well developed, participants are usually very hazy about how their LEA will use their training skills. Despite the importance of evaluation, providers do not always make it an integral part of the course, or involve the participants in managing the process. Some courses lack coherence; in an attempt to cover the whole spectrum of school management, topics are included which do not link together well, giving the impression of a disjointed series of lectures. When there is no full-time course director, it is particularly difficult to pull all the threads together. Above all, there is generally poor integration between management development and organisation development; if this is the case, what will the course do for the school or for the LEA?

Useful advice on the design of management learning events is available from the Centre for the Study of Management Learning (see, for example, Binsted 1980), but has largely been ignored in school management training. Some of the tests that might be applied to judging the effectiveness of one-term or basic courses are as follows (Everard 1984):

1   Are the aims of the course sharp or vague? Do they suggest that the course is intended to inculcate specific competencies or simply to enhance general awareness of every current educational issue upon which leading professionals are expected to be knowledgeable? Are measures of attainment and criteria of success built in? Do these criteria include intended outcomes for the school and for the LEA from which the participants come?

2   Is the course directed by someone who is best known and esteemed as a good manager, or as a good professional or academic?

3   Are members of the course team thoroughly familiar with management learning processes, as distinct from the traditional teaching processes of secondary and tertiary education?

4   Has the course director, or members of the course team, had recent experience of successful headship or management at a senior level, and can he or she analyse the causes of that success?

5   Does the course focus on the work that heads and senior managers actually have to do? For instance, since the dominant activity of a head is

dealing with other people, does the course concentrate on the development of interpersonal skills and provide plenty of practice for their exercise, critical evaluation and improvement?

6 Does the design (especially of the one-term courses) recognise that the course members are already experienced managers and does it capitalise on this experience in the management of the course by encouraging them to be active managers of their own learning?

7 Are appropriate training technology and supporting resources used in the course (for example, video, film, problem-solving workshops, management style inventories etc.) or does the lecture/discussion/case study/guided reading approach dominate?

8 Does the course provide plenty of effective help at a practical level in tackling some of the nagging problems that most heads face, for example, dealing with the inadequate head of department, coping with falling rolls, managing time, managing change (in the curriculum etc.), selecting staff, appraising staff, developing staff, dealing with interest groups outside the school, forward planning, and resource management (or stewardship)? Or is it dominated by sessions on welfare policies, statutory frameworks, democratic decision-making, parental rights, gender and multicultural education?

9 Does the course pay more than lip-service to the requirement that management outside the education service should be studied? Are such management training methods experienced as well as studied?

10 To what extent does the course design identify and respond both to the particular training needs and learning styles of the individuals who come on it and the training requirements (if any) of the employing Authority?

11 Is the course dynamically evaluated; that is, is it an integral part of the design that there is a feedback loop to tell the organisers how effectively it is meeting its objectives and what needs to be done to improve it as it goes along?

12 Does the course measure up to the relevant criteria that are now being used to judge school curricula (for example, coherence, block time-tabling, negotiation with students, open learning, learning outside the institution, congruence of the overt and hidden curriculum)? Or is it just 'a search for a better yesterday'?

One basic course that came closer than most to meeting these tests has been the subject of a detailed evaluation report (Ballinger 1985b). Ballinger, who has an MA in management learning, was a member of the course design team, which was directed by two practising heads. As well as the 14 heads who joined the course there were two education officers and two advisers. The participants worked on real problems in real time, which greatly facilitated the application of the learning to their jobs; this was monitored as part of an evaluation period that extended for nine months after the end of the course. Transfer from the programme to the workplace was the fundamental organising principle and many outcomes were demonstrated. Participative group work was the main learning process, especially for action learning and visits; reviewing experience was an integral part of this process. The course evoked exceptionally high commitment from the participants, whose responses to its design and structure were glowing.

As described in the evaluation report, the quality of this course bears favourable comparison with the best of those available to industrial managers, and it embodies similar principles of course design. Only by exploring the subsequent outcomes of courses can their effectiveness really be assessed and only by identifying what school improvements the heads are expected to achieve, can the training be properly focused. Although it is my impression that the general quality of management training provision is still appreciably lower in education than in industry, the spread of good practice through the NDC could well result in education catching up.

4.7 Education management provision

Award-bearing courses in education management are now a well-established approach to developing management in schools. The 1970s saw impressive growth in the provision of such courses yet the demand for places often outstripped the supply. Although the development took place in an *ad hoc* manner, useful foundations were laid for what later became a more concerted effort on the part of government to improve the way in which educational institutions were run.

The Hughes Report *Professional Development Provision for Senior Staff in Schools and Colleges* (Hughes, Carter and Fidler 1981), commissioned by the DES, gave a generally favourable picture of the courses on offer in 1979–1980, but as a former industrial training manager reading between the lines, I gained a less favourable impression. If I had been advising the head of an independent school, which is in a sense a 'business', whether to use such courses to improve the quality of school management, there are few indeed that I could have recommended with any confidence. In this section I shall explain why, by reference to public sector courses validated by the CNAA. I have insufficient knowledge of similar courses offered by universities (which according to Hughes represented 45 per cent of the total) or validated by them, but I have no reason to suppose that they would be significantly different.

As a member of the CNAA Educational Organisation and Management Panel (later, Board) from its inception until 1984, I was involved in scrutinising voluminous course documents, visiting institutions to talk to staff and students, and contributing to decisions on validation and approval. Twenty courses were involved at 18 institutions, mostly intended for school teachers. Academic colleagues on the Board were better able to comment on the academic respectability, rigour and rubric of these courses and the acceptability of the student selection and assessment processes; I concerned myself more with assessing the likely practical outcomes in terms of student performance in school. I judged that the primary purpose of attending a course on education management is to become a more competent and effective manager of an educational institution; and that the main reason for funding such courses and the state sector students on them, out of the public purse, is to help to upgrade the quality of management as it is practised in such institutions. This criterion for judging courses was very superficially explored in the Hughes Report.

Such a pragmatic, instrumental purpose was rather offensive to some course staff I encountered, and indeed to some students, who felt it was perfectly proper for a management course simply to provide opportunities for *studying* management from an abstract or theoretical point of view, without actually attempting to improve managerial skills. Indeed, the popular Open University course on Management and the School, for example, does not pretend to advise heads on *how* to manage, but simply to give students an *understanding* of management (Hughes, Carter and Fidler 1981: 54). Likewise some students are satisfied with getting a qualification in education management for its own sake, perhaps in the hope that the mere possession of a degree or diploma will enhance their career prospects, regardless of whether that which they learned is capable of being applied or whether they acquire the skills to apply it to the performance of their managerial function.

This view, that management, which is a practical subject like medicine and engineering, can properly be studied in the abstract, without reference to any behavioural outcomes, save possibly that of becoming a more trenchant armchair critic of the way one is managed by the head or by the LEA, is not supported by Principle 3 of CNAA's regulations, to which it runs counter:

The direction of the student's studies must be towards greater understanding *and competence*. Thus, while it may be appropriate for a programme to include the acquisition of techniques or skills, or the learning of data, these must lead to a higher level of intellectual and creative *performance* than that intrinsic in the learning of the skills, techniques or facts themselves' (CNAA 1985; my italics).

A similar principle may not formally apply to university courses on management, in which case there may be more justification for a non-instrumental approach. But for CNAA courses, an explicit criterion for judgement is whether the student's competence and performance as a manager is likely to be improved as a result of his studies. If a course is not directed to this end, such performance may actually be impaired (Everard 1982).

Evaluation of courses is seldom taken to the point of ascertaining afterwards whether performance is improved; there are almost insuperable practical difficulties in doing this, especially when throughout the education service performance is seldom systematically assessed. Even if it were, it is difficult to establish a causal relationship between improved or impaired performance and attendance on a course; there are too many confounding variables (section 3.10).

In these circumstances we are reduced to making subjective judgements about the probability of whether a particular course will change performance, either because the student has acquired and learned how to practise new skills, or because the enhancement of his self-esteem and self-confidence as a result of obtaining a paper qualification leads to higher motivation. Sometimes the students themselves are asked if they can detect any improvement in their job performance; on one such course, reviewed by CNAA in 1984, between 24 and 34 per cent of past students could not. Perhaps their performance did improve, but subliminally; or perhaps it did not. So how should courses be judged in terms of the likelihood that they will lead to improved managerial performance? The main tests I apply are:

1   Are the course aims and objectives soundly formulated?

2   Does the course team understand the process by which managers learn to manage? Have they, for example, ever heard of Kolb, or the Centre for the Study of Management Learning?

3   How many of the course team have ever managed an organisation or a substantive part of one?

4   What evidence is there that the staff development policy of the institution (if there is one) requires teaching staff to develop their *pedagogical* skills (as distinct from acquiring new knowledge of their subject)?

5   Do the elements of the course relate closely to the principal skills that managers need, the work they do and the problems they face?

6   Is the terminology in the course description predominantly management-oriented, with active verbs like 'do', 'improve' and 'practise', or academically oriented, with passive words like 'consider', 'examine' and 'analyse'?

7   Is the bibliography dominated by theoretical, philosophical or ideological books, or is it balanced by the kind of practical books published by the Institute of Personnel Management, the British Institute of Management, the Industrial Society and BACIE?

8   Do the learning methods used on the course incline towards the experiential (remembering that management is a practical subject) or to the didactic?

9   Do the staff practise what they preach (or is the medium consistent with the message)?

10   Is there an effective feedback loop to enable students' perceptions of

how the course will help them to manage more effectively to be translated into action for improving it?

Very few courses pass all these tests; numbers 2, 3, 4 and 10 are the most severe. Not many more do so in the case of award-bearing courses in industrial management (I was also on the CNAA Postgraduate Courses Board and the Committee for Business and Management Studies), which is one of the reasons why many private sector employers make comparatively little use of such courses.

Most courses submitted to the CNAA EOMB for validation did, however, get approval, though often with riders and recommendations for improvements. These judgements were of necessity largely based on a study of the course documentation and its discussion with the course team, rather than on observation of what happens to students in the lecture room. Hence they are not as well founded as is desirable.

Without identifying the institutions involved (attributive comments will be found in the Hughes Report), let me exemplify some of the salient features, especially those relating to aims and objectives and beginning with examples of courses that meet many of my criteria.

1 A course leading to a master's degree in education management

Another department in the same institution has developed a good reputation in industry for running very practical courses in management. The institution is itself regarded as particularly well-managed, and has a good staff development policy. The preamble to the course description displays a good understanding of what management is, and is for: 'Managing is simply "getting things done through other people within organisations". Management within education has no value or purpose except insofar as it helps, directly or indirectly, to further the educational process. In that sense it is indeed part of the education process'. The theme of the degree is the notion of effectiveness, and there is a strong focus on the *processes* by which this is achieved. The course puts students into situations in which they have to experiment with their behaviour. The units deal with behavioural aspects of management, including skills development, resource management, policy formation, organisational design and management of change. Bibliographies contain good examples of practical books.

2 A course leading to a diploma in educational organisation and administration

Although based on a faculty of education rather than of management, the course is led by someone with substantive management experience. The course rationale talks about developing competence, and the three aims are soundly formulated with active words:

1 Deepen knowledge and understanding of the context and functions of educational management and human behaviour;
2 Enable students to ... strengthen attitudes conducive to professional responsibility and managerial effectiveness;
3 Develop the technical and social skills required for effective management.

Very few of the course aims recognise the importance of affective learning, in heightening students' determination to manage more effectively. The teaching methods are consistent with the aims, with an emphasis on practical, participative, problem-solving activities, simulations and role-play. On evaluation, the brochure says 'The evaluation must concern itself also with the final product, that is, whether the student is better able to recognise and respond to management problems and to manage change successfully.'

3 A course leading to a diploma in education management.

Although this is an 'educational' course, its aims and objectives use the language of training, and the learning methods are predominantly those associated with training. The aims begin with 'to improve managerial effectiveness. . .' and go on to 'develop management skills relating to the achievement of educational objectives in the context of economic constraints. . .'. The objectives constantly refer to active verbs, competences and skills; for example, for one unit, on managing people, one objective is 'to train students in a range of staff recruitment, selection, appraisal and development techniques in the settings of schools and colleges. Another objective refers to 'demonstrating skill in counselling'.

4 A course run by a department of management leading to a diploma in educational management

The course director has made a particular study of management in manufacturing industry, but the course staff are short on practical experience of management, and this shows. The institution's staff development policy is backward. The general aims of the course are concerned with studying management concepts, applying techniques and skills and grasping the implications for oneself of so doing. The success criteria state what the student will be able to do at the end of the course. The exam questions are designed to test the students' capacity for applying their learning to a new problem, rather than simply testing their knowledge; this causes the students consternation! The course evaluation protocol tests student interest, challenge and relevance, but not perceived effect on performance.

5 A course leading to a bachelor's degree in the management of education and curriculum change

It aims to develop a conceptual knowledge of organisation and management, and although said to be contributing to the professional competence of teachers, there is hardly any mention of skills development. Objectives are mainly about reflecting and considering the use of (as distinct from applying) concepts, and developing a broad knowledge of issues. The approach is almost wholly analytical, and the pedagogy dominated by seminars, lectures and tutorials, rather than the practice of skills. In particular, despite the title of the course, the management of change is not a skill that the course sets out to develop; in this area the bibliography is incomplete and dated. The course staff are unfamiliar with recent work on how managers learn and on educational change, and have had little exposure to management philosophy and practice outside education. Some students reported that there were one or two abysmal lecturers who bored everyone to tears.

6 A course leading to a diploma in primary school organisation

The aims of this course are formulated in abstract and analytical terms:

1   To enable course members to become more informed about, and to debate, discuss and offer informed comment on, problems of primary education [not *solve* them];
2   To examine a range of patterns of school organisation [not *decide between* them];
3   To analyse and assess management processes. . . [not learn to *operate* such processes];
4   To encourage an appreciation of the need for staff development [not learn how to *set up and operate* a scheme];
5   To examine the relationship between senior staff and outside agencies [not to *manage* the interface between];
6   To examine the processes involved in decision making [not to *develop skill in*].

7 A course leading to a master's degree in education organisation and administration

The course aims were not explicit, but a clue to its nature is given by the sentence 'the content of all the units owes more to educational than to management studies.' In the description the course team went out of their way to stress the difference between educational and commercial institutions, and the need for a very different approach to management. One unit 'introduces a deliberately sceptical note, in the form of a sociological critique of management perspectives'; the bibliography had a distinctly 'left wing' flavour not only in this unit but even in that relating to staff development and appraisal. Whilst it is quite proper to give managers an understanding of radical approaches to management and organisation, if this dominates a course at the expense of the practical skills that are needed to manage existing institutions, there is a risk that the behavioural outcome of the students' studies will be more to help them to withstand management than to practise it. An employer who supports a teacher going on a management course is entitled to know what it is trying to achieve, and has to judge whether it is likely to serve the organisation's (school's) interests if it is successful.

8 A course leading to an MA in management education and development

This was offered as a qualifying course in management *teaching,* as distinct from management *subjects.* Its primary aim was to develop the effectiveness of management teachers, that is, those who design and lecture to award-bearing courses on management, including education management. Whilst the need for such a course was correctly identified, the course design came nowhere near to meeting such a need. It was curriculum-dominated, whereas the focus should clearly be on helping participants to facilitate the processes by which managers learn. The objectives, where stated (and one of the units had no stated objectives!), were framed in terms of understanding theories, criticising theories, analysing data, acquiring an awareness of a variety of social research procedures and developing teaching sessions to enable students to analyse current and future trends. Little reference was made to the practice of pedagogical skills, to reviewing the effectiveness of such practice in terms of behavioural outcomes, to recent research on management learning, to books about the design of learning situations, to transference of learning from a course to the workplace, to the assessment of teaching competence or even to the processes of management. This particular course submission (which was not approved by the CNAA) was made jointly by two well-established institutions, both with a good reputation in their fields. It is sad that such a course, designed to improve the quality of management education, should itself fall so far short of the very pedagogical standards that it was intended to raise. By contrast, the MA course in management learning at Lancaster University is very much directed at the process and outcomes of learning; it is based on sound and extensive research as well as practical management training experience, and it significantly influences the subsequent behaviour of those who take the course.

These examples illustrate what different courses appear to be trying to achieve, and could be further extended by examining and comparing the different curricula. However, course curricula have many commonalities, and can no doubt be used in different ways by different staff. Waitt and

Parry even write of *the* management curriculum and see some DES 3/83 courses as hand-me-down versions of the standard curriculum used on award-bearing courses (Waitt and Parry 1985). They draw attention to the huge power of institutional inertia and conservatism to protect the management curriculum, which in their view offers little, if anything, that any manager really needs to know. 'It is all too easy to become better informed but none the wiser', they say. For them it is important to agree the outputs of a course, rather than the inputs, with heads and LEAs, or consortia of LEAs, and to be very clear what management education is for. They adduce this as an argument for project-based learning, and indeed their institution (North East London Polytechnic) is one of the few that have obtained CNAA validation for action-learning courses, which have no standard curricula.

Whilst I would not recommend that all institutions go as far as this in designing award-bearing courses in education management, I do think that designers should pay far more attention to identifying what educational outcomes are desired by students and employers alike. Courses are still too teacher-centred, pedagogy too didactic, objectives too woolly, curricula too topic-based rather than problem-centred and too differentiated rather than integrated. Process should come before content and affective learning given as prominent a place as cognitive learning. Some education management courses are moving in this direction, but most have a long way to go.

4.8 Higher education institutions

Section 4.7 described some of the education management courses provided by institutions of higher education and questioned how far some of these courses really led to more competent management. Now I turn to the question of whether these academic institutions are set up to be effective agencies for developing management generally. Doubts have been raised about the appropriateness of some of them to support development of management in schools. As institutions, many of them suffer from exactly the same shortcomings as schools; the more practical concepts of management have fallen on the stony ground of academic culture. Sometimes departments of education keep at arm's length from departments of management and departments of management have little to do with departments of business. The synergy that comes from a well-integrated organisation is often missing. Industry, which can choose where to go for support in developing management, is far from enthusiastic about most higher education institutions.

Within the public sector, it is understandable that LEAs would wish to use for school management training the institutions they maintain, and also the university institutes of education that have established a reputation for training teachers to teach. Moreover, unlike tertiary sector education management, they have no Further Education Staff College to which they can turn. The Secondary Heads Association has advocated the setting up of an equivalent college as a centre for promoting management development in schools, but there is no sign of this being provided from central funds and it is unlikely that industry would provide the money. Regional centres exist at Padgate and Wakefield and although they have achieved some success, their influence has been limited. They attract plenty of people to their courses, both as participants and speakers, but neither has established a strong consultancy or research base, such as that built up by the Centre for the Study of Management Learning and other departments in the school of management at Lancaster University. This is the largest in the country and ranked fourth out of 64 United Kingdom schools of management for its research, as well as being generally highly regarded in a recent national survey. The Centre focuses on the industrial sector and although the Department of Educational Research has set up an interdepartmental Management in Education Group, with external representation, to foster school management development by means of jointly supported research, consultancy and training, it is far too early for this to make any real impression on the national scene.

The Centre for the Study of Comprehensive Schools, with its links to the Department of Education at York University, does not have management as the main thrust of its activities, although it has been assiduous in identifying and spreading good practice in all sorts of ways.

The University of London Institute of Education is by far the largest in the country and has a sizeable research budget, but here again educational *management* is not the main focus of its work, although one of its departments DEAPSIE (Department of Economic, Administrative and Policy Studies in Education) specialises in management and offers DES 3/83 one-term courses. The University's Centre for Staff Development in Higher Education also contributes to the development of management skills and the separate University Centre for Teachers runs short courses on management (including basic DES 3/83 courses). Although DEAPSIE uses skilled resources from outside education, and has many contacts with industrial management, it is not well-resourced enough to make much of an impact on the national scene. The Institute is, however, re-organising and is setting up a new Education Management Unit (1985).

Other university centres for school management education and training (for example, Exeter, Nottingham, Sussex and Warwick, which latter has close contacts with industry) have their strengths, but none stands head and shoulders above the rest. Of Bristol, more is said in section 4.11.

There is nothing to correspond with the International Management Centre from Buckingham, a private institution which operates in industry out in the field and establishes good learning bridges between theory and practice.

Of the polytechnics and colleges of higher education, Sheffield and Brighton seem to have made the most impact, but stand nothing like so high as centres of excellence in school management development as the leading business schools stand in industrial management development (London, Manchester, Cranfield, Oxford, Bradford, Henley, Durham and Ashridge). By comparison with education, such centres are well resourced, and the Foundation for Management Education (funded by industry and run by managers rather than academics) has played an invaluable catalytic and pump-priming role over a number of years in stimulating improvements in the provision and quality of management education and training. Since almost any major activity requires development funds for supporting change and building on success, it may be questioned whether a high enough proportion of the total expenditure on education management in higher education institutions is earmarked for such developments as FME has pioneered to good effect in the industrial management field. I guess not. The new education management unit in NFER may help to expand the research base but this still leaves a gap in the provision of a well funded and competently managed *development* agency. Much reshaping in the outlooks of existing higher education institutions will be needed before they can give schools what they need.

4.9 Private sector institutions

Few people are aware of the huge variety of management courses on the market, most of which are used by some part of industry. The London Regional Management Centre commissioned a study which revealed that there were in 1978 over 1000 institutions providing such courses in London and the Home Counties alone. The choice is utterly bewildering. Courses have mushroomed over the last twenty years, and for every one that disappears, new ones spring up.

Most of these courses are offered by private sector institutions and there are many companies that will naturally turn to these rather than to public sector provision because they believe the quality of the courses is more reliable when agencies stand or fall according to whether they can sell an acceptable product. By contrast, it is suspected that at least some public sector institutions get funded regardless of the product they offer. Certainly many public sector courses, especially those aimed at education, are cheaper, and this appeals to schools, but the most expensive element in training is not the fee but the value of the trainees' time. The most cost-effective decision on the choice of a training course is therefore seldom to go for the cheapest.

It is sometimes suspected that agencies selling high-priced courses must be fleecing their customers and making enormous profits. Some of these suspicions may be justified but by no means all. High staff:student ratios cost money, yet may be needed for the particular course design. Really competent trainers are in such demand that they tend to ration their time by charging high fees.

In the education field, there is one agency, ISTC, that was identified in an ILEA research study (Jayne 1982) as offering courses that scored unusually highly in teachers' estimation, yet their charges are remarkably modest; so there are bargains to be had, but not many. ISTC is run by an ex-head who calls on the services of a network of colleagues and contacts who have been identified as good practitioners and leaders in their field. He runs his courses residentially at venues which are somewhat less well-appointed than industrial managers would readily accept but still offer good service, accommodation and food. Among the reasons he gives for the high regard in which ISTC courses are held are (apart from those mentioned) efficient administration, immediate attention to complaints or difficulties, high participation by course members, mainly on directed tasks with some end-product, careful choice of course directors and lecturers, clear aims and objectives for each course and careful planning to achieve them (Stibbs 1984).

Industrial training managers are greatly helped in the selection of effective courses by a private sector organisation known as the National Training Index. The NTI collects critical information about over 3000 institutions and 10 000 lecturers in both the public and the private sector. It also issues a quarterly newsletter, including a section on 'high spots' and 'low spots', and provides a commentary on general trends in management training. Most large firms subscribe to the NTI and ensure that their managers who attend courses complete evaluation forms, which are then collated by the Index and used as a basis for their reports. The Index thus not only records what is available, in two loose-leaf binders (each two inches thick) but also responds to written and telephone enquiries about the quality of courses and lecturers. The service is extended also to management films and venues for training. Although it is costly to subscribe to the Index, it can be consulted in the BACIE library which is probably the best in the United Kingdom specialising in books on training. BACIE* has among its institutional members a number of LEAs, and heads who have visited the library have found it very useful.

---

* The British Association for Commerical and Industrial Education, 16 Park Crescent, London W1N 4AP; telephone 01 636 5351.

A selection of the names and addresses of the most reputable private sector institutions offering short courses in management appears in my CSCS report (Everard 1984), together with comments on their strengths. Some of the institutions offer bursaries for teachers, for instance the Coverdale organisation. Institutions whose courses have been particularly praised by heads are Coverdale, the Industrial Society, Roffey Park Management College and Life Skills Associates. Some companies that run their own internal management courses (including those based on private sector 'packages' such as those of Hersey and Blanchard and of Adair) are prepared to accept teachers at marginal cost. Details of such companies can be had from the CBI subsidiary, UBI*.

Whether the growth of school management training will add to the number of private sector institutions offering courses suitable for teachers and give rise to a consumers' guide to these, is doubtful; although the market is a large one, it can hardly be described as remunerative. In my view, however, the development of school management training would be helped by a 'mixed economy' of providers. There is room for more institutions like EIS (the educational arm of The Industrial Society) and ISTC to supplement the public sector courses.

4.10 Publishers: books, journals, video and computer programs

The printed word and magnetic tape enjoy the great advantage of being inexpensive ways of developing management and they can be used at a time that suits one's convenience. Although teachers may understandably jib at paying some £50 for a handbook of management training which can be used in schools, and may think £15 too much to pay for any book on management, it does not require much improvement in performance before such an investment pays off. The question is whether the books are written in such a way as to make changes in management behaviour likely. This book is not aimed directly to that end, whereas my earlier book was (Everard and Morris 1985); it was planned to be practical, stimulating and interactive. It is sometimes cynically said that most books on management are written by academics for academics; the practising manager looks for something that speaks directly to his condition and rings bells right, left and centre.

* Understanding British Industry, Sun Alliance House, New Inn Hall Street, Oxford OX1 2QE; telephone 0865 722585.

Of the many books and articles I have read on management, most appear to be aimed at stimulating the intellect by developing one's philosophy, understanding and constructs of thought about management. They operate sometimes exclusively in the cognitive domain. In terms of behavioural change, this is a distinct limitation; learning has to take place at the affective level also. Nor is it enough to *enjoy* reading a good book; unless it moves one along the dimension of will and commitment to action, it is unlikely to be instrumental in breaking through one's settled ways of doing things.

Just as evaluation is the Achilles' heel of training, so of publishing. What sound evidence is there that schools actually become more effective institutions as a result of teachers reading about management issues? What statistical evidence is there that many teachers read books and articles about management anyway? Regrettably few of those whom I have interviewed are in the habit of actively studying from the printed word and the same applies to industrial managers. So what can be done to stimulate the habit of guided, planned, purposeful reading, leading to an evaluative review of what (if anything) happened as a result of the reading, with conclusions being drawn about why it happened (or did not, as the case may be) and how the process of learning from the printed word could be improved in future? Who will sift through the mountain of paper to find the bits that are the most powerful instigators of more effective behaviour? Who will carry out consumer tests on management books and articles, will identify the best sellers (or the most photocopied articles) and will warn managers off the dross? I have not found good answers to these questions, but I can give some pointers here and a bibliography on page 245.

Books written by trainers like Mager, Honey, Mumford, Boydell and Hague tend to be oriented towards inducing a behavioural outcome, whereas those written by educationists tend to be slanted towards producing enlightenment.

Notwithstanding this, there are a few management classics such as McGregor's *The Human Side of Enterprise* (McGregor 1960) which, by opening up a whole new way of construing the concept and practice of management, has undoubtedly had a significant effect on developing management in the western world. *Understanding Organisations* (Handy 1976) probably qualifies; it is to be hoped that its sequel *Understanding Schools,* to be published in 1986 by Penguin, will also do so (Handy and Aitken 1986).

Succinct booklets that slip into the pocket or handbag and are clearly aimed at people who are busy are more likely to gain the attention of managers unaccustomed to study than long, heavy hardbacks. Education for Industrial Society has published a series of such booklets on school management topics; BACIE, the IPM and the BIM perform a similar service for managers in general. Although only a few concern management, the compilers of the CSCS leaflets on key issues also play a valuable role in condensing wisdom and specifying actions.

Some journals appear to be edited as though the editor is setting out to induce change, rather than simply to inform or to chronicle developments. Until his retirement, John Wellens had this reputation with his *Industrial and Commercial Training,* which has significantly affected the development of management and youth training in the United Kingdom over the last decade; a selection of articles from this journal which have proved particularly interesting to heads on an OTTO course is given in the bibliography. Of the educational journals none quite fills this bill but *School Organisation* possibly comes nearest. BEMAS's *Educational Management and Administration* is too intellectual to do so. *Educational Change and Development* is not journalistic and punchy enough and its circulation is too small. Managers are not looking for academic respectability so much as for instrumental effect.

Although some people have the self-discipline and learning style that enables them to work alone (especially from such books as *A Manager's Guide to Self-Development,* Burgoyne, Boydell and Pedler 1978; Pedler, Burgoyne and Boydell 1978), there is much to be said for creating a reading circle of people who are oriented towards self-development and who will support and encourage one another in the use of the printed word for this purpose. Members can meet over a beer or cup of tea to discuss a book or article they have all read and they can develop a plan for implementing what they agree to be useful. They can also scan, review or even précis new books or articles for one another, though the objective must not be taken as mere literary criticism but rather the active, creative plagiarism of good ideas. A head, or deputy with special responsibility for staff development, might lead a group of this kind, as part of a coherent INSET programme. A lot of energy is needed to sustain such activity.

Turning to video, there is now a huge range of video and cinematographic material about management. An index and compendium of reviews has been published and is available from BACIE (Management Update 1985). Some of the John Cleese series such as 'Meetings, Bloody Meetings' have been widely used in developing management in schools. As with books, there is a dearth of systematic information about the behavioural outcomes of watching these videos, which make important points in entertaining ways. Since it is more effective to use more than one of the senses in order to communicate, the impact of videos may well be greater than that of the printed word and for many people this medium is more agreeable. The use of a film followed by a skilfully led group discussion is a well tried technique in management training, and when the hire cost is spread over a dozen or more people, it is by no means astronomical.

As distance learning methods in management are developed by the

Centre for the Study of Management Learning at Lancaster and the Henley Management College (both of which are pioneering in this field), we can expect to see more sophisticated multi-media packages, including video, being marketed to facilitate learning in-company and in-school. However, apart from the Open University course material on education management, this is still a few years away as far as schools are concerned.

With the increasing availability of computers in schools, we can eventually expect to see them being used in (or after) school for staff development. Dispersed organisations like banks and building societies which have many computer terminals are leading the field here and may eventually have something to offer to the equally dispersed network of schools. The development of the technology is being accelerated through the MSC's Open Tech programme and is proving very helpful in training people who find it difficult to get away from their jobs except in odd moments (see for example, case studies from ICI and Austin Rover (Chapman and Blackwell 1985). The large potential market for school management development and the need for finding cost-effective methods for carrying it out, suggest that there will be developments in the use of computer-managed learning over the next decade, but at the time of writing, computer programs are playing a negligible part in school management development.

4.11 The National Development Centre for School Management Training

The NDCSMT is a joint enterprise of the School of Education, Bristol University and the South West Regional Management Centre at Bristol Polytechnic. It was funded by the DES from September 1983 for three years. Its purpose was to improve the effectiveness of school management training for heads and senior staff in primary, secondary and special schools in England and Wales. It does not itself provide training; it has five major functions of information gathering, evaluation, development, dissemination and support for implementation. Although its brief includes all forms of school management training, it focuses particularly on DES 3/83 provision. It has operated with about eight staff, including secretarial, some of them part-time.

Together with the DES 3/83 grants, the NDC has become the main institutional spearhead for developing management in schools, but its influence was weak in the early part of its existence when it did not have very much going for it. It was pitched into a task that was already underway when it was formed; some of the DES 3/83 courses had got off the ground earlier in the year of its formation and the providers of courses elsewhere in the country (some of which had bid for its role) were not well disposed to accept the authority of its leadership. Moreover, its brief from the DES was predicated on a narrow concept of management training and development, as became increasingly apparent during the first year.

The LEAs were sharply critical of the hasty implementation and inadequate planning of the whole initiative; one chief adviser summed it up as 'a good example of mismanagement' (Earley and Weindling 1985). He was right.

When a group of industrialists was invited to comment on the situation in March 1984, they felt the NDC was trying to 'get the solution right before they had defined the problem'. The initiative lacked coherence; school management training had got detached from management development and staff development policies in general. The emphasis seemed to be on course providers and their offers, rather than on the client system (the LEAs). *Ex cathedra* judgements on courses were expected by the DES rather than the development of better evaluation procedures by providers. There were the usual difficulties of collaboration across the transbinary divide between the university (the senior partner, with a well-established research reputation) and the polytechnic (which possessed some valuable resources in terms of practical training materials, contacts and experience). The will and mechanisms to tap the extensive industrial experience of management development were none too strong, and indeed the Centre staff had some very ill-founded ideas about industry and industrial management. There was a danger of the Centre becoming a sink rather than a source of information and to some extent this is still true of its resource bank.

From this unpromising start the Centre has recovered. The first year's progress report (Bolam 1984) recorded a number of worthwhile initiatives and drew forcible attention to deficiencies in management training provision. However, the criteria at first produced for recognising effective courses were full of holes and the quality of support that the NDC offered to providers was widely criticised, as were some of the regional conferences it ran. On the positive side, there was some useful sharing of experience and understanding at the national conferences and the autumn 1984 newsletter signalled the most significant development of all — 'A major shift in our thinking... from course development towards finding ways of improving performance in the job itself. Management training is thus a part of the wider process of management development.' This led Centre staff to become involved at a much more strategic level with LEAs, namely in planning, implementing and evaluating LEA-wide management development policies and programmes for heads and senior staff with eight pilot authorities. If early promise is fulfilled, this initiative should lead to a more supportive context in which management development and training can flourish, although in 1985 the climate for development was unhelpfully vitiated by the teachers' industrial action.

By 1985 the Centre was beginning to be helpful to course providers, having produced two sound reports on evaluation. Despite their looseness, use of the criteria for course recognition has apparently led to improvements in the less well-conceived courses, though the leading providers perceive that they still have more to give than to learn from Bristol – a situation that parallels the position of the more progressive companies formerly or currently responding to Industrial Training Boards.

Because of its information collection function, the Centre can pinpoint areas requiring special attention, such as the need to cater for management development in special schools and the need to ensure that management development is ultimately aimed at producing improvements in the quality of learning in all the country's schools. To this end their most important role is probably to stimulate the progress of LEAs towards the fourth stage of management development which they have identified in Table 4.1.

Although in autumn 1985 the future of the National Development Centre is not assured beyond 1986, in my view the need for its existence (or that of something like it) has been proven. It is in the business of changing attitudes towards management development and growing a culture in which it can thrive. Neither the DES nor most LEAs have a reliable understanding of what needs to be done and why, for their decision-makers mostly come from a tradition that neither grasps nor promotes the development process. The NDC is coming to grips with and explaining the true meaning and significance of management development for the education service. It has shown itself to be a learning system, able to adapt to its changing environment. It has the potential to continue playing a change agent role. The system in which it is operating displays all the charactistics of inertia that Pettigrew observed in his 20-year study of ICI (Section 3.8) – and more. Three years is therefore an impracticably short time in which to achieve a similar kind of cultural change. The early adopters (LEAs, providing institutions, schools, heads) of progressive management development policies need continuing support. Willing plagiarists of good practice need to be welcomed on board. If schools are to become more effectively managed, the catalytic role of an NDC will be

Notes on Table 1
* Comparable tables could be produced for schools and providers, both of which display analogous features at roughly similar stages.
** One important complicating feature, stressed at the regional conferences, is that each LEA has to consult and collaborate with several providers and with other LEAS, and that each provider has to work with several LEAS which are located in more than one sub-region.
*** LEAS at Stage 3 have emphasised the importance of having a shared understanding and a clear vision of what kind of school the management development strategy is designed to achieve.

Table 4.1 Possible stages in the adoption of a management development approach by LEAs

Stage	Main observable features	No. of LEAs
1	The LEA makes little management training provision of any kind for heads and senior staff. Its use of external courses is small.	A diminishing minority
2	The LEA makes considerable use of internal and external courses but on an *ad hoc* basis and without any clear policy framework. It is only just becoming aware of the 'development' approach.	The majority
3	The LEA has been working for several years on the evolution of a management training policy related to school improvement. The pattern of activities is varied, vigorous and well-established but still consists mainly of courses. Most heads and senior staff have experienced them and, occasionally, so too have officers and advisers. In consequence, there is a reasonably common understanding in the LEA of the possibilities and limitations of training and, accordingly, of the need to adopt a 'development' approach.	A growing minority
4	The LEA has a coherent and explicit policy for management development aimed at school improvement. Procedures and staff exist for implementing the policy in the form of a regular programme. This includes the use of job descriptions, development interviews and other methods of diagnosing needs at individual, school and LEA levels, and a varied range of on-the-job, close-to-the-job and off-the-job activities. Off-the-job courses are one component in the programme and the LEA has an infra-structure and personnel capable of supporting course participants during the preparatory and following stages, and of relating such courses to the identified needs of the LEA and its schools. Heads, senior staff, advisers and officers regularly engage in the programme which is systematically monitored and evaluated in terms of school improvement.	None at present.

needed for many years to come, before change becomes self-sustaining. Indeed, a regional constellation of catalytic agencies is also required; and the title NDC should be widened to embrace development as well as training and the education service as well as schools.

A question of priorities then arises; should such agencies be 'missionaries to the poor', a scourge for backsliders, or should they run with success? The ICI experience suggests that it is better to put scarce change agent resources with the early adopters, and to leave unaided the subsystems, where change is blocked from the top, till they really hurt. Identifying, encouraging, supporting and spreading good practice has its limitations as a strategy and requires much patience, but eradicating bad practice meets too many brick walls.

Another lesson from ICI experience is the importance of seeing the wood as well as the trees. Not only did the network of change agents work in particular divisions, departments and works, but they were linked to work going on at company level as far up as the main board. There was an awareness of total system change, as well as subsystem change, and the people facilitating each met and talked about their work. Of course, there were risks of breaching confidentiality in sharing information about top level change, but these were outweighed by opportunities for synergy.

The NDC appears to operate in a more compartmentalised fashion. If there is any thinking going on about the future organisation development of the education service of which schools are a part (for example, in the Cabinet 'think-tank'), the Centre should be part of it; otherwise its work with school management development cannot be properly integrated with work on the management (or governance) of the service as a whole. The total system is then sub-optimised.

For too long the development of education has been influenced by political thinking, with its concepts of ideology and power, and by administrative thinking, with its concepts of command and bureaucratic procedures. It is time that *managerial* thinking, with its concepts of problem-solving, practicality, effectiveness and getting things done, played a greater part in steering the development of education, and an NDC with an expanded role and terms of reference could make a useful contribution to bringing this about.

Appendix 1

Particulars of schools visited

	Type	Ages	Numbers
A	Mixed comprehensive	11–18	1200
B	Mixed comprehensive	11–19	1400
C	Mixed county secondary	11–16	1000
D	Mixed comprehensive	12–16	1350
E	Boys comprehensive	11–19	1200
F	Mixed comprehensive	11–18	1000
G	Mixed comprehensive	11–18	1090
H	Village college	11–16	940
I	Boys comprehensive	11–18	1460
J	Mixed comprehensive	11–19	1100
K	Voluntary controlled mixed comprehensive	11–18	1100
L	Mixed comprehensive	11–18	1200
M	Independent boys boarding	11–19	550
N	Mixed comprehensive	11–18	700
O	Mixed comprehensive	11–18	450
P	Independent boys boarding	11–19	700
Q	Mixed comprehensive	11–16	500

R	Mixed comprehensive	11–19	2200
S	Infant		200
T	Independent girls grammar with junior and preparatory	3–18	900

Appendix 2

Research methodology

The aim of the research was to characterise the content and context of the problems that schools face in terms that enable links to be made with similar problems in industry, and then to describe the solutions that industry has developed in terms that relate to the culture, language and practice of schools and local education authorities. All organisations encounter problems. They have various sources. Management responds to try to ameliorate them. How effectively is this management energy applied (a) in schools and (b) in business and industry? What can each learn about the other's approaches? What are the obstacles to the transfer of learning? How can they be overcome? The research model used in addressing these questions is shown in Figure 1. The research was carried out in four stages as follows:

Figure 1 The research model

```
   School concepts and language          Business concepts and language

                Management                             Management
                energy                                 energy

       culture      P   R   A                 culture      P   R   A
       values           E   M                 values           E   M
       goals        R       E                 goals        R       E
                        S   L                                   S   L
       structure    O       I       G         structure    O       I
       roles            P   O                 roles            P   O
School{ work       B       R   Business{ work           B       R
       organi-            O   A   A  organi-                    O   A
sation              L       N   T  sation                  L       N   T
       people               S   I            people               S   I
       relationships E           O           relationships E           O
                                P                                          
       environment M   E   N                 environment M   E   N
       plant            S   S                 plant            S   S
       finance                                finance

                        Learning
                        bridge
```

1   Gather data that help to identify and categorise the main obstacles to improved effectiveness in schools;

2   Identify corresponding situations in industry where management has secured improved effectiveness;

3   Describe the successful approaches, techniques and practices adopted by industrial managers, which could also be applied, with appropriate modifications, in schools;

4   Elucidate the conditions under which the transfer of such approaches has proved successful and unsuccessful in the past.

Stage 1 was essentially investigative and descriptive. With limited resources of time and funds, clearly a choice had to be made between visiting relatively few schools and studying the problems of management in some depth, and carrying out a general trawl over a larger number of schools. In both cases the question of selection arose.

For the first few visits I kept an open mind about the number of schools to aim to visit, but it soon became apparent that there was much diversity between schools. Moreover, I was conscious of the interference that my visits were causing to the normal work of the school, and I did not wish to trespass unduly on the goodwill that heads extended to me by allowing me to pay a visit. Thirdly, I saw problems of preserving confidentiality in publicly reporting on a small number of schools, each studied in depth. Pett, for example, on secondment from the Midland Bank, spent half a term in a comprehensive school but his report had to remain confidential to the school, so his findings cannot be put to use elsewhere (Beloe 1985). Consequently, I decided to make the normal encounter a full day's visit (that is, covering pre-school activities and evening meetings), which enabled me to cover 20 schools.

The schools could not be randomly selected because I could not expect every school to be willing to co-operate in the research. Besides, a judicious selection of schools was likely to be helpful in revealing a richer variety of problems and practices. I wanted to visit at least one of the following types of school, but to concentrate on those in the left hand column:

mixed		single sex
comprehensive		selective
state		independent
day		boarding
secondary		primary
English		Scottish
changing		stable
plus inner city	urban	rural

In making the final choices, I sought advice from the Centre for the Study of Comprehensive Schools, Understanding British Industry, Education for Industrial Society, the University of London Institute of Education and ICI. I received unsolicited suggestions from Dr Alan Paisey of Bulmershe College and Mrs Maureen Norton of Woolley Hall. In one case I wrote to a head who had published an article in the *Times Educational Supplement,* and in another case a head who had heard of what I was doing asked me to pay a visit.

Clearly such a sample is biased, but this does not invalidate the research results, provided that they are not claimed as fully representative of schools in general. A particular bias is that there is an above-average number of schools that have had some kind of encounters with industry; given the nature of the project, this is a helpful feature. Another bias, which certainly expedited and enriched data collection, was towards schools that were at least incipiently conscious of the importance of management, so that they were able to use higher level language in describing their management problems. A similar bias was deliberately built into the choice of interviewees; I particularly asked to meet any senior staff who had had experience of industry, or who had received some kind of training in management. Interviews with such staff covered a good deal more ground in a given time than those with staff who had a relatively naïve approach to management.

I usually carried out separate interviews with all the members of the school's senior staff (head, deputy heads and bursars where appropriate) and with the head's own selection of other staff. Heads of science, CDT, commerce and careers were often chosen, especially those with industrial contacts. Not all heads selected staff likely to convey a favourable impression of the management of the school; in fact, a few deliberately chose a 'maverick' and I was glad to enjoy the confidence of a number of interviewees who were prepared to 'wash dirty linen' in discussion. Given understandable feelings of loyalty towards one's organisation and one's head, it was particularly helpful to hear about the 'alternative prospectus' of the school.

The first approach to the school was by letter. In the vast majority of cases this produced a favourable response, and details of the visit were then negotiated. Only two schools did not reply, and one declined on the grounds that a major reorganisation was about to take place. Another school had to cancel arrangements for the visit because of the consequences of industrial action. A few schools were visited more than once.

Although I used a prepared checklist (Figure 2) for the interviews, I followed it heuristically; my strategy was to feel my way as quickly as possible towards fruitful lines of enquiry, and to get interviewees talking about matters that they felt to be significant. The opportunity was taken to cross-check data given in previous interviews; for example, if the head claimed to have a participative style of management, I asked subsequent interviewees to give examples of how they were involved in decisions affecting the school.

Figure 2 Schedule of questions

1   Have you any concerns about confidentiality?

2   Do you have any useful documents to show me, for example, a prospectus, an organisation chart or a job description?

3   How would you describe your management responsibilities?

4   Have you had any management training? If so, what helped and what didn't?

5   When you first had significant management responsibilities, what situations most concerned you, in case you could not handle them to your satisfaction? How did you feel at the time?

6   What obstacles and constraints are hindering improved effectiveness?

7   Describe some significant situations that you think were well managed. What was the setting, what occurred and what was the outcome? Why was it regarded as successful? What were the causes of success?

8   Describe similarly some situations that have been relatively poorly managed, or have not achieved the desired outcome.

9   How do you categorise management situations of this kind?

10   As you have watched others managing (your former heads, your deputies), what conclusions have you drawn about the causes of success and failure, about training needs etc.?

11   What managerial qualities do you think most important in schools?

12   Have you any views about what managers in industry, commerce and the armed services might have to offer to schools in terms of management attitudes, skills and techniques? And vice versa?

13   How do you feel about learning to improve your management?

14   What methods do you use, for example, books, courses, videos, meetings with peers?

15   Are there any difficulties or obstacles in getting help?

16   Are there any other points you want to put to me about management in schools?

17   How can I best observe management in action in your school?

Management research can be divided into two paradigms, 'hard' and 'soft' (Easterby-Smith 1985). The hard researcher goes for facts and figures and believes that knowledge is cumulative; the soft researcher believes that facts and knowledge cannot exist independently of the knower, and therefore goes for the meanings and interpretations that people attach to their experiences. My viewpoint and approach approximated to the latter. I recognise that those coming from different walks of academic life tend to disparage a holist approach, but I believe that research methods should be adapted to the nature of the subject, and 'management' does not lend itself to a reductionist approach.

However, I did gather some statistical material, for example on budgets and examination results. I also obtained copies of relevant internal documents such as prospectuses, staff manuals, organisation charts, committee structures and minutes of meetings. In some schools I attended a variety of assemblies, meetings, disciplinary interviews and other events that happened to be taking place during my visit. Of these, the daily meeting of senior management was the most common. In the case of staff meetings I particularly observed the process of the meeting, the style of the chairman and the extent to which there were clear objectives and a set of priorities.

With this type of research it is difficult to convey the full richness of one's findings without breaching the code of confidentiality. Earley and Weindling, who carried out research of a similar kind into the first years of headship (Earley and Weindling 1985), faced the same problem. They decided not to give the schools they visited the opportunity to vet the write-up or the analysis of their findings before publication, but instead to rely on their own skill in avoiding breaches of confidentiality and in accurately interpreting data. I decided to allow each school three months in which to vet the draft of Chapter 2, but not to send them a copy of my visit report. My contract with the school guaranteed that data would be treated in confidence and any account of my findings would be non-attributive. A particular problem arises in drafting an account in the form of a case study of a particular school; it must be based on data obtained from several interviewees, some of whom have provided information about which they might not like the head to know. With the few schools on which I decided to report in case study form (three of which are in Everard and Morris 1985, Chapter 18), these problems were averted, in some cases by suppressing data; even so there was one school where regrettably my draft was held to overstep the boundaries of confidentiality in a way that I had not foreseen.

The best way round the problem of confidentiality, and the one adopted in recording most of the results in this book, was to take all the visit reports and carry out a thematic cluster analysis of the contents, with the help of a BBC computer. This yielded the classification on which Chapter 2 is based, and enabled a place to be found for all the data that could not be safely included in case study form. Each paragraph was labelled with one of the categories and the whole data rearranged by theme rather than by school. Some contextual information had to be added for clarification. The draft was then revised in narrative form, with additional checks to see that confidentiality was still being preserved. It was this draft that was then sent to schools for vetting, together with a copy of Appendix 1 giving the bare details of each school. Where it was felt important to draw the head's attention to particular passages, these were noted in the covering letter.

Special provisions applied to ILEA schools, since permission for visits for research purposes is in the hands of the Research and Statistics Branch, which requires a separate copy of drafts for vetting purposes, independently of the school concerned.

No special problems arose in responding to the comments on the draft.

Bibliography

Books

The following books are judged to be useful to policy-makers, advisers, heads and school management trainers. A brief description of each is provided.

Management development

Barrington, H. 1984: *Learning about Management*. Maidenhead: McGraw-Hill.
A readable account of how Lever Bros. managers are trained.
Blumberg, A. and Greenfield, W. 1980: *The Effective Principal*. Boston, Mass.: Allyn and Bacon.
An American commentary on developing school management.
Buckley, J. 1985: *Training of Secondary Heads in Western Europe*. Windsor: NFER-Nelson.
An interesting study sponsored by the EEC.
Burgoyne, J. and Stuart, R. 1978: *Management Development: Context and Strategies*. Aldershot: Gower.
Good material from the Centre for the Study of Management Learning.
Huczynski, A. 1983: *Encyclopaedia of Management Development Methods*. Aldershot: Gower.
A comprehensive compendium of approaches to management development, with references to articles and books that explain how to use the methods. Will widen horizons about the huge range of methods available.
Nixon, B. (ed.)1981: *New Approaches to Management Development*. Aldershot: Gower.
A useful series of essays by practising members of the Association of Teachers of Management. Berger and Nixon's chapter on 'Training for Skills and Attitude Change' is particularly useful.
Randall, G., Packard, P. and Slater, J. 1984: *Staff Appraisal*. London: Institute of Personnel Management.
A guide to practice outside education.
Taylor, B. and Lippitt, G. (eds) 1983: *Management Development and Training Handbook*, 2nd edn. Maidenhead: McGraw-Hill.

State-of-the-art essays by some leading management development thinkers and practitioners in the UK and the USA.
Woodcock, W. and Francis, D. 1982: *The Unblocked Manager.* Aldershot: Gower.
Helps you to identify what stops you from being a more effective manager, and what to do about it.

Management of schools

Bush, T. and Glatter, R. (eds) 1980: *Approaches to School Management.* London: Harper and Row.
A series of essays by leading thinkers, for the Open University course.
Everard, K. B. and Morris, G. 1985: *Effective School Management.* London: Harper and Row.
A practical guide with many exercises.
Frith, D. (ed.) 1985: *School Management in Practice.* Harlow: Longman.
Essays by practitioners.
Galton, M. and Moon, B. (eds) 1983: *Changing Schools. . . Changing Curriculum.* London: Harper and Row.
A helpful book in encouraging managers to think about the future of schools.
Hargreaves D. 1982: *The Challenge of the Comprehensive Schools.* London: Routledge.
Helps teachers think what these schools are for.
Morgan, C., Hall, V. and Mackay, H. 1983: *The Selection of Secondary School Headteachers.* Milton Keynes: Open University Press.
Depressing!
Paisey, A. 1984: *School Management: A Case Approach.* London: Harper and Row.
A good list of school management problems written up in case study form for use on training courses.
Rutter, M., Maughan, B., Mortimore, P. and Ouston, J. 1979: *Fifteen Thousand Hours.* Shepton Mallet: Open Books.
Demonstrates the importance of managing the ethos of a school.
Sayer, J. 1985: *What Future for Secondary Schools?* Lewes: Falmer.
The former principal of Banbury School proposes radical reforms in secondary education.
Trethowan, D. M. 1983: *Management in Schools: Target Setting.* London: Education for Industrial Society.
Warwick, D. 1983: *Management in Schools: Staff Appraisal.* London: Education for Industrial Society.
Two of a series of inexpensive booklets on school management topics.
Waters, D. 1979: *Management and Headship in the Primary School.* London: Ward Lock.
A readable book by an experienced primary head turned management trainer.

Managerial roles and tasks

Lyons, G. 1976: *The Head's Tasks: A Handbook of Secondary School Administration*. Windsor: NFER.
A major diary study of what managers do in 33 schools.
Matthew, R. and Tong, S. 1982: *The Role of the Deputy Head in the Comprehensive School*. London: Ward Lock.
Intended to make deputies think about what they should be doing.
Mintzberg, H. 1973: *The Nature of Managerial Work*. New York: Harper and Row.
Explains what managers do, based on observation of them at work.
Peters, R. S. (ed.) 1976: *The Role of the Head*. London: Routledge Kegan Paul.
Essays by leading educationists.

Management style and leadership

John, D. 1980: *Leadership in Schools*. London: Heinemann.
A book that teachers like.
Mant, A. D. 1983: *Leaders We Deserve*. Oxford: Martin Robertson.
A stimulating book, with a chapter on schools, describing a theory of leadership.

Organisation and team management

Belbin, M. 1981: *Management Teams: Why They Succeed or Fail*. London: Heinemann.
An engrossing account of some excellent research.
Gray, H. L (ed.) 1982: *The Management of Educational Institutions*. Lewes: Falmer.
Specially commissioned papers about the theory of organisational management.
Gray, H. L. 1985: *The School as an Organisation*, 2nd edn. Stoke-on-Trent: Deanhouse.
Applies organisation theory to schools.
Handy, C. B. 1978: *Gods of Management*. London: Pan.
An analysis of organisational culture, which should appeal particularly to classical scholars.
Handy, C. B. 1984: *Taken for Granted: Looking at Schools as Organisations*. York: Longman.
A 'must', at least until his next appears:
Handy, C. B. and Aitken, R. 1986: *Understanding Schools*. Harmondsworth: Penguin (to be published).
Hanson, E. M. 1979: *Educational Administration, Organisation and Behaviour*. Boston, Mass.: Allyn and Bacon.
Application of behavioural science.

Hersey, P. and Blanchard, K. H. 1977: *Management of Organisational Resources: Utilising Human Resources.* Englewood Cliffs, N.J.: Prentice-Hall.
An approach used in IBM and transferred to some UK schools.
Owens, G.R. 1981: *Organisational Behaviour in Education.* Englewood Cliffs: Prentice-Hall.
Application of behavioural science to management.
Paisey, A. 1981: *Organisation and Management in Schools.* London: Longman.
Good on principles of management and the importance of objectives.
Reddin, W. J. 1970: *Managerial Effectiveness.* New York: McGraw-Hill.
A punchy, but at times over-elaborate, account of a theory of effectiveness.
Reddin, W. J. 1985: *The Best of Bill Reddin.* Institute of Personnel Management.
Collected articles by a stimulating author which capture some of the essence of modern management. Advanced.
Reynolds, D. 1985: *The Effective School.* Lewes: Falmer Press.
A survey of what leads to effectiveness in schools.
Saunders, G. 1984: *The Committed Organisation.* Aldershot: Gower.
How to get organisations to develop a vision of the future and be committed to attaining it.
Woodcock, M. 1979: *Team Development Manual.* Aldershot: Gower.
Forty-five activities for improving teamwork.

Management of change

Fullan, M. 1982: *The Meaning of Educational Change.* New York: Teachers College Press and Ontario Institute for Studies in Education.
The best book on the nature and implementation of organisational and curricular change in education.
Gray, H. L. 1985: *Change and Management in Schools,* 2nd edn.
An analytical book by an 'experiential' author with radical views.
Leithwood, K. A., Holmes, M. and Montgomery, D. J. 1979: *Helping Schools Change: Strategies Derived from Field Experience.* Ontario Institute for Studies in Education.
Intervening in schools to improve effectiveness. Useful for advisers.
McLean, A., Sims, D., Mangham, I. and Tuffield, D. 1982: *OD in Transition: Evidence of an Evolving Profession.* Chichester: John Wiley.
A well-researched study of what really happens in the management of change in the UK.
Schmuck, R. A., Runkel, P. J. and Arends, R. I. 1977: *The Second Handbook of Organisation Development in Schools.* Palo Alto: Mayfield.
A classic American book, useful for advisers and consultants.

Stewart, V. 1983: *Change: The Challenge for Management*. Maidenhead: McGraw-Hill.
One of the best British books, by a psychologist, on the management of change. Reasonably down-to-earth.

Self-development for managers

Francis, D. and Woodcock, W. 1982: *50 Activities for Self-development*. Aldershot: Gower.
A practical manual, suitable for schools, good on identifying training needs and on describing useful techniques.
Hague, H. 1979: *Helping Managers to Help Themselves*. Oxford: Context.
A partly descriptive and partly practical approach to self-development by a well-known trainer.
LGTB: *The Effective Manager: A Resource Handbook*. Luton: Local Government Training Board.
A similar handbook to the MSC's:
MSC: *Management Self-development: A Practical Manual for Managers and Trainers*. Sheffield: Manpower Services Commission.
Full of useful practical exercises; not industry-oriented.
Mumford, A. 1980: *Making Experience Pay*. London: McGraw-Hill.
A practical guide to using everyday experience in developing management.
Pedler, M., Boydell, T., Leary, M., Carlisle, J. and Cranwell, B. 1984: *Self-development Groups for Managers*. Sheffield: Manpower Services Commission.
Practical advice on how to get a group started in managing its own development. The authors have the right ideas about how people develop, and the importance of affective learning.
Pedler, M., Burgoyne, J. and Boydell, T. 1978: *A Manager's Guide to Self-Development*. London: McGraw-Hill.
Full of practical exercises.

Interactive skills

Honey, P. 1980: *Solving People Problems*. Maidenhead: McGraw-Hill.
Although the case studies are taken from industry, the problems have their parallels in schools.
Hopson, B. and Scally, M. 1981: *Lifeskills Teaching*. Maidenhead: McGraw-Hill.
Explains some of the differences between didactic and experiential learning.
Rackham, N., Honey, P. and Colbert M. 1971: *Developing Interactive Skills*. Northampton: Wellens Publishing.
A good book by leading practitioners, well-researched and practical.

Training, coaching and learning methods

Binsted, D. 1980: *Design for Learning in Management Training and Development: A View*. Bradford: MCB Publications.
An excellent monograph for course designers, based on research at the Centre for the Study of Management Learning.
Goad, T. W. 1982: *Delivering Effective Training*. San Diego: University Associates.
A well-organised book for practitioners, giving plenty of practical help and useful checklists. Helpful for the academic who wants to learn about training pedagogy.
Honey, P. and Mumford, A. 1982: *Manual of Learning Styles*. Maidenhead: Honey.
Useful for course designers.
Kolb, D. 1984: *Experiential Learning*. Englewood Cliffs, New Jersey: Prentice-Hall.
This is a classic, which should be compulsory reading for anyone designing management training courses. Some parts are a little heavy.
MacKay, I. 1980: *A Guide to Asking Questions*. London: BACIE.
Helpful booklet for interviewing situations.
MacKay, I. 1984: *A Guide to Listening*. London: BACIE.
Especially useful for the talkative manager.
Megginson, D. and Boydell, T. 1979: *A Manager's Guide to Coaching*. London: BACIE.
An inexpensive handy booklet explaining how to coach people into more effective performance.
Pfeiffer, J. W. and Jones, J. E. 1974 and annually: *A Handbook of Structured Experiences for Human Relations Training*. San Diego, Ca.: University Associates. Also (with Goodstein, L. D.) *Annuals for Facilitators, Trainers and Consultants*.
An Aladdin's cave of practical exercises devised by behavioural scientists for changing behaviour. Useful for course designers.
Rae, L. 1983: *The Skills of Training – A Guide for Managers and Practitioners*. Aldershot: Gower.
Reviews main techniques used in training and development. More modest than Huczynski. Not a practical manual.

Industry

Everard, K. B. 1984: *Management in Comprehensive Schools: What Can Be Learned from Industry?* 2nd edn. York: Centre for the Study of Comprehensive Schools.
Largely applicable to primary schools too.
Jamieson, I 1985: *Industry in Education: Developments and Case Studies*. Harlow: Longman.

A useful account of industry-education liaison, sponsored by the Schools Council.

Open University 1976: *A Case Study in Management: Sidney Stringer School and Community College. E321 2.* Milton Keynes: Open University.

How a former industrial manager sets about managing the school of which he is appointed head, and successfully applying principles from industrial management.

Peters, T. J. and Waterman 1982: *In Search of Excellence.* New York: Harper and Row.

A best-seller, useful in disabusing educationists of myths about industry.

Pettigrew, A. M. 1985: *The Awakening Giant: Continuity and Change in ICI.* Oxford: Basil Blackwell.

A long book with a good state-of-the-art commentary on the practical application of OD. Offers plenty of insights into the problems of large complex organisations.

Psychometric tests

Kiersey, D. and Bates, M. 1978: *Please Understand Me: Character and Temperament Types.* Del Mar, Ca.: Prometheus Nemesis.

An account of the Myers-Briggs test.

Management research

Hammond, V. 1985: *Current Research in Management.* London: Frances Pinter.

A report of a conference on recent research.

Journals

This section is representative rather than comprehensive. It lists useful articles from *Industrial and Commercial Training* only. For the last decade or more, this has been one of the leading journals for up-dating management trainers in the state of the art. The following articles are among those that have been made available to heads on the University of London Institute of Education OTTO programme. One secondary head categorised them according to their usefulness: M = must be read; S = should be read; W = worth reading.

1 Overviews and trends

Honey, P. 1982: *What I Believe about Management Training.* 14, 112–16 (W).

A leading practitioner in management training distils his experience.

Nixon, B. 1980: *Recent Trends in Management Development*, 12, 374–380 (W).
How Sun Alliance opposed management development and view recent techniques.

2 Management style

Back, K. and K. 1980: *Assertiveness for People and Organisations*, 12, 22–27 (M).
A useful analysis of an aspect of management style.
Wellens, J. 1982: *What is Meant by a Modern Management Style*, 14, 74–80 (W).
Participative (democratic?) management and how it can go wrong.

3 Coaching and learning

Attwood, T. 1983: *Achieving Results?* 15, 345–8 (M).
Some hints from a well-known management trainer on how to get things to happen.
Honey, P. 1981: *Shaping Behaviour*, 13, 306–11 (S).
An analysis of how one sort of contribution to a discussion triggers another, and how you can shape other people's responses.
Mumford, A. 1983: *Emphasis on the Learner: A New Approach*, 15, 342–4 (M).
A professor of management development analyses some causes of ineffectiveness in management learning.
Singer, E. 1981: *Forum: the Insiders' Debate*, 13, 166–8 (M).
An experienced management trainer describes how to coach and set up learning situations.
Smith, P. 1978: *Working and Learning in Groups*, 10, 322–4 (M).
How groups work and how to use them for learning.
Tierre, J. 1979: *Experiential Learning: A Follow-up*, 11, 151–61 (W).
Reports by people who have received experiential training and identified its strengths and weaknesses.
Wright, D. 1978: *Transactional Analysis*, 10, 238–44 (W).
A simple explanation of an approach often used in management training.

4 Repertory grid

Honey, P. 1979: *The Repertory Grid in Action: How to Use it as a Pre/Post Test to Validate Courses*, 11, 358–69.
A detailed account of an approach to course evaluation and how to use it.
Honey, P. 1979: *The Repertory Grid in Action: How to Use it as a Self-insight Exercise*, 11, 407–14 (S).
A practical exercise for use during a management course.

Honey, P. 1979: *The Repertory Grid in Action: How to Use it to Conduct an Attitude Survey*, 11, 452–9 (S).
A practical account of surveying attitudes towards management.
Neal, M. and Tyrrell, F. 1979: *Sharing Meanings: An Introduction to the Repertory Grid Technique*, 11, 327–34 (S).
An introduction to a technique that has broad application in management training.

5 Team-building

Maude, B. 1980: *Training in Team-building*, 12, 460–62 (M).
A good review of the training methods used in team-building.
Smallwood, A. 1976: *Coverdale training*, 8, 12–16 (S).
An explanation of the philosophy and approach of Coverdale training, widely used in industry.

6 Management of time

Tierre, J. 1981: *Awareness of Time and Space*, 13, 350–51 (W).
Hints for the manager who is always pressed for time.

7 Self-development

Delf, G. and Smith, B. 1978: *Strategies for Promoting Self-development*, 10, 494–501 (S).
What a top manager or trainer can do to encourage people to develop themselves.

8 Staff appraisal training

Whitfield, I. 1980: *Staff Training for Appraisal Interviewing*, 12, 366–8 (M).
A realistic account of staff appraisal schemes and training in their operation.

References

Aitken, R. 1985: Week by Week. *Education,* 166, 411,439 and 463.

Allsop, P. 1985: Leadership Training in Indutry. *Contributions,* 8, 17–20.

Ascher, K. 1983: *Management Training in Large UK Business Organisations.* London: Harbridge House Europe.

ATM 1985: *Newsletter,* London: Association of Teachers of Management.

Attwood, L. T. 1979: *Management Development in British Companies.* Bradford: MCB Publications.

Ballinger, E. 1984: *Management Development Outside Education: Some Implications for the NDC.* Bristol: National Development Centre for School Management Training.

Ballinger, E. 1985a: *An Interim Analysis of Available Evaluation Reports on Basic and OTTO Programmes.* Bristol: National Development Centre for School Management Training.

Ballinger, E. 1985b: *Headship in the 80s: Evaluation Report.* Bristol: National Development Centre for School Management Training.

Bancroft, Lord and Harvey-Jones, J. 1984: Cantor Lectures. *Journal of the Royal Society of Arts,* 132, 367–89.

Barrington, H. 1984: *Learning about Management.* Maidenhead: McGraw-Hill.

Beckhard, R. 1969: *Organisation Development: Strategies and Models.* Reading, Mass.: Addison-Wesley.

Belbin, M. 1981: *Management Teams: Why They Succeed or Fail.* London: Heinemann.

Beloe, M. 1985: Fly on the Wall: An Outsider in the School. *Contributions,* 8, 38–42.

Beynon, H. 1984: 2nd edn. *Working for Ford.* Harmondsworth: Penguin.

Binsted, D. 1980: *Design for Learning in Management Training and Development: A View.* Bradford: MCB Publications.

Bolam, R. 1978: School Focused INSET and Consultancy. *Educational Change and Development,* 1, 25.

Bolam, R. 1984: *First Year of the NDCSMT: A Progress Report.* Bristol: National Development Centre for School Management Training.

Bolam, R. 1985: *Director's Report No. 4.* Bristol: National Development Centre for School Management Training.

Bone, T. 1982: Problems of Institutional Management in a Period of Contraction. In H. L. Gray (ed.), *The Management of Educational Institutions*. Lewes: Falmer Press, 263–83.

Bookman, D. 1985: *Newsletter No. 3*. Bristol: National Development Centre for School Management Training.

Bowden, D. 1985:*Prepared to Manage*. Cheshire County Council.

Bridgwater, P. 1980: A Conceptual Basis for Management Training. *Journal of European Industrial Training*, 4, 17–21. Also: Making the Most of Our Managers. *Albright World*, September, 6.

Buckley, J. 1985: *The Training of Secondary School Heads in Western Europe*. Windsor: NFER-Nelson.

Buet, P. 1985: A Working Secondment – A Case History. *BACIE Journal*, 40, 108–9.

Bullock, A. (chairman of committee of inquiry) 1975: *A Language for Life*. London: HMSO.

Burgoyne, J. G. 1976: *A Taxonomy of Managerial Qualities as Learning Goals for Management Education: Development and Initial Testing*. Lancaster: Centre for the Study of Management Learning.

Burgoyne, J., Boydell, T. and Pedler, M. 1978: *Self Development: Theory and Applications for Practitioners*. London: Association of Teachers of Management.

Burgoyne, J. G. and Stuart, R. 1978: *Management Development: Context and Strategies*. Aldershot: Gower.

Chapman, P. and Blackwell, L. 1985: Bringing Learning into the Factory. *Transition*, October, 18–21.

Chater, R. 1984: Learning from the Other Side. *Education*, 7 December, 469.

CIPFA 1981–2: *Handbook of Education Unit Costs*. CIPFA Statistical Information Service.

Cooper, C. L., and Marshall, J. (eds) 1978: *White Collar and Professional Stress*. Chichester: Wiley.

CSCS/BP 1984: *School Industry Links: Leaflet No. 6*. York: Centre for the Study of Comprehensive Schools.

Dean, J. 1985: *Managing the Secondary School*. Beckenham: Croom Helm.

Derr, C. B. and DeLong, T. J. 1982: What Business Management Can Teach Schools. In H. L. Gray (ed.), *The Management of Educational Institutions*. Lewes: Falmer.

DES 1985: *Better Schools*. London: HMSO.

Diffey, K. 1985: Who Appraises Whom? *SHA Review*, 79, 911–3.

Dimmock, C. 1985: communicated at NDC Annual Conference, July.

Duffet, R. H. E. 1982: *Study of Devolution of Managerial Responsibility to Heads of Schools*. Cambridgeshire County Council.

Dwyer, J. 1984: *Preparation for Secondary Headship*. Whitley Bay High School.

Earley, P. and Weindling, D. 1985: Training of Heads. The Local Authorities Make a Positive Response. *Education,* 17 May, 439.

Easterby-Smith, M. 1985: Management Research: Paradigms, Purposes and Issues. In A. Chapman (ed.), *What Has Management Research Got to Do with Managers?* London: Association of Teachers of Management.

Evans, K. 1985: Letter to the Editor. *Contributions,* 8, 1–2.

Everard, K. B. 1974: Mutual Monitoring. *Industrial and Commercial Training,* 6, 304–8.

Everard, K. B. 1982: Higher Education: Should Industry Be Concerned? In D. Anderson (ed.), *Educated for Employment?* London: Social Affairs Unit, 23–37.

Everard, K. B. 1983: Commercial and Industrial Education in China. *BACIE Journal,* 38, 13–15.

Everard, K. B. 1984: *Management in Comprehensive Schools: What Can Be Learned from Industry?* 2nd edn. York: Centre for the Study of Comprehensive Schools.

Everard, K. B. 1984–5: Teachers as Managers. *Contributions,* 7, 43–8.

Everard, K. B. 1985a: OD in Education. In H. L. Gray (ed.), *Organisation Development (O. D.) in Education.* Stoke-on-Trent: Deanhouse.

Everard, K. B. 1985b: The Management of Schools – An Industrialist's View. *SHA Review,* 79, 899–909.

Everard, K. B. and Marsden, C. L. 1985: Industry's Contribution to School Management Training: A Matter of Mutual Interest. *BACIE Journal,* March/April, 49–52.

Everard, K. B. and Morris, G. 1985: *Effective School Management.* London: Harper and Row.

FEU 1981: *How Do I Learn?* Project Report No. 9. London: Further Education Unit.

Fletcher, C. A. 1973: *An Evaluation of Job Appraisal as it Operates in the Welsh Office.* Civil Service Department.

Fullan, M. 1982: *The Meaning of Educational Change.* New York: Teachers College Press and Ontario Institute for Studies in Education.

Gill, D. 1977: *Appraising Performance.* IPM Report No. 25. London: Institute of Personnel Mangement.

Graham, D. G. 1985: *Those Having Torches – Teacher Appraisal: A Study.* Ipswich: Suffolk County Education Offices.

Gray H. L. and Heller, H.: *Problems in Helping Schools.* Occasional Paper no. 18. Stoke-on-Trent: Deanhouse.

Gray, H. L. 1985: *Problems in Helping Head Teachers to Learn about Management.* University of Lancaster: unpublished.

Haigh, G. 1985: Exterminate! *Times Educational Supplement,* 18 October, 27.

Handy, C. B. 1976: *Understanding Organisations.* Harmondsworth: Penguin.

Handy, C. B. 1984: *Taken for Granted: Looking at Schools as Organisations*. York: Longman.

Handy, C. B. and Aitken, R. 1986: *Understanding Schools*. Harmondsworth: Penguin (to be published).

Hancock, D. 1985: Lecture to Industrial Society Conference, 25 February.

Harding 1872: *Practical Handbook of School Management for Teachers, Pupil Teachers and Students*. Thomas Laurie.

Harris, N. D. 1985: Why Not Try Triads? *Industrial and Commercial Training*, March/April, 7.

Hartles, R. 1982: Week by Week. *Education*, 10 December, 451.

Hegarty S. (ed.) 1983: *Training for Management in Schools*. Windsor: NFER-Nelson.

Hersey, P. and Blanchard, K. H. 1977: *Management of Organisational Resources: Utilising Human Resources*. Englewood Cliffs, N.J.: Prentice-Hall.

Herzberg, F. 1966: *Work and the Nature of Man*. Cleveland, Ohio: World Publishing.

HMI 1977a: *Modern Languages in Comprehensive Schools*. London: HMSO.

HMI 1977b: *Ten Good Schools*. London: HMSO.

HMI 1979: *Aspects of Secondary Education in England*. London: HMSO.

HMI 1985: *Effects of Local Authority Expenditure Policies on Education Provision in England*. London: Department of Education and Science.

Holroyde, G. 1985: Learning the Lessons of the Sixties. *Education*, 22 February, 172.

Honey, P. and Mumford, A. 1982: *Manual of Learning Styles*. Maidenhead: Honey.

Hughes, M. G., Carter, J. and Fidler, B. 1981: *Professional Development Provision for Senior Staff in Schools and Colleges*. University of Birmingham.

Humble, J. W. 1971: *Management by Objectives in Action*. London: McGraw-Hill.

ICI 1985: Citation. *Newsline*, 27 September.

IFF Research 1985: *Adult Training in Britain*. Sheffield: Manpower Services Commission.

ILEA 1983: *Keeping the School under Review*. London: ILEA.

Industrial Society 1985: *Survey of Training Costs. New Series No. 1*. London: The Industrial Society.

Jackson, A.: *Heading for What?* Leeds University: Counselling and Careers Development Unit.

Jamieson, I. 1981: Schools and Industry: Some Organisational Considerations. *School Organisation*, 1, 309–15.

Jayne, E. 1982: Survey of Opinions of Management Training Courses by Senior Staff of Secondary Schools. *British Journal of In-service Education*, 8, 151. Also 1980: *Survey of Management Training Courses for Senior Staff of Secondary Schools.* ILEA Research Report No. 771/80; and 1982: *Management Training for Senior Staff. Trained for the Job?* ILEA Research Report No. 794/82.

Jenkins, H. 1985: Perceptions of Senior managers in Schools and Manufacturing Industry. *Educational Management and Administration*, 13, 1–12.

Johnson, S. 1983: Week by Week. *Education*, 28 October, 343.

Kempner, T. 1984: How to Keep up with the Other Leaders. *Times Educational Supplement*, 9 March, 4.

Kolb, D. A. 1984: *Experiential Learning: Experience as a Source of Learning and Development.* Englewood Cliffs, N.J.: Prentice-Hall.

Lavelle, M. 1984: The Role of Consultancy and OD in Innovation in Education. *School Organisation*, 4, 161. Also lecture to ISTC course on School Organisation, April 1984.

Legon, P. 1981: Staff Working Parties: A Policy for Increased Productivity. *School Organisation, 1, 335.*

Likert, R. 1967: The Human Organisation. New York: McGraw-Hill.

Lusty, M. 1983: Staff Appraisal in the Education Service. *School Organisation*, 3, 371.

Makin, V. 1984: Giving the Customers a Say in How the Store is Run. *Times Educational Supplement*, 23 November, 14.

Management Update 1985: *Knowing Your Training Films: Index and Reviews.* London: Management Update Ltd.

Mant, A. D. 1969: *The Experienced Manager: A Major Resource.* London: British Institute of Management.

Marsden, C. L. 1983: Management Training: An Experience. *Contributions, 5,* 14–16.

Maw, J., Fielding, M., Mitchell,P., White, J., Young, P., Ouston, J. and White, P. 1984: *Education plc?* London Institute of Education: Heinemann.

Maxon, J. 1985: Personality Type and Personal Development. *Industrial and Commercial Training,* January/February, 21–27.

McGregor, D. 1960: *The Human Side of Enterprise.* New York: McGraw-Hill.

McHale, J. 1984: 'Read, Write and Keep Rabbits'. *People and Jobs,* March, 10.

Milsten, M. 1985: Stress Management in Schools: The Organisation is the Problem and the Solution. *Educational Change and Development,* 6, 12–20.

Mintzberg, H. 1973: *The Nature of Managerial Work.* New York: Harper and Row.

Morgan, C., Hall, V. and Mackay, H. 1983: *The Selection of Secondary School Headteachers.* Milton Keynes: Open University Press.

Mumford, A. 1980: *Making Experience Pay.* London: McGraw-Hill.

Murgatroyd, S. and Reynolds, D. 1984: The Creative Consultant: The Potential Use of Consultancy as a Method of Teacher Education. *School Organisation,* 4, 321.

Nichols, T. and Beynon, H. 1977: *Living with Capitalism.* London: Routledge and Kegan Paul.

Nisbet, J. W. 1982–3: *Director's Report.* Oxford: Understanding British Industry.

NDCSMT 1984: *3/83 Courses: A Descriptive Survey. Report No. SC/84/2P.* Bristol: National Development Centre for School Management Training.

NDCSMT 1985: *Evaluation Advice.* Bristol: National Development Centre for School Management Training.

Ordidge, P. 1985: Delegation – Is It Different for Managers in Education? *Educational Management and Administration,* 13, 13–16.

Paisey, A. 1981: *Organisation Management in Schools.* Harlow: Longman.

Pateman, T. 1980: Accountability, Values and Schooling. In T. Bush, R. Glatter, J. Goodey and C. Riches (eds), *Approaches to School Management.* London: Harper and Row.

Pedler, M., Burgoyne, J. and Boydell, T. 1978: *A Manager's Guide to Self-Development.* London: McGraw-Hill.

Peel, M. 1984: *Management Development and Training: A Survey of Current Policy and Practice.* London: British Institute of Management/ Professional Publishing Ltd.

Peters, T. J. and Waterman 1982: *In Search of Excellence.* New York: Harper and Row.

Pettigrew, A. M. 1983: Patterns of Managerial Response as Organisations Move from Rich to Poor Environments. *Educational Management and Administration,* 11, 104.

Pettigrew, A. M. 1985: *The Awakening Giant: Continuity and Change in ICI.* Oxford: Basil Blackwell.

Plowden, W. 1985: What Prospects for the Civil Service? *Journal of the Royal Society of Arts,* 133, 526–43.

Randall, G., Packard, P. and Slater, J. 1984: *Staff Appraisal.* London: Institute of Personnel Management.

Reddin, W. J. 1970: Managerial Effectiveness. New York: McGraw-Hill.

Rée, H. 1985: Letter to the Editor. *Contributions,* 8, 3–5.

Reynolds, D. 1983: What Makes a Good School? *Education,* 30 September, 271.

Reynolds, D. 1985a: The Effective School. *Times Educational Supplement,* 20 September, 25.

Reynolds, D. 1985b: *The Effective School*. Lewes: Falmer Press.

Rutter, M., Maughan, B., Mortimore, P. and Ouston, J. 1979: *Fifteen Thousand Hours*. Shepton Mallet: Open Books.

Sayer, J. 1984: *Survey of School Management Courses*. London: Secondary Heads Association.

Schein, E. H. 1969: *Process Consultation: Its Role in Organisation Development*. Reading, Mass.: Addison-Wesley.

Schofield, J. 1980: *The Creation of a Good Comprehensive School*. Spurley Hey High School.

Slater, D. 1985: in M. Hughes, P. Ribbins and H. Thomas (eds), *Managing Education: The System and the Institution*, London: Holt, Rimehart and Winston.

Stewart, R. 1982: *Choices for the Manager. A Guide to Managerial Work and Behaviour*. London: McGraw-Hill.

Stibbs, J. L. 1984: Private communication, 26 March.

Stoner, F. 1984: private communication.

Taylor, K. 1983: Heads and the Freedom to Manage. *School Organisation*, 3, 273.

Taylor, W. 1976: The Head as Manager: Some Criticisms. In R. Peters (ed.), *The Role of the Head*. London: Routledge and Kegan Paul.

Torrington, D. and Weightman, J. 1983: Why Heads Should Not Be Seen as Managing Directors. *Times Educational Supplement*, 9 December, 16.

Trethowan, D. M. 1983a: *Management in Schools: Target Setting*. London: Education for Industrial Society.

Trethowan, D. M. 1983b: Managing to Learn. *Times Educational Supplement*, 25 November, 21.

Trethowan, D. M. 1985: Industrial Means to Educational Ends. *Contributions*, 8, 6–11.

Waitt, I. and Parry, G. 1985: Teaching Management: The Project Approach. *Education*, 14 June, 533.

Walker, G. 1985: The Head's Tale. *Steam*, 4, 3. ICI.

Warwick, D. 1983: *Management in Schools: Staff Appraisal*. London: Education for Industrial Society.

Weindling, D. and Earley, P. 1986: *The First Years of Headship in the Secondary School*. Windsor: NFER-Nelson. Interim report, 1984: From Research to Practice. *Proceedings of the 1984 Members' Conference*. NFER. Supplemented by private communication.

West-Burnham, J. 1983: The Implications for Secondary Schools of a Static Career Structure. *School Organisation*, 3, 255–261.

Yates, E. 1981: A Survey of Opinion on Methods of Professional Development for Secondary Heads. *School Organisation*, 1, 243–254.

Yates, E. 1983: *Professional Development for Secondary Headteachers*. City of Wakefield Education Department.

Index

Action learning, 166, 213, 225
Activities of heads, 112
Adair, 162, 170, 229
Administration, 127
Administrative problems, 34, 41, 50, 91
Advisers, 7, 63–4, 207–9
Ageing staff, 36–7, 173
Aims and objectives, 28, 30, 33, 48, 70, 83, 96, 100, 104, 111
Aitken, 205–6
Albright and Wilson, 173–4
Appraisal, 4, 9, 25, 47, 57, 64–8, 75, 82–3, 103–4, 107, 109, 112, 122, 133, 136, 141, 143–59, 166, 168, 253
Apprenticeship model, 6, 10–12, 25, 71, 75, 121, 141
Army Apprenticeship College, 22
Ascher, 166
Association of Teachers of Management, xi, 212
Attwood, 89, 166
Autonomy, 52, 105, 112

BACIE, xi, 220, 228, 230–1
Ballinger, 167, 201, 215, 217
Barrington, 125, 129
Beckhard, 172, 203
Behaviour on courses, 93
Belbin, 89–90
BEMAS, 212, 231
Blake and Mouton, 162
Bolam, 208, 210, 214, 233
Bone, 179
Books, 229
Bowden, 95, 106, 169
Brainstorming, 161
Brighton Polytechnic, 26, 70, 72, 84
British Institute of Management, 161, 165, 197, 204, 220, 230
Buckley, 116, 163, 197
Budgets, 51
Burgoyne, 55, 130
Bursar, 12, 13, 17, 43, 52–4, 100, 102, 180
Butcher, 89

Cambridgeshire LEA, 52, 107

Capitation, 51–2
Career aspirations, 38
Centre for the Study of Comprehensive Schools (CSCS), x, xi, 5, 85, 226, 231, 241
Centre for the Study of Management Learning (CSML), 216, 220, 226, 232
Change, 3–5, 47, 71, 75–9, 81, 92, 113–4, 116, 119, 132, 163, 167, 194, 248
Chater, 169
Classrooms, 22
Cleveland LEA, 181, 207
CNAA, xi, 207, 218–25
Coherence, 49, 205–7
Collegiality, 9
Communication, 19, 20, 24, 45, 113
Complexity, 119
Components of management, 130
Computers, 14, 17, 43, 53, 54, 75, 179, 232
Consultants, 54, 164, 196, 207, 209–11
Consultation, 13, 21, 24, 38, 113
Contraction, 119
Control, 47, 105, 115
Cost-effectiveness, 43, 44, 50, 53, 54, 119, 228
Courses, 69–75, 84, 161, 214–24
Coverdale training, 72, 80, 97, 162, 169–70, 198, 229, 253
Culture, 17, 22, 101, 106, 181–3
Curriculum, 16, 44, 75, 82

Dean, 130, 207
Decisions, 17, 36, 109, 134
Defensiveness, 115
Delegation, 104, 109–10, 134
Department of Education and Science, 205, 208, 232, 234
Deputy heads, 10, 12, 55
Derr and de Long, 110
Development, 75
Development training, xi, 4
Devolution of responsibility, 42, 44, 52
Diploma in Management Studies, 6, 161, 173
Discipline, 13, 25, 29, 34, 47, 92, 109
Duffet, 102
Dwyer, 110

Education Committee, 44, 45, 49, 58, 76, 120, 205
Education for Capability, 4
Education management, 218
Effectiveness, 22, 66, 101, 103, 107, 163, 178, 203, 208, 214, 221–2, 232, 236
Efficiency, 103, 176
Ethos, 21–33, 136
European school management, 116
Evaluation, 60, 68, 164, 168, 197, 230, 232, 234
Exams, 76
Exchange of jobs, 62
Expenditure, 44, 50, 198
External relations, 25, 92, 105

Feedback, 95, 141
Fielding, 188, 192
Filing systems, 16
Films, 231
Financial control and management, 13, 21, 43, 49, 50–54, 82, 105, 112
Foundation for Management Education, 227
Fullan, 116
Fund-raising, 44, 51
Further Education Unit (FEU), 98

Governors, 9, 52, 58, 92, 103, 153, 197
Graham report, 159
Gray, 114, 209
Group dynamics, 161
Grubb Institute, 6, 70, 74

Handy, 101, 182, 203, 230
Harbridge House, 166
Harrison and Berlew, 170
Harvard Business School, 161
Heads of Departments etc., 11–13, 55, 64
Heller, 181, 207, 209
Henley Management College, 6, 57, 72, 161, 169, 232
Hersey and Blanchard, 89, 229
Herzberg, 121
Hidden curriculum, 22
Hidebound behaviour, 35, 38, 39, 50, 137
Higher Education institutions, 225
HMIs, 2, 205
Holroyde, 164
Housemaster, 8, 11
Hughes Report, 2, 71, 84, 218–9, 221

IBM, 193
ICI, ix, x, 1, 3, 71, 77, 79–81, 123, 137, 147, 152–3, 161–2, 165, 170, 176–8,
180–86, 189, 194, 199, 212, 232, 234, 236, 241
ILEA, 6, 10, 52, 214, 228
Images, 85, 103, 117
Independent schools, 13, 15, 25, 42, 46, 50, 52, 59, 69, 119, 179
Induction, 8, 12, 114
Industrial action, 35, 49
Industrial contacts, 61, 64, 68–70, 76, 78–84, 112
Industrial experience, 7, 11, 16, 43, 52, 53, 77, 106, 250
Industrial relations, 35, 37, 45, 105, 170
Industrial Society, 25–27, 72, 164, 229, 230
Industrial Training Research Unit, 98
Information flow, 20, 21
Innovation, 13, 49, 75–9, 103, 137
INSET, 2, 4, 38, 44, 49, 60, 64, 69, 70, 170, 201, 210, 231
Inspectors, 18, 21, 36, 38, 63–4, 68, 103, 194
ISTC, 214, 228
Institute of Personnel Management, 143
International Management Centre from Buckingham, 227
Interpersonal relations, 23, 43, 104, 117, 215
Interviewing, 58, 61, 133

Jackson, 131
Jamieson, 104
Jenkins, 104
Job descriptions, 9, 13, 24, 25, 45, 52, 75, 108–9, 141
Job exchange, 62
Job rotation, 141, 161, 166
Journals, 231
Judgement and feedback, 95, 100

Kempner, 169
Kepner-Tregoe training, 162, 174
Kolb, 89, 220

Leadership, 49, 57, 88, 111, 117, 122, 128, 133, 170, 247
Leading professional/chief executive tension, 94, 100, 102
Learning from industry, 186, 192
Learning styles, 90
LEAs, 41–6, 50, 76, 82, 103, 111, 160, 179, 201, 208, 215–6, 225, 233–5
Legislation, 2, 39, 53, 92
Leverhulme Trust, x
Life Skills Associates, 229
Likert, 24, 29, 61
Local Government Training Board, 205–6
Loneliness of heads, 23, 111, 116

Management by objectives, 97
Management development, 10, 103–4, 141, 159–74, 245
Management of change workshops, 172, 186
Management training, 214–18
Managerial grid, 162
Manpower planning, 145, 160, 205
Manpower Services Commission, 51, 232
Mant, 9
Married Women's Protection Act, 35
Marsden, 195
Master of Business Administration (MBA), 167
Matrix organisation, 12, 20
Meetings, 13, 17, 43, 70, 83, 102, 104, 108, 133–4, 163, 177, 243
Middle managers, 11
Mintzberg, 105, 131
Minutes, 13, 18, 21, 70, 104
Morale, 20, 39, 43, 49, 57, 76, 89, 108, 175
Morality, 188
Morris, xi, 84
Motivation, 38
Myers-Briggs Type Indicator, 89–90

National Development Centre for School Management Training (NDCSMT), xi, 2, 151, 167, 194, 204–5, 215, 232
National Training Index, 215, 228
National Training Laboratories, 161
Network for Organisation Development in Education (NODE), 213
Networks, 212
NFER, 227

Objectives, 28, 30, 33, 48, 70, 83, 96, 100, 110, 133, 141
Ordidge, 110
Organisation, 12, 21, 24, 83, 102, 104, 134, 247
Organisation development (OD), 78, 81, 117, 120, 141, 162, 169, 198, 205, 209, 216, 236
Osmosis, 71
OTTO courses, 2
Oxford Centre for Management Studies, 173

Paisey, 98, 175
Parents, 76, 92
Pedagogy, 76, 83, 98, 100
Peel, 161, 197, 214
Performance, 46, 61, 83, 105, 108, 138, 145, 175
Personnel management, 121

Persuasion skills, 171
Peters and Waterman, 102, 189, 192, 203
Pettigrew, 3, 153, 162, 172, 178, 181, 208, 234
Philosophy, 6
Planning, 57, 82–3, 98, 105, 109, 133
Policy, 102, 205
Political influence, 37, 40, 41, 58, 61, 92, 119–20, 169, 205, 223, 236
Polytechnic of Central London, 161, 212
POST Report, 9, 58
Potential, 145
Power, 105–6
Prefects, 15
Preparation for headship, 114
Private sector institutions, 227
Proactivity, 57
Problems, 33–50, 90–3, 108, 133, 139, 180
Productivity, 175
Professional associations, 212
Professional tutor, 211
Prospectus, 17, 22, 25
Psychometric tests, 89, 100, 108, 166
Public relations, 92, 109, 123, 136
Publishers, 229
Pupil involvement, 15, 21, 31, 59, 68, 77, 101, 152, 211

Qualifications, 6, 10, 71
Qualities, 54, 113
Questionnaires, 16, 24, 29, 61, 64, 84, 100

Rank Xerox, 194
Reading, 99–100
Recognition, 136–7
Reddin, 89, 97, 162, 170
Ree, 188
Relationships with LEA, 43, 50, 92
Research methodology, 239
Resource management, 174
Resources, 34, 43, 92, 105
Reviews, 60–4, 68, 133
Rewards, 46, 50, 92, 106, 136–7, 145
Reynolds, 22
Ring-fence policies, 39, 45, 58
Roffey Park, 25–6, 72–3, 229
Role conflict, 40, 94, 101
Role models, 7, 55, 71
Role of head, 117
Royal Society of Arts, 4

Salaries, 34, 46, 52, 91
Scale points, 46
Schofield, 113

School secretary, 16, 21, 36, 63, 211
Schools Council Industry Project (SCIP), 15, 26, 62, 71, 104, 207
Secondary Heads Association, 212, 215
Secondments, 64, 195
Selection, 58, 100, 109, 113, 122, 149, 166
Self-development, 10, 12, 99, 142, 231, 249, 253
Senior managers, 9, 13, 18
Sensitivity training, 161
Skills, 55, 111, 113
Staff development, 9, 27, 82, 105
  manuals, 13, 21
  meetings, 13, 55
  problems, 34–5, 91
Staffrooms, 13, 22, 41
Stress, 35–6, 40, 50, 75, 83, 91, 107, 114, 138, 212
Style, 21, 23–4, 29, 33, 40, 46, 70, 77, 88, 100, 104–5, 109, 113, 122, 247, 252
Success criteria, 95–6
Suggestion schemes, 176
Support, 100, 104, 107, 109, 111, 121, 204ff.
Surveys, 106, 164–70, 198, 214–5, 226
Systematic approach, 95, 115, 139, 163, 184
Systems approach, 120

Tavistock Institute of Human Relations, 161
Taylor, 40, 87
Teacher training institutions, 73
Teamwork, 96, 107, 113, 247
Templeton College, 173

Time structuring, 14, 104, 134
Torrington and Weightman, 106, 187
Training, 61, 69–75, 83, 88, 103–5, 107, 109, 111, 141
  for appraisal, 150
  packages, 162, 232
Trebor, 194
Trethowan, 97, 148, 188
TVEI, 39, 49, 51, 180

Understanding British Industry (UBI), 229, 241
Unions, 36, 40, 45, 49, 119
University College Cardiff, 89
  of London Institute of Education, x, 89, 187, 194, 226, 241
Unsatisfactory performers, 25, 35, 50, 109, 137

Video 231

Walker, 5
Weaknesses, 109, 146
Weindling and Earley, 113
Western Europe comparisons, 116, 197
Woolley Hall, 25
Word processing, 17, 25, 54, 83, 179
Work flow, 16, 21, 134
  study, 170, 177
Working parties, 77–8

YMCA, 163